THE AFTERMATH OF SLAVERY

A STUDY OF
THE CONDITION AND ENVIRONMENT
OF THE AMERICAN NEGRO

BY

WILLIAM A. SINCLAIR, A.M., M.D.

WITH AN INTRODUCTION BY

THOMAS WENTWORTH HIGGINSON, LL.D.

ISBN: 978-1-63923-832-3

Printed: March 2023

Published and Distributed By:
Lushena Books
607 Country Club Drive, Unit E
Bensenville, IL 60106
www.lushenabks.com

ISBN: 978-1-63923-832-3

WHO BELIEVE THAT THE FLAG SHALL BE
THE SYMBOL OF LIBERTY UNDER LAW
AND OF EQUAL RIGHTS BEFORE THE LAW
FOR ALL AMERICANS

CONTENTS

A BIOGRAPHICAL NOTE

WILLIAM A. SINCLAIR, the author of this book, was born in slavery at Georgetown, South Carolina. When about four years of age, in the early part of the Civil War, he was sold with his mother, from his home; but about a year after the close of the war, after many trying experiences, they returned to his native place, where a partial reuniting of the family was effected. William's father died shortly after this, and the widowed mother became responsible for the boy's maintenance and education. He attended the local schools and prepared himself to enter upon a higher course of study at Claflin University, Orangeburg, South Carolina. Thence he went to the well-known South Carolina College at Columbia, that venerable institution of learning, which, in the days of slavery, had been patronized by the aristocracy of the state including Haynes, Rhett, McDuffee, Barnwell, and Calhoun, and which, under Republican administration of the state after the close of the war, had been thrown open to colored as well as white students. Colored students were debarred from this college in 1877, and Mr. Sinclair entered Howard University, Washington, D. C., where he graduated from the college and theological departments and where he later received the degree of Master of Arts. The next step in his educational development was post-graduate study at Andover Theological Seminary, where he won a prize for a dissertation and delivered an address at the commencement exercises.

For six years he devoted himself to missionary work, under the auspices of the American Missionary Association, at Nashville, Tennessee, and here he improved the opportunity to study medicine at the MeHarry Medical College of Central Tennessee University (now Walden University of Nashville), where he took his medical degree, being also the salutatorian of his class.

A BIOGRAPHICAL NOTE

During his college vacations Mr. Sinclair taught school, and he has filled, with credit and success, the positions of principal of the graded school at Georgetown, South Carolina, and professor of natural sciences in Livingstone College, Salisbury, North Carolina; and for the past sixteen years he has been financial secretary of Howard University, Washington, D. C.

Throughout the period of his education he displayed unusual powers of oratory, and in his labors for Howard University he has been heard in the pulpit and on the platform throughout the United States, and in the United Kingdom as well. In this field his natural abilities and his evident learning have everywhere procured him distinctive recognition among thinking people.

Throughout his travels Dr. Sinclair has discussed the race question, publicly and at the fireside, with persons of every degree and station in life, and in the following pages he gives to a wider circle than he can reach by personal discourse the information that has been required of him concerning the condition and environment of the American negro.

INTRODUCTION

N OW that so many authors, Southern and Northern, have suddenly broken out into the discussion of the so-called negro problem, it is nothing more than fair that another negro author should have his word to say. The very fact that these Southern contributions cover a very wide range in quality, from the really high-toned and enlightened work entitled Problems of the Present South, by Edgar Gardner Murphy, down to the demagogic glorification of the Ku Klux Klan by the Reverend Thomas Dixon, Jr. — this range of thought makes it only right to recognize the effort of a colored man to be fair and plain-spoken in doing justice to his side of the house.

The attempt to do this, at least, is visible in every page of the book to which this is a preface. One who like myself has visited within nine months the heart of the former slave states, who has seen the strong effort made by so many of the Southern whites to do justice to the negro and who has talked freely with Southern public men — in my own case, for instance, with the governors of three different states — must needs feel an impulse to take a hand when a colored writer enters on a manly and courageous argument for his own side, such as may be found in the volume which follows ; and I cannot decline his request to write a preface for him.

Reading the book with some care, I could point out a few passages with which I disagree, but surprisingly few; and in some of these cases the disagreement proceeds from the fact that I am a man old enough to recall a time when there existed all around us at the North instances of the same kinds of injustice of which we now properly complain when we see it at the South. It seems like a bit of Egyptian darkness to Dr. Sinclair for those states to have entirely separate schools for the two races, but that does not seem so hopeless an evil to me, who more than fifty years ago in two different cities in New

England took a hand in abolishing just such schools. The first great step is to have public schools at all, either for white or black. In the same way men justly complain of the "Jim Crow" cars, as they call them; but I, who can remember the time in my childhood when a colored woman was taken out of a stage-coach opposite what is now Cambridge Common, because other passengers objected to her color, cannot feel the evil to be so hopeless as he does. The South is merely passing through a period such as Massachusetts passed through long ago, and the great fact of importance is that it is being passed through and men will get beyond it sooner or later.

I can remember, in the same way, when every Boston Directory separated the two races, putting the colored families at the end of the book; and I can remember when the very editor who first made the change told me of it beforehand, begging me to keep it secret that the newspapers might not get hold of it. "When the people once see it done," he said, "they will soon forget that it ever was otherwise." Thus much I say of the execution of the book, which is in almost all respects admirable and shows much more thoroughness in dealing with both sides than any book recently produced by a Southern white man, except that of Mr. Murphy, which is a model to all in its tone, though even that, I think, does here and there a little less than justice to the negro.

Even this book does not fully bring out the utter injustice done by Mr. Thomas Nelson Page when he ignores plain facts in the following charge against the Southern negro: "In 1865, when the Negro was set free, he held without a rival the entire field of industrial labor throughout the South. Ninety-five per cent of all the industrial work of the Southern States was in his hands. And he was fully competent to do it. Every adult was either a skilled laborer or a trained mechanic. It was the fallacious teaching of equality which deluded him into dropping the substance for the shadow." (Page's The Negro: The Southerner's Problem, p. 127.) Mr. Murphy

INTRODUCTION

himself incautiously says: " The South has sometimes abridged the negro's right to vote, but the South has not yet abridged his right, in any direction of human interest or of honest effort, to earn his bread." (Murphy's The Present South, *p. 187.*)

Yet if the reader of the present volume will turn to Chapter II he will find many pages showing, on the authority of Mr. Blaine and of Vice-President Henry Wilson, that there was a long period of years when the legislation of state after state prohibited every black citizen from earning his living by these higher forms of labor which Mr. Page now blames a generation of negroes for having lost from their grasp. Were it for these pages only, the perusal of the present work may be urged upon every fair-minded man. It is nothing less than ludicrous to complain of a generation of negroes for not bringing up their boys to be mechanics when, as in South Carolina, the legislature enacted that no person of color should pursue any work other than husbandry without a special license from the judge of the district court, this license being good for one year only, and the boy aiming at it having to pay a license fee of ten dollars. No such fees had ever been exacted from white men, nor even from the free black man during the days of slavery.

THOMAS WENTWORTH HIGGINSON.

Cambridge, Mass., Jan. 11, 1905.

xiii

The Aftermath of Slavery

CHAPTER I

THE INSTITUTION OF SLAVERY AND ITS ABOLITION

THERE is to-day a New South, and the colored people are a material part of it. The Old South, with its gruesome and unholy institution of human slavery, has passed out of existence, never to return. It has, however, left a heritage of complicated and vexatious problems, the just and righteous solution of which will tax to the uttermost the resources of the statesman, the fidelity of the church, and the patience and firmness of the nation. It is of prime importance to note that the existing blighting evils which are an infliction to both the white and the colored people are not inherent in either people, but have their roots in the essential barbarism of the slave system.

The Proclamation of Emancipation issued by the immortal Abraham Lincoln was intended to break the fetters of the slave; but now it can be seen that it was also an emancipation of the white people of the South. For slavery manacled the conscience of the master as completely as it did the body of the slave. Unhappily, neither the white nor the colored people are yet fully set free from the brutalizing evils of the system. It would seem that emancipation of the body can be more readily accomplished than the emancipation of the conscience.

In the spirit of liberty, however, the colored people are farther removed than the whites from the old régime. To the colored people freedom came as a boon from heaven, a special gift of God, an answer to the agonizing prayers of centuries. It was a treasure above all price. But the white people of the South took a different view of it. They loved freedom for themselves and would die in defence of it; unfortunately, however, they regarded the freeing of the colored man as a wrong to the white man. The virus of slavery was

3

present in the brain! And so the chief efforts of Southei ι leadership have been to curtail the freedom of the colored people, to minimize their liberty and reduce them as nearly as possible to the conditions of chattel slaves. These efforts, unremitting and sometimes violent, tremendously affect every phase of Southern life.

In general, a spirit of cruel intolerance dominates the white population of the whole Southland. Its church life, despite the many excellent and truly Christian members, both men and women, betrays strange deformities and inconsistencies; in large measure ignoring alike the golden rule, the Sermon on the Mount, the divinely beautiful lesson of the Good Samaritan, and, in short, the more vital and central truth of the entire teaching of Jesus himself — the fatherhood of God and the brotherhood of man. Christ's saying, " All ye are brethren," is not interpreted with sufficient breadth to include the negro.

" Free government " in the South means, in the attitude of the whites toward the negro, disregard of the law, the repudiation of the orderly processes of the Courts of Justice, the rule of the mob, and cruel proscription. President Lincoln declared that "those who would deny liberty to others are not worthy of it themselves." The white people of the South, still clinging to the traditions of the slave system, have continued to deny liberty to the colored man ; and to this attitude is due the existence in that section of a state of lawlessness with its long train of evils.

It has thus come to pass that mobs torture human beings and roast them alive without trial and in defiance of law and order ; mobs shoot down women and children who have never been charged with crime, and against whom there is no suspicion, — it is enough that they are negroes. Mobs take possession of the streets of great cities and assault and shoot down innocent colored people, driving them from their homes and burning their property, — in one instance more than a thousand

4

colored people, men, women and children, being driven from their homes in a single day. Mobs intercept and hold up the regularly constituted officers of the law, take prisoners from their possession and shoot them to death. Mobs break into jails and take out prisoners and hang them, sometimes in the jail yard, and riddle their bodies with bullets. Mobs even invade the sacred precincts of the court-room, and during the actual process of the trial, take prisoners from the custody of the lawful authorities and shoot them in the very temple of justice, or hang them in the court-yard in the presence of judge, jury, and court officers, amid the shouts and cheers of hundreds, and, at times, thousands of people. In one instance sixteen colored men were shot to death on the floor of the court-room in Mississippi, during the actual process of the trial of two colored men charged with a minor offence. And these things are done, not in a corner, but under the full glare of the noonday sun.

The white people of the South have taken pains to declare through their public press and public men — as if to mitigate national indignation and forestall condemnation — that all these things were committed by their "best citizens." This is a most startling indictment of the South, and by the South itself, and is an apt illustration of the saying, "Who excuses, accuses." It is not contended in these pages, however, that all the white people of the South, or the most of them, or even the " best " of them, are given over to unrighteous or riotous proceedings. For the whole, or even the majority of a people are not bad. There are always men and women, true and good, as honest as the day is long, who "love mercy, do justice, and walk humbly" as in the sight of God.

But that there is a prevalence of inconsistencies and barbarities and a reign of terror and blood which darken the sky of the Sunny South, the land where

"Everlasting spring abides
And never withering flowers,"

is as clear as the light of the sun. The white people of the South, however, are descended from noble and honored ancestors, who were imbued with the highest ideals of liberty, humanity, righteousness, and orderly government. Many of these were originally opposed to the introduction of the institution of human slavery, while others were sceptical or indifferent about it, and still others accepted it in the spirit of liberal toleration. It is a generally acknowledged fact that slavery at first existed in a mild and not very offensive form, practically devoid of the barbarities and brutalities which later characterized it, — the slave owner being somewhat like a feudal lord of more or less power and dignity, and the slave holding a relation not far removed from that of a liege. It is indisputable that the white people of the South carried on among themselves for years an agitation for the abolition of slavery, and that they probably would have abolished slavery, or eliminated it by colonization or some other means, but for the determined minor element composed of slaveholders, whose influence was greatly reinforced by the invention, in 1793, of the cotton gin, which while a most useful invention yet has proved a curse and scourge as well as a profit and blessing to mankind. This invention gave a tremendous impetus to the demand for slave labor by vastly increasing its commercial value ; it put new life and vigor into the slave trade, creating a limitless demand for slaves, and making the abolition of slavery practically impossible save by a national upheaval.

Through the extension of the interests in the slave trade and slave labor, and the realization of the enormous profits resulting from these sources, came the Southerner's dream of wealth, power, and dominion, which turned any general sentiment for the abolition of slavery in the South into a demand for more slaves. Thenceforth the white people of the South dedicated themselves, not to the development of their free institutions, but to the building up of a slaveholding oligarchy, overbearing and cruel, which was yet to challenge the nation itself to mortal combat, to cover the land with mourning, and to redden a continent with blood.

This invention of the cotton gin raised the Cotton Industry to such supreme importance that cotton became king of the products in the world's market. And King Cotton, like Satan in the temptation of the Christ on the Mount, said to the Southern whites : " All these things will I give thee, if thou wilt fall down and worship me, — the kingdoms of the world and the glory of them." The white people of the South did not resist this appeal to their greed and love for gilded luxury ; this promise of untold wealth, power, and dominion that was held forth to them. They betook themselves to the worship of King Cotton.

Truly COTTON was KING. It became their worshiping fetich. They were lured from their high ideals, and even threw to the winds those basic principles, those very fundamental truths of Christianity, the fatherhood of God and the brotherhood of man.

" Am I my brother's keeper ? " asked one of old. The white people of the South were no longer their " brother's keeper," certainly not the keeper of their " brother in black."

The institution of slavery increased and expanded by leaps and bounds, and became more and more debasing to the whites and blacks alike. The slave trade was stimulated as never before, and those engaged in it became brutal beyond description. The appalling sacrifice of human life, and the wide-spread desolation incident to its operation were matters of public knowledge. Scores of African villages might be laid waste, fire and sword work havoc, and thousands of old and young people killed in order to secure one cargo of slaves ; but what of that ? It was not worthy of a moment's consideration that to deliver a single slave on a plantation might cost the lives of half a hundred of Africans. What concern was it to them if a thousand lives were sacrificed, since they obtained that one slave ?

7

The ghastly horrors of " the middle passage "; the clanking of chains; the wild and deep groans of men; the heart-rending weeping and wailing of women and children; the cruel floggings; the agonizing cries of despair from the dying, to whom the visit of death was as the visit of an angel; the dumping of the dead into the sea by hands dyed with human blood; the crowding of these ill-fated and hapless creatures of all ages and both sexes into the dark and filthy pest holes of slave ships, and all the terrible, unspeakable agonies of body and anguish of spirit which they endured — all this and more caused the slaveholder no worry, no loss of sleep. The conscience was seared. Remorse was dead.

They had no time for maudlin sympathy. Slaves they wanted. Slaves they must have. The cost in horror and blood; life, pain, and devastation; ruin and desolation were as nothing. The cotton fields must be developed, extended, and expanded; the malarial swamps and marshes must be redeemed and made to yield their harvest of golden sheaves laden with the pearly grains of rice; all the land, the field and forest, and even the earth beneath must be made to yield their increase, and the labor of slaves must accomplish this. So the white people of the South cried out for slaves — *and more slaves* — AND STILL MORE SLAVES.

It was impossible that these things could have other than a disastrous effect on public morality. The white South had indeed fallen from its high estate. Its great ideals had gradually faded away.

In an article in the *Atlantic Monthly* for September, 1901, Mr. Thomas Nelson Page, speaking of the condition of the South at the time of the War of the Rebellion, says that the South was " without ships, without money, without machinery that could produce a knife, a blanket, or a tin cup; without an ally, without even the sympathy of a single nation, without knowledge of the outside world, or indeed of her able and determined opponent."

Does he realize the cutting irony, the bald satire of his own statement? For he is pleading, as he always does, in season and out of season, for the white people of the South; apologizing for, or justifying, the many hardships imposed on the negro, and seeking always to discredit and prejudice him in the eyes of the nation. His is indeed a pitiful description of a pitiful civilization; and the pity of the pity is, that it is pitifully true.

The worse than ghoulish horrors commonly practised by the brutal kidnappers, or African slave traders; the ghastly spectacle of the slave auction-block, where slaves, men, women, and children were examined and sold as though they were cattle, and the heartrending, inhuman, and disgusting scenes attendant thereon, — these things had caused throughout the civilized world such a revulsion of public sentiment against the institution of human slavery that the South in the moment of its great extremity was indeed absolutely "without an ally, without even the sympathy of a single nation." It was these ghastly abominations of the slave auction-block, which on one occasion Abraham Lincoln witnessed as a young man when on a visit to New Orleans in 1831, that moved him to declare eternal war against the system of slavery.

The incident as reported is this: "He saw a slave, a beautiful mulatto girl, sold at auction. She was felt over, pinched, trotted around to show to bidders that said article was sound. Lincoln walked away from the sad, inhuman scene with deep feelings of unsmotherable hatred. He said to John Hank, who was with him: 'If I ever get a chance to hit that institution, I'll hit it — hard, John.'" He got the chance, and did "hit it"; how hard, the world knows.

It is worth while to point out the cause of the backward and pitiable condition of the South in 1861, which Mr. Page, with lamentations, so accurately and pithily depicts. The institution of slavery laid tribute on the talent, the

9

statesmanship, the loyalty, and all the vital forces — moral, spiritual, and material — of the South.] It was the all-absorbing topic ; it monopolized the brain and heart of the South. All other subjects converged into it.

The South had for years devoted, even dedicated its genius, its strength, its energies, to the institution of human slavery, and to the development, protection, expansion, and perpetuation of the system. Its genius and talent for other things simply shrivelled up. It devoted itself so completely to the institution of slavery that the South made, what William Lloyd Garrison declared slavery to be, " an agreement with death and a covenant with hell." It was death to the public morals and conscience of the South ; and it was hell to the ill-fated, helpless, down-trodden slave.

The institution of slavery, as bad and debasing as it was for the negro in one way, was probably even worse for the whites in another. It so stupefied the conscience of the whites that even now, forty years after the destruction of the system, they show but few signs of recovery from its baneful effects. It so twisted and perverted their moral conceptions that they cannot view rationally or with justice the simplest question affecting the manhood rights of the negro.

This fact was demonstrated when President Roosevelt simply recognized the eminence and worth of a colored American citizen, in the person of Principal Booker T. Washington, by inviting him to dinner. What was all the consequent furor, denunciation, and display of bad temper and worse judgment but the manifestation of the entailed, unpitying consequences of the barbarism of slavery ? France honors a member of the colored race as a general in her army ; another has been vice-president of her Chamber of Deputies ; others occupy high stations in the life of the nation ; a number are in her leading schools. England's gracious sovereign, the late Queen Victoria, repeatedly entertained colored persons at breakfast or luncheon, extending, for instance, such courtesy to the whole company of the famous Fisk University Jubilee Singers ; but there was not a person in the whole British Empire who protested against it.

The most powerful emperors, kings, and rulers of Europe have extended such courtesies without having public decency shocked or violated by ribald protestations. Prince Henry, the brother of the German Emperor, while on a visit to the United States, and when every minute of his time was at a premium, denying himself to many prominent people, especially commanded that the Hampton Jubilee Singers, colored, be presented to him at the Waldorf-Astoria Hotel. Such instances render the more pitiable, if not ridiculous, the spectacle that the South made of itself in regard to the Roosevelt-Washington dining incident. But this " may be set down to the not yet closed account of " the barbarism of slavery.

This system of slavery, as it existed in the South, was as black as moral turpitude could make it. The fond words mother, home, and family were devoid of their high and real meaning to the slave. For he lived, moved, and had his being in the ever-present, dismal, and benumbing shadow of the auction-block. His was a life approaching moral desolation ; a life in which the great moral incentives begotten of the ties, honor, and blessedness of the family life, blood, and name, were absent. There was next to nothing in the family life of the slave to inspire him to noble purpose and endeavor. There could be no legal marriage; the constant separation of those who had entered into the marriage relation, by the sale of either husband or wife, made this impossible. For the wife or husband, if sold every day in a week, could marry anew after each sale.

Uncle Tom's Cabin, that wonderful work of Mrs. Harriet Beecher Stowe, did not depict, nor even scarcely hint at, some of the grosser evils and barbarities of the system ; and yet the white South winces over it. These people should not be blamed for being so sensitive over Mrs. Stowe's incisive and luminous protrayal of the life and civilization of the South, although the worst was not told. Much in connection with the treatment of slaves and the raising of them for the home market was really unprintable.

The buying and selling, the separation and breaking up of negro families were common all over the South. Neither age nor sex were regarded. The infant was snatched from the mother's arms; the father and mother of a family were torn from each other; they were sold, each in a different direction, never more to meet on earth. Strange, passing strange, that it never dawned on the white people of the South that

> " The black mother who rocks her boy
> Feels in her heart all a mother's joy."

It is unquestionably true that there were good and humane masters. There were some, indeed, who were most considerate to their slaves; and others who never even became reconciled to the system of slavery, but rather hated it to the end, and rejoiced at its destruction. But this was the exception, and did little to change the general conditions and lessen the evils inherent in the system. Neither Washington, the father of his country, nor Thomas Jefferson, the author of the Declaration of Independence, believed in human slavery; Madison is credited with keeping the word *slavery* out of the Constitution; while Mason, Tucker, Randolph, and others opposed the institution.

Thomas Jefferson, the father of Democracy, both spoke and wrote against slavery. He foresaw that there would be a great national convulsion over it, and counselled its elimination. He left on record these prophetic words, " Nothing is more certainly written in the book of fate than that these people shall be free." The South did not take heed. If Thomas Jefferson were living to-day in the dawn of the twentieth century, with the immense strides of mankind taken since his time, he would tell the white people of the South that "nothing is more certainly written in the book of fate than that these people shall enjoy equal rights and privileges before the law." The white people may disregard the warning now as they did under the slave régime, but infidelity to truth, justice, and good order, and the dragon teeth of unrighteousness and oppressive laws will bring a bitter harvest to their children, and may long plague the land.

There were other Southerners, some notable ones, who from time to time, because of their conscientious scruples against human slavery, set their slaves free. Like Abraham Lincoln, their souls burned within them with righteous indignation against the unspeakable iniquities of the system; and they sincerely felt that "no man was good enough to own another man." Some even left the South to avoid identification with the abominations of slavery, and took up their residence in the free North. Some sent their children by colored mothers North to be educated and to live, and also set the mothers free and removed them to the North as well. There were, and still exist, instances of tender and even affectionate regard between the master class and the slave class. Since emancipatiou there have been some of the master class who have been devotedly interested in the welfare of their former slaves, and have been both a help and a protection to them; in some instances rescuing them from unjust treatment and the fury of lawless mobs. Nevertheless, the plain, unvarnished truth remains, that the great body of slave owners were either inconsiderate or cruel themselves, or put their slaves into the hands of heartless slave-drivers, overseers, and hard task-masters. And these made the life of the slaves a burden, grievous and hard to bear.

Some apologists seek to gloss over the iniquities of this system and even give it a patriarchal tinge with divine virtues; they would make it appear as though American slavery was established for the "benevolent assimilation" of the African negro. It is true that the white men of the South did ac-

13

complish a large measure of " assimilation," the manifold evidences of which are to be seen in every city, town, village, and country district throughout the South ; but there are grave, very grave reasons for doubt as to the " benevolent " character of this "assimilation." What good the milder slavery actually did for the negro was in spite of its barbarity and was due to his great powers for absorbing civilization. Slavery was in no sense whatever a philanthropic or humanitarian enterprise, but was developed and conducted on the low plane of avarice, greed, and bestiality. There seem to be no grounds on which it can be claimed that it was intended for the good of the negroes, who in their low estate were but chattels to be marketed and sold, and at their best were but as beasts of burden to toil and moil in order that the master class might live in comfortable ease and luxury.

The wide-spread and brutal floggings on the bare body continued in some cases until the blood flowed ; the bathing in salt water to increase the agony ; the general use of bloodhounds, in some instances making them lacerate the flesh of the slaves to give them a taste for human blood and make them more ferocious and thus a greater terror to the slaves ; the devices for torture such as the stocks, the thumbscrew, the pillory ; and the varied methods of stringing up, — are some of the " fascinations " and " beauties " of the slave's life which the apologists of the system ignore. There are well authenticated cases of slaves being whipped to death, and of others dying from the effects of the floggings. But notwithstanding, to borrow the title of one of the beautiful plantation melodies, their " Hard Trials and Great Tribulations," the slaves continued to increase in numbers.

They learned how to use the title of another of their sweet melodies, — to " Steal Away, Steal Away, Steal Away to Jesus," and find strength, comfort, and sustaining help in every time of need. They seem also to have demonstrated that liberty is an instinct of the human heart ; for in the blackest hour of the long night of their gloomy bondage, they sang most gleefully and with joyous, hopeful hearts, another of their soul-inspiring melodies:

> "One of these days I shall be free,
> When Christ the Lord shall set me free."

This song was forbidden by the slave owners, because its spirit would tend to keep alive the thirst for liberty. It is but another illustration of the wisdom of the man who said: "Let me write the songs of a people, and I care not who may write their laws."

The negroes hoodwinked the master class by humming the music of this particular song, while the words echoed and re-echoed deep down in their hearts with perhaps greater effect than if they had been spoken. These melodies were to them the Incarnation — God with them; and to their keen and simple faith He seemed to be visible and tangible, ever present and ever blessed. These songs had a meaning and power which all men may appreciate, but which the negro alone could fully comprehend. Songs are the heart-language of a people; and as the negro heart-language it is not surprising that these melodies should touch and melt human hearts the world over. Queens, emperors, and potentates of the Old World; the President in the White House; the most cultured and fashionable audiences everywhere have been moved and melted to tears by their rendition. Of a truth as a heart-language they are at once the interpretation and exemplification of that wondrous touch of nature "which makes the whole world kin." In them was the secret of the sustaining power which enabled the negroes to weather the storms of their bitter afflictions and sing: —

> " Nobody knows the trouble I see,
> Nobody knows but Jesus ;
> Nobody knows the trouble I see,
> Glory in my soul.

15

" I'm sometimes up, and sometimes down,
O! yes, Lord!
Sometimes almost to the ground,
O! yes, Lord!

"Nobody knows the trouble I see,
Nobody knows but Jesus;
Nobody knows the trouble I see,
Glory in my soul!"

It was this "glory in the soul" that enabled them not only to withstand all the grinding experiences, tribulations, and bestialities of the slave system, but even to flourish and multiply. Only the strongest of races could have survived this wasting and agonizing strain of centuries.

The following table shows the increase in slaves by decades:

YEAR.	NUMBER OF SLAVES.
1800	1,002,037
1810	1,377,808
1820	1,771,658
1830	2,328,642
1840	2,873,648
1850	3,638,808
1860	4,441,830

A factor of great yet weird significance in Southern life may be referred to here. During all the years of slavery, the amalgamation of the races, though practically one-sided, was going on with ever-increasing pace. The overwhelming evidence of this widely diffused amalgamation which can never be blotted out was written and bleached indelibly in the faces and features of the servants in the dining-room, in the chambers, in the nurseries, in the sewing-rooms, in the laundries, in the kitchens, in care of horse and stables, of servant gardeners, messengers, and plantation hands; it was to be seen in servants in every sphere and vocation in Southern life.

The white men of the South had endowed and were still endowing the negro slave with their best blood and greatest

16

names. Some of these slave owners, be it said to their credit, did treat their own offspring of a negro mother with consideration. But the great body of these slave owners would sell their own offspring and their mothers, together or separately, without the least show of compunction of conscience. For a man to sell his own children and the mother of his children, even though they were not legitimate heirs at law, into a bondage where hope hardly abideth, is a monstrous act of hard-heartedness. But such monstrous acts were common.

These slave owners well knew to what a horrible life their own daughters of negro mothers would be subjected, a life worse than death ; but this, too, was of little or no concern to them. The touching lines of Longfellow's " The Quadroon Girl " are painfully illuminating on this point.

In this connection, it may be remarked that an exceedingly strange phenomenon, and one that will require the utmost resources of the sociologists for a rational explanation, is that the white people of the South, who under the degrading influences of the slave régime sold their own children and the negro mothers of their children into a bondage black, bitter, and brutalizing, are to-day, forty years after the destruction of slavery, and under the benign light of a more advanced civilization, ostracizing and outlawing by legislative acts and otherwise disfranchizing, lynching, and burning at the stake their own children of negro mothers, and the children of their fathers and grandfathers and more remote ancestors.

It is interesting to note, in connection with this thought, that the three colored persons — Principal Booker T. Washington, who was invited to dine at the White House by the President ; Dr. William D. Crum, who was appointed collector of the port of Charleston, South Carolina ; and Mrs. Cox, the capable and accomplished postmistress at Indianola, Mississippi, who was driven from her position and virtually expelled from the town by a brutal and lawless mob of the much-vaunted superior whites — these three colored persons, bearing the very best character, educated, cultured, property-owners, and in all the essentials of life superior to many white people of the South, — have actually more Caucasian than African blood in their veins. And notwithstanding which, their recognition by the President as American citizens fit to hold office threw the people of the South into hysterics, and brought about the most bitter denunciation of them and the President; and some Southern whites have even publicly demanded their assassination. For lack of a more intelligent and plausible reason, this, too, " may be set down to the not yet closed account of " the barbarism of slavery.

As slavery became more intrenched in the South, the opposition to it became more pronounced and determined in the North. The people of the North, having voluntarily set free their own slaves, were practically united against the institution of slavery, or at least were uncompromisingly opposed to its further extension. Thus, the North and the South faced each other on the slavery question; the South demanding an extension of the system, and the North its limitation, if not destruction. Robert Toombs of Georgia, a leading slave owner and statesman of the South, declared that he would never be contented " until he could call the roll of his slaves at the foot of Bunker Hill monument in Massachusetts." Slavery became the paramount issue in national politics, in great religious bodies, social circles, at the fireside, everywhere. It was the all-absorbing subject.

While many of the antislavery leaders stood firmly and unequivocally upon a broad foundation of liberty, humanitarianism, or the ethics of the gospel of Christ, yet it should not be overlooked that they were strongly urged by the fact that the slave labor at the South had already exerted a degrading influence on the white free labor at the North and was an ever-increasing menace to it. The white free labor of the North, in order to maintain its own dignity, and preserve its rewards, must perforce join in the crusade against slave labor at the South. This positive peril of the great masses of white toilers in the North being reduced to conditions approaching those of the slave in the South became a factor of great importance. Moreover, the aggressions and intolerance of Southern leaders and their plainly expressed contempt for the laborer greatly increased sectional animosities and augmented the ranks of the abolitionists.

In the fierce and bitter conflict of words that arose, the South scored signal victories.

It obtained the Missouri Compromise, but repudiated the compact when it served its interest to do so.

It obtained the Fugitive Slave Law, which imposed on Northern white men, under heavy penalties, the duty of hounding down the fugitive slave, a fellow-man who was guilty of no crime save that of fleeing a bondage which was as black as midnight and more cruel than the grave.

It obtained the Dred Scott decision from the Supreme Court of the United States. Chief Justice Taney, speaking for the Court, declared that negroes " had no rights which the white man was bound to respect."

It obtained, through Preston S. Brooks of South Carolina, *the silencing* of slavery's greatest foe, and humanity's greatest advocate, Charles Sumner of Massachusetts, — not by argu-ment, but by blows of a loaded cane stealthily given on the floor of the United States Senate.

Various counties in the State of South Carolina presented Brooks with gold-headed canes for his chivalrous and gallant act of thus assaulting, in behalf of his State and people, a man who was unsuspectingly writing at his desk.

It brought John Brown to the gallows, but " his soul goes marching on."

19

The slaveholders were aggressively domineering. They seemed to be "spoiling for a fight," and yet they felt sure that there would be no fight. Was cotton not king? Besides, the South controlled other great staples of the world's commerce, and millions of hardy and faithful slave laborers. This was the source of their confidence and the strength of their intolerance.

Mr. Hammond of South Carolina, in the United States Senate on March 4, 1858, said: "Without firing a gun, without drawing a sword, should the North make war on us, we could bring the whole world to our feet. What would happen if no cotton was furnished for three years? I will not stop to depict what every one can imagine, but this is certain, England would topple headlong and carry the whole civilized world with her. No, you dare not make war on cotton. No power on earth dares to make war on cotton. Cotton is King." War did, however, go on for *four* years, but England did not *topple*.

These and other events of more or less national import crowding thick and fast on each other fired into a white-heat the two great sections of the country, the North and the South. When the memorable year of 1860 came, it found the nation a seething caldron of political, social, and religious excitement. The time for the election of a President was at hand. "The irrepressible conflict" was on: it was to be a duel to the death between the pro-slavery and the antislavery forces.

The forces of liberty and righteousness were triumphant. Is it too much to say that God sent confusion into the councils of the slaveholding oligarchy, which, instead of nominating one candidate who might easily have been elected, nominated four candidates and was defeated?

"Whom the gods would destroy, they first make mad."

The course of events solidified the antislavery forces, and served to crystallize the antislavery sentiment. These forces and sentiment found expression through the Union Republican party, — a new organization with potentialities for achievements far beyond the ken of the men who stood sponsors at its birth: a party born unto grand moral ideas, and reviving and holding fast to the fundamental principles of liberty, equality, fraternity, to which the republic was dedicated. This was a party whose supreme services to the nation and whose beneficent and lasting work for humanity and the cause of liberty, could hardly have been conceived by its founders. It was a party ordained of God not only to break the galling fetters of the slave, crowning him with manhood, and emancipating the conscience of the master, freeing him from blood-guiltiness, but also destined to lift the nation itself out of its circumscribed provincialism into the sphere of the broadest nationality, giving the republic a foremost place among the great nations of the earth. It was destined even to carry the blessings of liberty to other peoples and climes. Cuba and Porto Rico now rejoice, as the Philippines certainly will later on.

The standard bearer of this party in this historic campaign, Abraham Lincoln, was raised up, equipped, and called to the Presidency of the republic, as providentially as Moses was called to lead Israel out of Egypt. He was the ideal man for the hour.

The slaveholding oligarchy interpreted Lincoln's election to mean that their power was broken, their dominion overthrown, and that the institution of slavery was no longer safe, within the Union. The reasoning was swift and direct. But slavery must be saved at any price; if not in the Union, then out of it; peacefully if possible, by war if necessary. It was but a step to the plunge into the dark abyss of secession. Secession and the founding of a great slaveholding empire, which had been an open threat for decades, now seemed imminent. The clouds of war were gathering. The murmurs, rumblings, and heated utterances were so foreboding that it

21

was deemed wise and prudent for President-elect Lincoln to go secretly a portion of the way from his State of Illinois to the seat of government at Washington, because of well-grounded fears of assassination.

Lincoln's inaugural address was pacific, but firm. He declared that his most solemn obligation and paramount duty was to enforce the Constitution and preserve the Union. Whether the leaders of the South did, or did not commit treason when they took up arms and sought to overthrow the government of their country is not a part of this discussion. There seems to be no ground for doubt, however, that many who had taken the oath of office to uphold and defend the Constitution and government of the United States were actively engaged in planning and plotting to overthrow the Constitution and to destroy the government to which they had plighted their word and honor. It is enough to say that the secession of Southern States followed the inauguration of Lincoln. These leaders plunged the nation into the bloodiest internecine conflict that history records. Amid the loud diapason of the cannonade the institution of human slavery went down forever, "and the government at Washington still lives."

The storm and stress of the antislavery agitation developed many magnificent characters who lend lustre and renown to the American name. Men and women of never dying fame, — Charles Sumner, John Brown, William Lloyd Garrison, Wendell Phillips, Dr. Gamaliel Bailey, Fred Douglass, Henry Highland Garnet, Lucretia Mott, Owen Lovejoy, Robert Morris, Ben Wade, Peter S. Porter, Henry Ward Beecher, John Greenleaf Whittier, Harriet Beecher Stowe, William Henry Furness, Henry Wadsworth Longfellow, and others — gave intellectual and moral splendor and grandeur to the cause, and quickened and lightened up the smoldering conscience of the people. They shared the feelings and were inspired by the brave words of William Lloyd Garrison, who said: "I am in earnest, I will not equivocate, I will not excuse, I will not retreat a single inch, and I will be heard. I solicit no man's praise, I fear no man's censure. The liberty of a people is the gift of God and Nature. Neither God nor the world will judge us by our profession, but by our practices."

In the great transformation which such persons wrought in public sentiment, they approach unto those, "who through faith subdued kingdoms, wrought righteousness, obtained promises, stopped the mouths of lions, quenched the violence of fire, escaped the edge of the sword, out of weakness were made strong, waxed valiant in fight, turned to flight the armies of the aliens."

Purely as a matter of history and not in a censorious spirit, it may be said that in the discussion of the prosecution of the war, the South can hardly escape free from blame for much that was rash, and some things that were needlessly cruel and inhuman. Its treatment of Union prisoners was often cruel, and sometimes deliberately and purposely so. The account of Andersonville, Libby, and other prison pens, where captured Union soldiers were held, disclosed an awful and most shocking story of their experiences and treatment. Mr. Blaine, in an address in Congress on this point, said: "I have read over the details of those atrocious murders of the Duke of Alva in the Low Countries, which are always mentioned with a thrill of horror throughout Christendom. I have read the details of the massacre of St. Bartholomew, that stand out in history as one of the atrocities beyond imagination. I have read anew the horrors untold and unimaginable of the Spanish Inquisition. And I here before God, measuring my words, knowing their extent and import, declare that neither the deeds of the Duke of Alva in the Low Countries, nor the massacre of St. Bartholomew, nor the thumb-screws and engines of torture of the Spanish Inquisition begin to compare in atrocity with the hideous crime of Andersonville."

The South's attitude towards colored soldiers and the white officers commanding them was indefensible. When a nation clothes a man with the uniform of its soldiers and puts a rifle into his hand, and sends him to the firing line, it is bound to protect him in all the rights of a soldier. To put a money reward on the head of white officers of colored troops, or to threaten to shoot or hang such soldiers, and shoot or punish their officers if captured is scarcely justifiable. The Confederate Congress enacted this extreme law: " That every white person, being a commissioned officer or acting as such, who, during the present war shall command negroes or mulattoes in arms against the Confederate States, or who shall arm, train, organize, or prepare negroes or mulattoes for military service against the Confederate States, or who shall voluntarily aid negroes or mulattoes in any military enterprise, attack, or conflict in such service, shall be deemed as inciting servile insurrection, and shall, if captured, be put to death or otherwise punished at the discretion of the Court." The law also provided for hanging or shooting colored soldiers captured, or for selling them into slavery.

But neither the colored soldiers nor white officers were daunted or terrified. The best exemplification of this is the favorite camp song of the Black Regiments, which ran in part as follows: —

> " Fremont he told us, when the cruel war begun,
> How to save the Union, and how it must be done;
> But ' Old Kentuck' swore so hard, father ' Abe ' had his fears,
> And wondered what to do with the colored volunteers.

> " Jeff Davis said he 'd hang 'em if he should catch 'em armed.
> That 's a mighty bad thing, but they ain't at all alarmed;
> First he 's got to catch 'em 'live, 'fore to hang is clear,
> And that 's what will save the colored volunteers.

> " Then give us the flag all free without a slave,
> We 'll fight and defend it, as the fathers did so brave ;
> So, forward, boys, forward ! 't is the year of Jubilee !
> God bless America, we 'll help to make her free."

The desecration of the body of Colonel Robert Gould Shaw was a dreadful mistake. This gallant young hero fell at the head of his black troops, the immortal 54th Massachusetts Regiment, on the parapet of Fort Wagner, near Charleston. When information was sought as to his body, the curt reply was: " He is buried with his niggers."

Colonel Norwood P. Hallowell of the 55th Massachusetts Regiment, in an address before the Military Historical Society of Massachusetts, says: "The manner of Colonel Shaw's burial has been circumstantially related by two Confederate officers, — Major McDonald, Fifty-first North Carolina, and Captain H. W. Hendricks, — both of whom were present at the time. Colonel Shaw's body was stripped of all his clothing save his undershirt and drawers. This desecration of the dead was done by one Charles Blake and others. The body was carried within the fort and there exposed for a time. It was then carried without the fort and buried in a trench with the negroes."

Colonel Shaw fell on July 18, 1863, and of him Colonel Hallowell further says: "Colonel Shaw was in the twenty-sixth year of his age, — how young it seems now! — and had seen two years of hard service in the Army of the Potomac. His clean-cut face, quick, decided step, and singular charm of manner, full of grace and virtue, bespoke the hero. The immortal charge of his black regiment reads like a page of the Iliad or a story from Plutarch. I have always thought that in the great war with the slave power the figure that stands out in boldest relief is that of Colonel Shaw. There were many others as brave and devoted as he, — the humblest private who sleeps in yonder cemetery or fills an unknown grave in the South is as much entitled to our gratitude, — but to no others was given an equal opportunity. By the earnestness of his convictions, the unselfishness of his character, his championship of an enslaved race, and the manner of his death, all the conditions are given to make Shaw the best historical exponent of the underlying cause, the real meaning of the war. He was the fair type of all that was brave, generous, beautiful, and of all that was best worth fighting for in the war of the slave-holders' Rebellion."

This recently made estimate of Colonel Shaw's character and place in history was shared by many notable Americans who were in the heat of the fray, some of whom have been gathered unto their fathers.

Charles Sumner said: "I know no soldier's death finer than that of a young commander, at the head of his men, on the parapet of an enemy's fort, which he had entered by storm."

Thomas Hughes declared: "It was the grandest sepulchre earned by any soldier in this century."

The New York *Times* said: "He was one of the young gentlemen whom this war has developed as a soldier and immortalized as a patriot and martyr. Of high social position, surrounded by everything to make life dear to him, he accepted the position of colonel of a colored regiment to help set at rest the question of respectability of that arm of the service."

Charles A. Dana wrote to Colonel Shaw's parents: "From the first I have watched his career as a soldier with a tender presentiment that he was to fill a bright place among the martyrs of liberty. With the grief of my love for him and for you, there is mingled a noble consolation, a thrill of almost joy, especially when I remember that he died a leader of the outcast and the oppressed. Such a death of such a man would renew my faith if I had doubted concerning the end. God governs, and the lives of so many among the best of his children are not offered up in vain."

Governor Andrew spoke of him in a message to the Massachusetts Legislature as "that gallant young American whose spotless life, whose chivalrous character, whose noble death there is no marble white enough to commemorate."

Henry Ward Beecher wrote from Europe, where he was upholding the cause of the Union: "I bear your burden with you and yours, and I cease not to bear all your pierced and sorrowing hearts to that wounded heart who consoles evermore with wonderful love and tenderness."

John Lothrop Motley wrote: "When we all of us have been long gathered into the common granary, sculptors, painters, and poets will delight to reproduce that beautiful vision of undying and heroic youth, and eyes not yet created will dwell upon it with affection and pride."

The New York *World* said: "The brutality which sought to wreak its vengeance upon the senseless clay of what had been a fearless foe, could not be more nobly chastised than it is by this lofty and living pride."

This had reference to Colonel Shaw's father's statement: "Our darling son, our hero, has received at the hands of the rebels the most fitting burial possible. They buried him with his brave, devoted followers, who fell dead over him and around him. The poor, benighted wretches thought they were heaping indignities upon his dead body, but the act recoils on themselves, and proves them absolutely incapable of appreciating noble qualities. They thought to give additional pang to the bruised hearts of his friends; but we would not have him buried elsewhere if we could. If a wish of ours would do it, we would not have his body taken away from those who loved him so devotedly, with whom and for whom he gave his life."

Ralph Waldo Emerson wrote tenderly of him, and dedicated a poem to him, closing: —

> "So nigh is grandeur to our dust,
> So near is God to man,
> When duty whispers low, 'Thou must,'
> The youth replies, 'I can.'"

James Russell Lowell said: "I would rather have my name known and blessed as his will be through all the hovels

of an outcast race than blazing from all the trumpets of repute." And in a poem on the heroism of Colonel Shaw,
Mr. Lowell also wrote:—

> " Brave, good, and true,
> I see him stand before me now,
> And read again on that young brow,
>   Where every hope was new,
> *How sweet were life!* Yet, by the mouth firm set,
> And look made up for Duty's utmost debt,
>   I could divine he knew
> That death within the sulphurous hostile lines
> In the mere wreck of nobly pitched designs
> Plucks heart's-ease, and not rue.

> " Happy their end
> Who vanish down life's evening stream
> Placid as swans that drift in dream
>   Round the next river bend !
> Happy long life, with honor at the close,
> Friends' painless tears, the softened thought of foes !
>   And yet, like him, to spend
> All at a gush, keeping our first faith sure
> From mid-life's doubt and eld's contentment. poor,
>   What more could Fortune send?

> " Right in the van,
> On the red rampart's slippery swell,
> With heart that beat a charge, he fell
>   Foeward, as befits a man ;
> But the high soul burns on to light men's feet
> Where death for noble ends makes dying sweet."

Why these splendid tributes to a young man not twenty-
six years of age ? It was recognized that he was " the
best historical exponent of the underlying cause, the real
meaning of the war "; " the figure that stands out in bold
relief," and dared all for liberty and country, justice and
humanity.

Colonel Robert Gould Shaw, waving his sword on the parapet of Wagner at the head of the 54th Massachusetts Regiment, thrust an idea and a force into the mighty conflict

which neither side had reckoned on at the opening of hostilities, and which many competent to judge declared turned the balance of the scales. It brought to the Union arms about two hundred thousand colored soldiers, and as many more colored men employed in various lines of labor and service.

When the war began, the South regarded the slaves as the strongest pillar of support in the Confederacy. These were to raise crops for feeding the armies, to build fortifications, to do other service in camp, and to care for the women and children. But as the war progressed, it developed that the negroes in the cotton fields, the rice swamps, the corn fields were quite a different factor from the negroes in uniform, with musket in hand and in battle array. What the South counted its greatest strength was in fact its greatest weakness.

The North was quick to seize the advantage. The negroes were equal to the emergency. " The grand historic moment which comes to a race only once in many centuries came to them, and they recognized it." The slaves were used most effectively against the masters. So that Colonel Shaw's larger service to his country and humanity was in demonstrating at a critical moment the availability and heroism of the negro as a soldier. It was at a time when the cause of the Union was wavering, and, as Colonel Hallowell says, " when volunteering had ceased, when the draft was a partial failure, and the bounty system a senseless extravagance." While it is true that the negro had rendered invaluable services in the Revolutionary War, and later in the war of 1812, yet practically, for three quarters of a century he had been under the lash of the heartless slave-driver, and had ceased to be an object of consideration except to a remnant of God-fearing philanthropists and courageous humanitarians. The organized government was his oppressor.

It is just to say that Colonel Shaw gave to the colored race a new status. He brought to the race the habiliments of manhood, and the race crowned him with immortal fame. He was the first to lead the negroes in large numbers into the baptism of fire and to prove their mettle. Thenceforth neither the North nor the South doubted. Colonel Shaw himself was not without some realization of the magnitude and glory of his mission, for in a letter to the lady he was to wed, he wrote: " I shall feel that what I have to do is to prove that a negro can be made a good soldier. . . . There is great prejudice against it, but now that it has become a government matter, that will probably wear away. At any rate I sha'n't be frightened out of it by its unpopularity. I feel convinced that I shall never regret having taken this step."

That he took great pride in his black troops and had full faith in their soldierly qualities may be evidenced by a letter he wrote of the first battle in which he led them against the Confederates on James Island, Charleston Harbor, July 16, 1863. He said: "You don't know what a fortunate day this has been for me and for all of us, excepting some poor fellows who were killed and wounded. General Terry sent me word he was highly gratified with the behavior of my men, and the officers and privates of other regiments praise us very much." He also wrote: " We hear nothing but praise of the 54th on all hands."

Two days after this he led the charge on Fort Wagner, saying to his friends these brave words: " We shall take the fort, or die there. Good-by."

His life blood was poured out on the soil of South Carolina and enriched it. His memory is a heritage to the nation.

The Shaw School at Charleston for colored youths was named in honor of him. The Shaw University at Raleigh, North Carolina, a flourishing institution for colored pupils, also commemorates his memory.

Harvard College has a bust of him in marble, carved by the colored artist Edmonia Lewis, once a slave, but now a

SLAVERY AND ITS ABOLITION

sculptor in Italy; and in Memorial Hall at Harvard there is also a life-size portrait of the hero of Fort Wagner.

Massachusetts has erected a monument in bronze and marble, on the Boston Common, directly in front of her State Capitol to perpetuate his memory, and that of "his brave and devoted followers." The inscription, composed by President Eliot of Harvard University, is as follows:—

TO THE FIFTY–FOURTH   OF MASSACHUSETTS
REGIMENT   INFANTRY
THE WHITE OFFICERS

TAKING LIFE AND HONOR IN THEIR HANDS CAST IN THEIR LOT WITH MEN OF A DESPISED RACE UNPROVED IN WAR AND RISKED DEATH AS INCITERS OF SERVILE INSURRECTION IF TAKEN PRISONERS. BESIDES ENCOUNTERING ALL THE COMMON PERILS OF CAMP MARCH AND BATTLE.

THE BLACK RANK AND FILE

VOLUNTEERED WHEN DISASTER CLOUDED THE UNION CAUSE. SERVED WITHOUT PAY FOR EIGHTEEN MONTHS TILL GIVEN THAT OF WHITE TROOPS. FACED THREATENED ENSLAVEMENT IF CAPTURED. WERE BRAVE IN ACTION. PATIENT UNDER HEAVY AND DANGEROUS LABORS. AND CHEERFUL AMID HARDSHIPS AND PRIVATIONS.

TOGETHER

THEY GAVE TO THE NATION AND THE WORLD UNDYING PROOF THAT AMERICANS OF AFRICAN DESCENT POSSESS THE PRIDE COURAGE AND DEVOTION OF THE PATRIOT SOLDIER. ONE HUNDRED AND EIGHTY THOUSAND SUCH AMERICANS ENLISTED UNDER THE UNION FLAG IN (M.D.C.C.LXIII–M.D.C.C.LXV)

But above all Colonel Shaw will live in the hearts of all his countrymen who appreciate noble manhood and the virtues of heroism, and especially in the hearts of the multiplying millions of colored people whose value and power as citizens and as soldiers he first conspicuously and convincingly impressed on the nation.

31

Of Fort Wagner, Colonel N. P. Hallowell says : "It was armed with eighteen guns of various calibres, of which number fifteen covered the only approach by land, which was along the beach and was the width of scarcely half a company front in one place. This approach was swept not only by the guns of Wagner, but also by those of Battery Gregg on Cumming's Point, the very northern extremity of the Island, and by those of Sumter, and it was enfiladed by several heavily armed batteries on James and Sullivan Islands. Our Fifty-fourth Massachusetts (Colonel Shaw at the head) led the column. In quick time that devoted column went on to its destiny, heedless of the gaps made in its ranks by the relentless fire of the guns of Wagner, of Gregg, of Sumter, of James and Sullivan Islands. When within two hundred yards of the fort, the rebel garrison swarmed from the bomb-proof to the parapet, and to the artillery was added the compact and destructive fire of fourteen hundred rifles at two hundred yards' range, a storm of solid shot, shells, grape, canister, and bullets, the two hundred yards were passed, the ditch was crossed, the parapet was gained, and the State and National Colors planted thereon."

The bearer of the State flag was killed and it fell into the fort, and its possession brought about one of the fiercest hand to hand struggles witnessed during the war. As the bearer of the national flag was killed, Sergeant William H. Carney sprang forward and grasped the flag. His valor was attested by wounds in both legs, in the breast, and the right arm. He won cheers from his comrades by shouting : "The old flag never touched the ground."

Lewis H. Douglass, the son of Fred Douglass, was praised by both white and colored for great heroism. He was among the first to mount the parapet, and shouted : "Come on, boys, and fight for God and Governor Andrew." Captain C. J. Russell and W. H. Simkins were especially mentioned among the brave officers killed. Among the officers wounded were

Lieutenant-Colonel E. N. Hallowell; Captains Appleton, Jones, Willard, and Pope; Adjutant James; Lieutenants Homans, Smith, Pratt, Tucker, and Emerson. Lieutenant Emerson sheathed his sword, picked up a musket of a fallen comrade, and used it effectively.

Private George Wilson was shot through both shoulders and yet refused to go to the rear.

Captain Emilio, and Lieutenant-Colonel E. N. Hallowell, in turn, succeeded Colonel Shaw in command.

Colonel N. P. Hallowell also says: "The regiment went into action with twenty-two officers and six hundred and fifty enlisted men. Fourteen officers were killed or wounded. Two hundred and fifty-five enlisted men were killed or wounded. Prisoners, not wounded, twenty. Total casualties, officers and men, two hundred and sixty-nine, or forty per cent. The character of the wounds attests the nature of the contest. There were wounds from bayonet thrusts, sword cuts, pike thrusts, and hand grenades; and there were heads and arms broken and smashed by the butt-ends of muskets."

General Hagood, the Confederate commander of the fort said: "It was a dearly purchased compliment to let them lead the assault. Their Colonel Shaw was killed upon the parapet, and the regiment almost annihilated." Lieutenant Iredel Jones, another Confederate officer, said: "The negroes fought gallantly and were headed by as brave a colonel as ever lived. He mounted the breastworks waving his sword, and at the head of his regiment, and he and a negro orderly sergeant fell dead over the inner crest of the works. The negroes were as fine looking a set as I ever saw — large, strong, muscular fellows."

General Strong — who, with the approval of General Seymour, offered the place of honor to Colonel Shaw and his men in leading the attack on Wagner — rode up to the regiment just before the assault and encouraged them, saying: "Boys, I am a Massachusetts man, and I know you

3   33

will fight for the honor of the State. I am sorry you must go into the fight tired and hungry." They had marched all night previously in a thunder-storm and had covered six miles that afternoon, subsisting scantily on the hard tack and coffee carried in their haversacks.

As a matter of history it must be stated that colored regiments had already been formed in South Carolina, in Louisiana, and in Kansas, and had been under fire, but on a comparatively small scale as yet, and had attracted little attention in the Northern mind. The First South Carolina Volunteers, under Colonel Thomas Wentworth Higginson, was the first colored regiment in the field.

The enlistment of Colonel Shaw's regiment was accompanied with grave apprehension, and John A. Andrew, the great war Governor of Massachusetts, voiced his deep concern in presenting the colors. Many prominent people were present. Governor Andrew said : " My own personal honor, if I have any, is identified with yours. I stand or fall as a man and a magistrate with the rise and the fall in the history of the 54th Massachusetts Regiment. I know not, sir, when in all human history to any given one thousand men in arms there has been permitted a work at once so proud, so precious, and so full of hope and glory as the work committed to you. And may the infinite mercy of the Almighty God attend you every hour of every day through all the experiences and vicissitudes of that dangerous life in which you have embarked.

" May the God of our fathers cover your head in the day of battle. This flag, sir, has connected with its history the most touching and sacred memory. It comes to your regiment from the mother, sister, and family relations of one of the dearest and noblest soldier boys of Massachusetts. I need but utter the name of Lieutenant Putnam in order to excite in every heart the tenderest emotions of fond regard or the strongest feelings of patriotic fire."

Happily indeed for the colored race, and for the republic, the soldier boys of the 54th Massachusetts Regiment not only met, but surpassed the highest expectations of friends, and put to confusion doubters, critics, and detractors.

Mr. Ezra A. Cook, now a publisher at Chicago, but then on the firing line says: " The bravery of this colored regiment was so conspicuous as to revolutionize the sentiment of the Federal soldiers, a majority of whom had been opposed to the colored soldiery up to that time. Those who had the most fiercely denounced their employment previously, after this assault expressed pleasure at being put into the same brigade with the colored troops."

Fort Wagner opened a new epoch in American history. It changed the thought and current of national life. It showed and sanctified the chattel slave — a MAN.

It only remains to be said that the broad mantle of charity now covers all these harrowing events. The experience was bitter, terrible; the cost, staggering. But they are thought of now only as matters of history. The lessons they teach, however, are not to be minimized or forgotten by either the North or the South. But the Civil War is a thing of the past. It should be and is regarded as a by-gone event. No Southerner is judged to-day by the part he took in it. So is slavery a by-gone condition. There is and can be no place in the life and government of this great republic for the retainment of its barbarous traditions and brutal ideals. It would make for the peace and well-being of the nation for the white people of the South to come to this realization. The God of the universe made the negro a man. The nation clothed him with citizenship. His services in peace and in war confirm unto him every right of an American.

Let the white people of the South cease to live in the past, and rather let them profit by the awful lesson with all its solemn and bitter warnings, that —

" Long trains of ills may pass unheeded, dumb,
But vengeance is behind and justice is to come."

Let them with conscience void of offence toward God and man face the future, and, " forgetting the things which are behind, and looking forward to the things which are before," let them establish law and order and demonstrate their capacity for self-government by working out a government which shall bestow no special favors or privileges on men because God made them white ; and which shall do no injustice to men because God made them black.

Then indeed shall righteousness set up her habitations ; truth and justice shall be enthroned ; and civilization, Christianity, and government in the Southland shall stand redeemed, regenerated, and disenthralled — a glory forever.

CHAPTER II

RECONSTRUCTION AND THE SOUTHERN "BLACK CODE"

THE close of the war was followed by the era of Reconstruction. The war suppressed the rebellion; reconstruction brought forth order out of the resulting chaos.

This era of Reconstruction witnessed the issue of the Proclamation of Amnesty by President Johnson, which pardoned all who took part in the rebellion, except a few thousands who held high civil or military or diplomatic positions before and during the war, and made provision that even these could obtain pardon by the mere asking for it and swearing allegiance to the Constitution and Government of the United States. This period also witnessed the enactment of the "Black Code" by the legislatures of the seceding states; the enactment by the Congress of the United States of the Thirteenth, Fourteenth, and Fifteenth Amendments to the Constitution; the overthrow of the "Black Code;" the final annihilation of the institution of human slavery in the South; the fixing forever the status of American citizenship; the rehabilitation of the seceding states, and the resumption of their autonomy in the Union; the mustering out and return to their homes and the marts of trade of more than a million "citizen soldiers," 200,000 of them colored, crowned with glory and honor, who counted it not dear unto themselves to offer their lives a willing sacrifice on the altar of their country, and who, by their deeds of valor and heroic sacrifices, smothered the rebellion, preserved the republic from dismemberment, and vindicated the sovereignty of the nation.

The era of Reconstruction was fraught with gravest solicitude and crowded with vital, complicated, vexatious, and far-reaching issues: issues that not only affected the status, liberty, and rights of the colored people, but were of equally supreme importance to the republic and to constitutional government, and in fact of greatest concern to the whole human family, since it seemingly involved the matter of the life or death of the experiment of self-government by the people.

It was an era which tried men's souls. Fortunately for the republic and the vast and far-reaching interests at stake, or hanging in the balance, there were at the helm and standing guard on the deck of the "Old Ship of State" men trained in self-mastery and self-restraint; men rooted and grounded in the principles of liberty and republican government; men responsive to the dictates of humanity and Christianity, sympathetic and charitable; men who faced with calmness and composure the passions within their own councils and the defiance hurled at them from the South; men broad in learning and culture; men with a genius for statecraft and masters in statesmanship; men who saw and knew the *right* and dared to do it.

In the foundation of the republic, as laid by the fathers, there was one radical, vital defect, which has ever remained a peril to the majestic structure of liberty and self-government which they built so well. It was the rotten stone of human slavery,— an ever present challenge and reproach to the Declaration of Independence, and always a menace to the peace and perpetuity of American institutions.

The leaders of the Reconstruction era dug out this rotten stone, and replaced it with indestructible foundation-stone: Equality of rights for all men before the law — the only safe and enduring foundation for the Temple of Liberty. Thus they crystallized into law the most glorious sentiment of the ages: "A government conceived in liberty and dedicated to the principle that all men are created equal." In placing the republic squarely, solidly, and for all time on this broad foundation, "which time cannot wither, nor age decay," they conserved the liberties won and progress achieved in centuries of struggles, and revived the drooping hopes of mankind by making it positive that "this nation, under God, shall have a new birth of freedom." Unholy is the hand that would remove this foundation-stone, hewn of Heaven, making all men equal under the law of the land, as they are equal under the law of nature and nature's God! Vile is the tongue that would assault the temple of the nation's liberty and the world's hope built thereon!

The white people of the South, wherever dominated in the main by unbalanced, superheated leadership, have been wrought into a frenzy,— a frenzy dangerous to themselves and to the best interests of their fair land; dangerous to civilization and to the peace and prosperity of the nation. Reason, common-sense, and the nobler instincts of humanity seem to have left them for the time. Primarily, this is due to the influences begotten of the barbarism incident to the institution of human slavery; for the barbarism of slavery has not even yet exacted its last penalty.

The nation accepted and nurtured slavery, and it is still suffering the consequences of its noxious poisons. Let the nation be warned of the more serious consequences which would follow the obliteration of the liberty and hope of the colored people, and the consignment of them to practical serfdom. It is an adage hoary with age that "the dancers must pay the fiddlers." Great wrongs are sure to bring great retributions. But it ought to be plain to every one, including the white people of the South, that the ideals and standards of the defunct slaveholding oligarchy can never again prevail in this land over the holy principles of liberty and free institutions.

The violent Southern leaders trace their grievances back to the events of the Reconstruction era. They make many misleading and mischievous declarations about the "damnable crime" committed on the white people of the South by giving the negro the ballot, and restoring to him the rights of "life, liberty, and the pursuit of happiness," the heritage of every human being. They exercise extraordinary care, however, to omit absolutely all reference to the causes and conditions which made negro suffrage a possibility, namely:

First, the war which the South waged against the nation in its desperate struggles for four years to rend and destroy it.

Second, the enactment by Southern legislatures — composed entirely of ex-Confederates, after the war had closed, and the white people of the South were given an absolutely free hand under the proclamation of President Johnson to reconstruct their respective States — of the "Black Code," the most barbarous series of laws ever written by a civilized people.

Third, the flat, defiant refusal of the white people of many Southern states to reconstruct their state governments in harmony with the changed conditions produced by the war, as embodied in the Proclamation of Emancipation and the Thirteenth Amendment to the Constitution of the United States, which abolished slavery.

Fourth, the curt and indignant refusal of the white people of some Southern states even to participate in such reconstruction unless they were permitted to have their own way in re-establishing a new form of slavery, — to be in some respects even worse than the system which the war had overthrown.

But if a crime was committed on the white people of the South, there must have been criminals who committed the crime. Who were these criminals? Among the great leaders of this era who had more or less to do in formulating and completing the measures of reconstruction, there may be mentioned, without any attempt at invidious distinction, Charles Sumner, Henry Winter Davis, William Pitt Fessenden, Benjamin F. Wade, Henry Wilson, Lyman Trumbull,

James G. Blaine, George S. Boutwell, Zachary Chandler, James A. Garfield, N. P. Banks, Lot M. Morrill, Roscoe Conkling, John Sherman, James W. Grimes, Ira P. Harris, Jacob M. Howard, Thaddeus Stevens, Elihu B. Washburn, Justin S. Morrill, John A. Bingham, Henry T. Blow, George F. Edmunds, Oliver P. Morton, Schuyler Colfax, Benjamin F. Butler, H. L. Dawes, W. B. Washburn, W. D. Kelley, Rutherford B. Hayes, Samuel Shellabarger, James M. Ashley, S. M. Cullom, John A. Logan, Thomas W. Ferry, W. B. Allison, Ignatius Donnelly, Philetus Sawyer, William Windom, G. M. Dodge, William Lawrence, C. C. Washburn, John A. Kasson, Russell Thayer, George F. Hoar, James Harlan, Matt. H. Carpenter, Hannibal Hamlin, Carl Schurz, Eugene Hale, O. D. Conger, Timothy O. Howe, and Noah Davis. Here is a roster of American statesmen the equal of any that ever faced a great crisis in the history of the nation. Shall the memory of these men and their compeers rest under the black imputation of criminality? What serious citizen would think of mentioning in the same breath these devoted patriots, well-poised and self-contained, with the leaders like Tillman, Money, McHenery, Vardaman, not to mention " Tray, Blanche, and Sweet-heart," et al., who to-day seek to dominate the fair Southland?

The Northern leaders of this era were supported in every step taken by the great commanders who suppressed the rebellion : Generals Grant, Sherman, Sheridan, Hooker, Howard, Hartranft, Chamberlain, Cox, Burnside, Meade, Miles, Hawley, Gresham, Anderson, Thomas, Birney, and their comrades of the land forces, and Admirals Farragut and Porter and others of the naval forces. The movement was also supported by the great leaders of public sentiment in the nation, headed by Henry Ward Beecher ; the whole being reinforced by the twenty millions of loyal Americans who willingly contributed the treasure and blood which saved the Union and emancipated the slave.

If the Northern civil leaders of this era were criminals, or committed a crime against the South, then the great commanders of the army and navy and the vast majority of the people of the loyal States were sharers in the crime. In such a case virtue and patriotism resided only with the men who used their might and main to destroy the republic, and afterwards to re-establish slavery. To lay the taint of criminality, directly or indirectly, by inference or otherwise, on the leaders of reconstruction, the saviors of the republic, the master builders who launched it on its "new birth of freedom" — is in itself a shocking offence to the patriotic citizen. Within a brief period General Sherman has been referred to by Southern leaders as the "brute who burned Columbia," and General Canby as the "scoundrel who fastened carpet-bag government on the Carolinas;" John Brown as "an old fanatic and murderer," and General Sherman's army as composed of "chicken thieves, robbers, bums, and the scum and filth of Northern cities," who preyed on the people of the South.

These charges are false. The memory of the great statesmen and leaders of the Reconstruction era, and as well the brave men who risked all on land and sea to save the nation's life, lies embalmed in the hearts of a grateful and loyal people, and should be held as a sacred legacy, free from detraction and defamation. They not only did not commit a crime against the white people of the South, but on the contrary displayed a gracious magnanimity and generosity in dealing with the people of that section; and in handling the delicate, perplexing issues of their day, they showed a conservatism that is unmatched in recorded history. Generously they offered the olive branch of peace and good-will; but the South rejected it with scorn and contempt.

Says Mr. Blaine, in his "Twenty Years of Congress": "A great opportunity was now given to the South. Only a few weeks before, they had all been expecting harsh treatment, many, indeed, anticipated punishment, not a few were dejectedly looking forward to a life of exile and want. The President's policy, which had been framed for him by Mr. Seward, changed all this. Confidence took the place of apprehension, the fear of punishment was removed, those who, conscious of guilt, had been dreading expatriation were bidden by the supreme authority of the nation to stay in their own homes and to assist in building up the waste and desolate places. Never in the history of the world had so mighty a rebellion been subdued; never had any rebellion been followed by treatment so lenient, forgiving, and generous on the part of the triumphant government. The great mass of those who had resisted the national authority were restored to all their rights of citizenship by the simple taking of an oath of future loyalty, and those excepted from immediate reinstatement were promised full forgiveness on the slightest exhibition of repentance and good works." And this before the ballot was given to the colored people and before the nation was ripe for its bestowal.

For a clearer understanding of this matter it may be well to explain here that there were three distinct efforts at reconstruction:

First: the effort at reconstruction during the war, directed by President Lincoln.

Second: the attempt at reconstruction immediately after the close of the war, directed by President Johnson, who succeeded Lincoln after the latter's assassination.

Third: reconstruction proper, when the Congress took the whole matter in hand, and not rashly or hastily, but after serious and extended deliberations, full and free debates in both Houses, and repeated endorsements by the people at' elections, covering a period of over five years from the adoption of the Thirteenth Amendment to the Constitution to the adoption of the Fifteenth Amendment, brought to a righteous and irrevocable settlement all of the pressing, complex, and absorbing questions involved in the war, in slavery, and in our constitutional government.

As indicating the easy stages and progression of reconstruction legislation, it may be stated that the Thirteenth Amendment was passed by the Congress January 30, 1865; the enlargement of the powers of the Freedmen's Bureau, July, 1865; the Act protecting the civil rights of the colored people, April 9, 1866; the Fourteenth Amendment, June 13, 1866; the famous Reconstruction Act, March 2, 1867; and the Fifteenth Amendment was ratified March 30, 1870.

We will now consider these three attempts at reconstruction, in the order named.

At the very opening of hostilities President Lincoln adopted the eminently sagacious and statesmanlike policy of cultivating, by every possible means and concessions, the friendship and loyalty of those slave states and parts of slave states bordering on the free states, including Maryland, West Virginia, East Tennessee, Kentucky, Missouri. By his wonderful tact and strategy he succeeded in holding them from open revolt against the Union, although the great body of their citizens sympathized with the Confederacy. This policy was invaluable, in that it nerved the loyalists in the South, kept many hesitating ones in line, brought valuable support to the Union arms, kept up representation from some of the slave states in Congress, and thus maimed the Confederacy. In furtherance of his policy to reconstruct the seceding states so far as possible and encourage the loyalists and hamper the Confederacy, he issued a proclamation to the effect that, in any state where ten righteous men out of a hundred could be found, — where "one tenth of the legal voters" were loyal to the Union,— they might reconstruct and reorganize the state government, and that such government would be recognized. Military commanders were instructed, wherever feasible, to assist and even to take the initiative in reconstructing such governments.

The state of Virginia adopted its ordinance of secession on the 17th of April, 1861. And in less than a month afterwards, on the 13th of May, the loyalists of the Old Dominion, residents largely of the western part of the state, met at Wheeling, and "denounced the ordinance of secession and pledged their loyalty to the national government and their obedience to its laws." It was but a little more than a month later that a delegated convention met, reconstructed the state government by the election of the usual officers, and senators and representatives were sent to Congress and were admitted ; and the reconstructed government of Virginia was recognized as the legal government of the state. But as the loyalists were domiciled almost entirely in the western section of the state and had no control or power outside of that section — the remainder of the state, and the great body of the people being hopelessly in the Confederacy, — the claim that they really represented the state of Virginia did not seem, as time went on, to be wholly tenable or satisfactory. So the loyalists went through the usual form and organized a new state, and there rose phoenix-like the progressive, prosperous, and rapidly developing commonwealth of West Virginia — which thus owes her existence as a sovereign state to the loyalty of her sons to the republic in this great crisis.

And so it came to pass that Virginia, the historic Old Dominion, in her gigantic efforts through her masterful Lee, her chivalric " Stonewall " Jackson, her redoubtable Johnson and Johnston, and her fighting legions, ever ready for the fray, was the most important factor in the attempt to dismember the Union ; but she alone, of all the states of the Confederacy, was dismembered. Much of the hardest fighting and wear and waste of war was on her soil ; she probably lost a larger proportion of her sons ; and the loss by the " partition " which carved out of her territory the great state of West Virginia probably represents a greater money value to-day than was placed on all the slaves in the South at the outbreak of the war. Is not this an impressive retribution?

The policy of reconstruction under Lincoln was also applied to Tennessee with such good recompense that one of her loyal sons, Andrew Johnson, was nominated for Vice-President by the Republican convention in 1864. Efforts at reconstruction were also made under his direction in Louisiana, with promising results, and in Arkansas and Florida with tentative though not very substantial results. To Governor Hahn of the reconstructed government of Louisiana, Lincoln wrote in March, 1864, advising that the ballot should be given to the colored men: "Let in, as for instance, the very intelligent, and especially those who have fought gallantly in our ranks. They would probably help in some trying time in the future to keep the jewel of liberty in the family of freedom."

This was probably the first utterance from a responsible source in favor of bestowing the ballot on the colored people of the South. It shows to splendid advantage Lincoln's great and noble heart. For the war was still in progress and destined to last, no one knew how long. It did continue for over a year longer. Lincoln's renomination and re-election were hanging in the balance. Serious reverses in the field might have defeated either or both. He was far in advance of the public opinion of the nation. For at this time it was not at all likely that a single Northern state could have been carried on the simple question of negro suffrage. Yet he plainly, positively, unmistakably indicated suffrage for the colored man as a part of his policy in reconstructing the Southern states. His generous nature, his great and noble heart, would have it known that the colored men "who have fought gallantly in our ranks" can be trusted to "help in some trying time in the future to keep the jewel of liberty in the family of freedom."

These words of Lincoln are dwelt upon because they are of deep significance and add to our opinion of his greatness, his fame, when it is considered that the validity of the Emancipation Proclamation was at that time a much debated question. Many strong and learned loyal men in the North doubted the legal right or power of the President alone, even as a war measure, to destroy or confiscate property by proclamation, especially when that property was beyond the control of the government. The slaves were at that time property ; they were also, with unimportant exceptions, within the bounds of the Confederacy and beyond the control of the government. Could the President alone, by mere proclamation, legally destroy and confiscate property which his government did not possess? Would Congress, the people, and the Supreme Court finally sustain him?

This question, pressed by influential sources in the North, weighed heavily on Lincoln. But he was equal to this, as he was to every emergency in the greatest conflict in history. He found strength and comfort in the "higher law" that "the negro was a man, and that no man was good enough to own another man and appropriate the fruits of his labor." And there was the feeling "that slavery drew the sword against the nation and that it should perish by the sword." To the realization of this "higher law" he hoped to bring the nation.

So important and pressing was this question that Lincoln dealt with it in his message to the Congress in December, 1864. In this message the President said : " While I remain in my present position I shall not attempt to retract or modify the Emancipation Proclamation. Nor shall I return to slavery any person who is free by the terms of that Proclamation or by any of the Acts of Congress. If the people should, by whatever mode or means, make it an executive duty to re-enslave such persons, another, and not I, must be their instrument to perform it."

Here is more than a veiled threat, it is an open defiance. Lincoln had just been re-elected to the presidency in November, a month before the message was sent to Congress; and he distinctly tells Congress and the people that he would give up the presidency rather than relinquish the principles of his Emancipation Proclamation; that he would resign his office rather than "return to slavery any person who is free by the terms of that proclamation or by any of the Acts of Congress."

Up to this date the Emancipation Proclamation was the only charter of liberty for the colored people in the South; and the all-important point is, that Lincoln regarded this as sufficient to enable the negroes to wear the uniform of a United States soldier, to be commissioned as officers, to be treated the same as white soldiers, to be protected as prisoners of war, to have common rights, and to vote at the ballot-box.

President Lincoln's deep solicitude for the colored soldiers, his profound interest in them, his unqualified respect for and appreciation of their invaluable services, and his determination that they should receive their full mete of justice, are made manifest in his state papers, public addresses and letters. In his message to Congress in December, 1863, less than a year after the first enlistment of colored soldiers, he said: "Full one hundred thousand of them are now in the United States military service, about one half of which number actually bear arms in the ranks, thus giving the double advantage — of taking so much labor from the insurgents' cause and supplying the places which otherwise might be filled with so many white men." In a speech at Baltimore, April 18, 1864, he said: "Upon a clear conviction of duty, I resolved to turn that element of strength to account; and I am responsible for it to the American people, to the Christian world, to history, and on my final account to God. Having determined to use the negro as a soldier, there is no way but to give him all the protection given to any other soldier."

In a letter of April 4, 1864, he says : "More than a year of trial now shows no loss by it in our foreign relations, none in our home popular sentiment, none in our white military force, — no loss by it anyhow or anywhere. On the contrary, it shows a gain of quite a hundred and thirty thousand soldiers, seamen, and laborers. These are palpable facts, about which, as facts, there can be no cavilling. We have the men, and we could not have them without the measure," — meaning the Emancipation Proclamation. At a public meeting in Baltimore he said : "The black soldier shall have the same protection as the white soldier."

He threatened retaliation, should the Confederates shoot black soldiers when captured, instead of treating them as prisoners of war. He refused to exchange a single Confederate soldier until colored soldiers were recognized by the Confederate government. Again, in a public address he declared : "Negroes, like other people, act from motives. Why should they do anything for us, if we do nothing for them ? If they stake their lives for us, they must be prompted by the strongest of motives, even the promise of freedom. And the promise, being made, must be kept."

In a general order, issued July 30, 1863, Lincoln said: "It is the duty of every government to give protection to its citizens, of whatever class or color or condition, and especially to those who are duly organized as soldiers in the public service. . . . The government of the United States will give the same protection to all its soldiers ; and if the enemy shall sell or enslave any one because of his color, the offence shall be punished by retaliation upon the enemy's prisoners in our possession. It is therefore ordered that for every soldier of the United States killed in violation of the laws of war, a rebel soldier shall be executed ; and for every one enslaved by the enemy, a rebel soldier shall be placed at hard labor on the public works."

In defence of the Emancipation Proclamation in a letter,

4   49

August 26, 1863, he said : " You are dissatisfied with me about the negro. Quite likely there is a difference of opinion between you and myself upon that subject. I certainly wish that all men could be free. . . . You dislike the Emancipation Proclamation. . . . You say it is unconstitutional. I think differently ; I think the Constitution invests its Commander-in-Chief with law of war in time of war. . . . The slaves are property ; . . . by the law of war property, both of the enemies and friends, may be taken when needed. Armies, the world over, destroy enemies' property when they cannot use it, and even destroy their own to keep it from the enemy. . . . But the Proclamation, as law, either is valid or is not valid. If it is not valid, it needs no retraction. If it is valid, it cannot be retracted, any more than the dead can be brought to life. . . . The Emancipation policy and the use of colored troops constitute the heaviest blows yet dealt to the Rebellion."　　　　　　　　　　　　　　　　/

Replying to an address from the workingmen of Manchester and London, England, who wished him success in conquering the rebellion, as by it slavery would be destroyed, and indicated their willingness to bear with patience all privations and sufferings, — for not only great hardships but even starvation faced many in England, owing to the fact that the blockade of Southern ports prevented the shipment of cotton, — Lincoln said : " It has been often ostentatiously represented that the attempt to overthrow this government, which was built upon the foundation of human rights, and to substitute for it one which should rest exclusively on the basis of human slavery, was likely to obtain favor in Europe. I cannot but regard your decisive utterance upon the question as an instance of sublime Christian heroism, which has not been surpassed in any age or country. It is indeed an energetic and reinspiring assurance of the inherent power of truth and the universal triumph of justice, humanity, and freedom."

To a Western delegation he said : " There are now in the service of the United States nearly 200,000 able-bodied colored men, most of them under arms defending and acquiring Union territory. The Democratic strategy demands that those forces be disbanded, and that the masters be conciliated by restoring them to slavery. The black men who now assist Union prisoners to escape are to be converted into our enemies in the vain hope of gaining the good-will of their masters. . . . Abandon all the forts now garrisoned by black men ; take 200,000 from our side and put them in the battle-field or corn-field against us, and we would be compelled to abandon the war in three weeks. We have to hold territory in sickly places. . . . There have been men base enough to propose to me to return to slavery our black warriors of Port Hudson and Olustee, and thus win the respect of the masters they fought. . . . Come what will, I will keep faith with friend and enemy. . . . Freedom has given us 200,000 men raised on Southern soil. It will give us more yet. Just so much it has abstracted from the enemy."

To a colored delegation at Baltimore, presenting him with a handsomely bound copy of the Bible, he said : " I can only say now, as I have often said before, it has always been a sentiment with me that all mankind should be free. . . . I have always acted as I believed was just and right, and done all I could for the good of mankind. . . . In regard to the great Book, I have only to say, it is the best gift which God has ever given to man. All the good of the Saviour of the world is communicated to us through this Book. . . . All those things desirable to men are contained in it."

In his inaugural address, March, 1865, President Lincoln said : " These slaves constitute a peculiar and powerful interest. . . . To strengthen, perpetuate, and extend this interest was the object for which the insurgents would rend the Union by war. . . . It may seem strange that any men should dare to ask a just God's assistance in wringing their bread from the sweat of other men's faces. . . . Fondly do we hope, fervently do we pray that this mighty scourge of war may speedily pass away. Yet, if God wills that it continue until . . . every drop of blood drawn with the lash shall be paid by another drawn with the sword, as was said three thousand years ago, so, still, it must be said that ' the judgments of the Lord are true and righteous altogether.' "

A fact of considerable interest is that the Confederate leaders, who dragged the South into secession with the alleged purpose of establishing a government whose very foundation-stone should be human slavery, should themselves have turned their eyes to these very enslaved negroes to save their cause. They were ever ready to use the negro for their selfish ends.

The Honorable Judah P. Benjamin, Secretary of State for the Confederacy, in a public speech at Richmond, advocating the arming of the negroes, said : " There are 700,000 males among the slave population capable of bearing arms — set them free and arm them and let them fight the Yankees." On the recommendation of General Lee and President Davis of the Confederacy, a bill to arm the slaves passed one House of the Confederate Congress, and lacked only one vote of passing the other House. Nevertheless, this same Confederate Congress actually passed a law to shoot white union officers commanding colored soldiers, and shoot colored soldiers when captured.

President Lincoln, in a public address in Washington, true to that humor and irony characteristic of him, said : " As they need only one vote, I would be glad to send my vote through the lines to help them out." He felt that they would certainly have so many more soldiers shooting at them. The well-grounded fear that the armed negroes would desert to the Union side defeated the measure. But if these 700,000 slaves had been thrown into the breach on the Confederate side, and had fought loyally, under promise of freedom, it does not seem possible that the Union could have been saved. But it was not to be so. God was leading on!

The feeling of love, gratitude, and reverence engendered towards President Lincoln by his championing of the negro cause is shown by the following incident. The Confederate government had scarcely evacuated Richmond before Lincoln, unheralded and unannounced, and accompanied by his young son and Admiral Porter, besides a few sailors from a man-of-war, entered the city and "like any other citizen, walked up the streets towards General Weitzel's headquarters, in the house occupied two days before by Jefferson Davis." The *Atlantic Monthly* thus describes the scene of the colored people coming from all sides to see their deliverer : " They gathered round the President, ran ahead, hovered upon the flanks of the little company, and hung like a dark cloud upon the rear. Men, women, and children, joined the constantly increasing throng. They came from all the by-streets, running in breathless haste, shouting and hallooing and dancing with delight. The men threw up their hats, the women waved their bonnets and handkerchiefs, clapped their hands and sang 'Glory to God! Glory! Glory!' rendering all the praise to God, who had heard their wailings in the past, their moanings for wives, husbands, children, and friends, sold out of their sight ; had given them freedom, and after long years of waiting, had permitted them thus unexpectedly to behold the face of their great benefactor. 'I thank you, dear Jesus, that I behold President Linkum!' was the exclamation of a woman who stood upon the threshold of her humble home, and with streaming eyes and clasped hands gave thanks aloud to the Saviour of men. Another, more demonstrative in her joy, was jumping and striking her hands with all her might, crying 'Bless de Lord! Bless de Lord!' as if there could be no end to the thanksgiving.

"The air rang with a tumultuous chorus of voices. The street became almost impassable on account of the increasing multitude, till soldiers were summoned to clear the way. . . . The walk was long, and the President halted a moment to rest. ' May de good Lord bless you, President Linkum!' said an old negro, removing his hat and bowing, with tears of joy rolling down his cheeks. The President removed his own hat and bowed in silence; but it was a bow which upset the forms, laws, customs, and ceremonies of centuries. It was a death-shock to chivalry, and a mortal wound to caste. ' Recognize a nigger! Faugh!' A woman in an adjoining house beheld it, and turned from the scene in unspeakable digust."

From this scene Lincoln returned to Washington, and on the 11th of April, 1865, just four days before his death, and two days after General Lee's surrender, he made his last public address, favoring, as a start in the right direction, the reconstructed government which the loyalists had organized in Louisiana, abolishing slavery, adopting the Thirteenth Amendment, providing schools for black and white alike, and providing for the franchise for the colored people.

In a letter April 4 he said: "I am naturally anti-slavery. If slavery is not wrong, then nothing is wrong. . . . I was, in my best judgment, driven to the alternative of either surrendering the Union and with it the Constitution, or of laying strong hands upon the colored element. I chose the latter." And the colored element did respond with great heartiness, and answering President Lincoln's call, they joyfully sang : —

> " We are coming, Father Abraham,
> Two hundred thousand strong."

If Lincoln was willing, as he proved to be, to use the great power of the United States government to guarantee that " the *black* soldier should have the same protection as the *white* soldier," then it defames his hallowed memory, and libels his nobility of heart to insinuate that he would not use the same powers to guarantee to the black citizen the same protection under the law as the white citizen. To him the Emancipation Proclamation meant freedom for the colored people ; and freedom meant citizenship ; and citizenship the ballot.

In his general order issued July 30, 1863, President Lincoln said : "It is the duty of every government to give protection to its citizens, of whatever class or color or condition."

In this general order, officially promulgated, he made direct intervention in behalf of colored men, and secured their protection by the exercise of governmental sovereignty in obliterating class distinctions. On this question his record is unmistakably clear. Sad, sudden, unexpected, and overwhelming as was the death of Lincoln, there were two events which immediately preceded it that must have been of supreme satisfaction and happiness to him. There were two overmastering emotions in his heart : one was to see the Union saved, and its supremacy made sure forevermore ; the other was to see slavery dead, and dead beyond a resurrection.

The God in whom he believed, whom he trusted, to whom he prayed, who sustained and led him " amid the encircling gloom" when he was weighted down to the earth with burdens greater than it seemed possible that man could bear, was merciful, gracious, and kind unto him. His eyes beheld the salvation of his country ! He saw the imperious, cruel, slaveholding oligarchy, which drew the sword against the nation, totter to its ruin ; its dreams of an empire on the Gulf of Mexico shattered and buried in the dust ; the Union saved.

He signed the death-warrant of slavery, which was embodied in the Thirteenth Amendment to the Constitution of the United States, and passed by the necessary two-thirds vote of both Houses of Congress : ⌈" Neither slavery, nor involuntary servitude, except as a punishment for crime, whereof the party shall have been duly convicted, shall exist in the United States, or any place subject to their jurisdiction."⌉ The final passage of this amendment, probably the most momentous legislative Act passed up to that time in the whole history of the American Congress, was not received in the rancor of party-spirit, nor with the huzzas of partisan triumph, but on the contrary with most profound, aye, holy emotions. Mr. Ingersoll of Illinois said : " Mr. Speaker, in honor of this immortal and sublime event, I move that this House do now adjourn."

Mr. Blaine said : " The action was of transcendent importance — lofty in conception, masterful in execution. Slavery in the United States was dead. To succeeding and not distant generations its existence in a republic for three-quarters of a century, the duration of the organized government of the United States up to that time, will be an increasing marvel."

When Mr. Lincoln was waited upon to be apprised of its passage, and was congratulated, he said : " In the midst of your joyous expressions, He ' from whom all blessings flow ' must first be remembered." Here is a true exhibition of the real spirit of the man ; his eyes beheld salvation for the negro ; the salvation of a race from a bondage of despair, black, bitter, brutal ; slavery dead and entombed — and he the master of the ceremonies. His joy was full, complete. So ever shall he wear the " crown, a martyr's diadem, his jewels millions of ransomed slaves."

> " Still strong he stood among the crowd,
> His head above the clamor loud,
> Unmoved by trial or dismay,
> The sunshine on his face alway.
> Like some firm cliff that guards the strand,
> So Lincoln stood to save the land."

THE SOUTHERN "BLACK CODE"

With the elevation of Andrew Johnson to the presidency after the death of Lincoln, there began the second effort at reconstruction. General Lee surrendered at Appomattox, April 9, 1865. President Lincoln, " the beloved of all hearts," expired on the 15th of the same month; Mr. Johnson took the oath of office just a few hours after Lincoln's death.

It was on the 29th day of May, 1865, that President Johnson issued his Proclamation of Amnesty and Pardon to all who took part in the Rebellion, except the few thousands who held high official positions in the civil, military, or diplomatic service of the United States at the breaking out of the war, or held similar positions in the Confederacy; but providing that such persons may receive full pardon by applying for the same to the President. Thus the rank and file of Southerners were let in, and the door kept ajar for the exceptions. The conditions imposed on the white people of the South were that they would henceforth " faithfully support, protect, and defend the Constitution of the United States and the Union of the States thereunder; abide by and faithfully support all laws and proclamations which have been made during the existing Rebellion with reference to the emancipation of slaves." Could there have been greater magnanimity, wiser generosity to the white people of the South?

The Emancipation Proclamation had been endorsed and confirmed by an overwhelming vote of the people of the loyal states, and by the sweeping and triumphant re-election of Lincoln in the preceding November.

The Thirteenth Amendment had passed both Houses of Congress by more than the necessary two-thirds vote, and had been signed by President Lincoln. The white people of the South were commissioned to reconstruct the seceding states and bring them back into their proper and normal relations with the Union. They were given an absolutely free hand;

their oath bound them to respect the changed conditions "with reference to the emancipation of slaves." But how did they use this high prerogative, this unfettered power, so graciously restored to their hands? They held, with lightning-like rapidity, state conventions, and their legislatures, composed entirely of ex-Confederates, were summoned in special sessions, within a few months immediately following the war ; and they proceeded forthwith to enact a Black Code of Laws, with reference to the colored people who were emancipated, and whose emancipation their Amnesty oath bound them to respect, that is the scandal and shame of civilization. Not a single right dear to a freeman did these men respect, "with reference to the emancipation of slaves." Not a single law or proclamation did they honestly observe. These men, in the language of one of old, practically said to the colored people : "My little finger shall be thicker than my father's loins. For whereas my father put a heavy yoke upon you, I will put more to your yoke ; my father chastised you with whips, but I will chastise you with scorpions."

We come now to the consideration of the specific points in this code of laws that the Southern whites considered proper for the government of the emancipated negro.

Mr. Blaine, in his "Twenty Years of Congress," gives such a masterly review of the Black Code of Laws passed by Southern legislatures after President Johnson's Amnesty Proclamation and when the ex-Confederates had unfettered power to reconstruct the Southern states, that it is reproduced here, as follows :

"That which was no offence in a white man was made a misdemeanor, a heinous crime, if committed by a negro. Both in the civil and criminal code his treatment was different from that to which the white man was subjected. He was compelled to work under a series of labor laws applicable only to his own race. The laws of vagrancy were so changed as, in many of their provisions, to apply only to him, and under their operation all freedom of movement and transit was denied. The liberty to sell his time at a fair market rate was destroyed by the interposition of apprentice laws. Avenues of usefulness and skill in which he might specially excel, were closed against him, lest he should compete with white men. In short, his liberty in all directions was so curtailed that it was a bitter mockery to refer to him in the statutes as a ' freedman.' The truth was that his liberty was merely of form and not of fact, and the slavery which was abolished by the organic law of a nation was now to be revived by the enactment of a state.

"Some of these enactments were peculiarly offensive, not to say atrocious. In Alabama, which might indeed serve as an example for the other rebellious states, ' stubborn or refractory servants ' and ' servants who loiter away their time ' were declared by law to be ' vagrants,' and might be brought before a justice of the. peace and fined fifty dollars ; and in default of payment, they might be ' hired out,' on three days' notice by public outcry, for the period of ' six months.' No fair man could fail to see that the whole effect, and presumably the direct intent, of this law was to reduce the helpless negro to slavery for half the year — a punishment that could be repeated whenever desired, a punishment sure to be desired for that portion of each recurring year when his labor was specially valuable in connection with the cotton crop, while for the remainder of the time he might shift for himself. By this detestable process, the ' master ' had the labor of the ' servant ' for a mere pittance ; and even that pittance did not go to the servant, but was paid into the treasury of the county, and thus relieved the white men from their proper share of taxation. There may have been more cruel laws enacted, but the statute books of the world might be searched in vain for one of meaner injustice.

"The foregoing, a process for restoring slavery in a modified form, was applicable to men or women of any age. But for 'minors' a more speedy and more sweeping method was contrived by the law-makers of Alabama, who had just given their assent to the Thirteenth Amendment to the Constitution. They made it the 'duty of all sheriffs, justices of the peace, and other civil officers of the several counties,' to report the 'names of all minors under the age of eighteen years, whose parents have not the means, or who refuse to support said minors,' and thereupon it was made the duty of the Court to 'apprentice said minor to some suitable person, on such terms as the Court may direct.' Then follows a suggestive *proviso*, directing that 'if said minor be the child of a freedman' (as if any other class were really referred to!), 'the *former owner* of said minor shall have the preference'; and 'the judge of probate shall make a record of all the proceedings,' for which he should be entitled to a fee of one dollar in each case, to be paid, as this atrocious law directed, by 'the master or mistress.' To tighten the grasp of ownership on the minor, who was now styled an apprentice, it was enacted in almost the precise phrase of the old slave code that 'whoever shall entice said apprentice from his master or mistress, or furnish food or clothing to him or her, without said consent, shall be fined in a sum not exceeding five hundred dollars.'

"'The ingenuity of Alabama legislators in contriving schemes to re-enslave the negroes was not exhausted by the odious and comprehensive statutes already cited. They passed an act to incorporate the city of Mobile, substituting a new charter for the old one. The city had suffered much from the suspension and decay of trade during the war, and it was in great need of labor to make repairs to streets, culverts, sewers, wharves, and all other public property. By the new charter, the mayor, aldermen, and common council were empowered 'to cause all vagrants,' . . . 'all such as have no visible means of support,' . . . 'all who can show no reasonable cause of employment or business in the city,' . . . 'all who have no fixed residence or cannot give a good account of themselves,' . . . 'or are loitering in or about tippling houses,' . . . 'to give security for their good behavior for a reasonable time and to indemnify the city against any charge for their support, and in case of their inability or refusal to give such security, to cause them to be confined to labor for a limited time, not exceeding six calendar months, which said labor shall be designated by the said mayor, aldermen, and common council, for the benefit of said city.'

"It will be observed even by the least intelligent that the charge made in this city ordinance was, in substance, the poverty of the classes quoted — a poverty which was of course the inevitable result of slavery. To make the punishment for no crime effective, the city government was empowered 'to appoint a person or persons to take those sentenced to labor from their place of confinement to the place appointed for their working, and to watch them while at labor and return them before sundown to their place of confinement ; and, if they shall be found afterwards offending, such security may again be required, and for want thereof the like proceeding may again be had from time to time, as often as may be necessary.' The plain meaning of all this was, that these helpless and ignorant men, having been robbed all their lives of the fruit of their labor by slavery, and being necessarily and in consequence poor, must be punished for it by being robbed again of all they had honestly earned. If they stubbornly continued in their poverty, the like proceeding (of depriving them of the fruit of their labor) 'may again be had from time to time, as often as may be necessary.' It would, of course, be found 'necessary,' just so long as the city of Mobile was in need of their labor without paying for it.

"It has been abundantly substantiated, by impartial evidence, that when these grievous outrages were committed, under the forms of law, by the joint authority of the Alabama legislature and the city government of Mobile, the

61

labor of thousands of willing men could be hired for the low wages of twenty-five cents per day, with an allowance of a peck of corn meal and four pounds of bacon for each man per week. It does not change the character of the crime against these humble laborers, but it certainly enhances its degree that the law-makers of Alabama preferred an oppressive fraud to the honest payment of a consideration so small as to be almost nominal. A man must be in abject poverty when he is willing to work an entire week for a sum usually accorded in the Northern states for the labor of one day. But only a community blind to public justice and to public decency as well could enact a law that in effect declares the poverty of the laborer to be a crime, in consideration of which he shall be deprived of the beggarly mite for which he is willing to give the sweat of his face.

" Apparently fearing that the operations of the law already referred to would not secure a sufficient number of laborers for the work required in the city, the law-makers of Alabama authorized the municipal government of Mobile to 'restrain and prohibit the nightly and other meetings or disorderly assemblies of all persons, and to punish for such offences by affixing penalties not exceeding fifty dollars for any one offence; and in case of the inability of any such person to pay and satisfy said fine or penalty and the cost thereof, to sentence such person to labor for said city for such reasonable time, not exceeding six calendar months, for any one offence, as may be deemed equivalent to such penalty and costs, which labor shall be such as may be designated by the mayor, aldermen, and common-council men of the city.'

" Power was thus given to consider any evening meeting of colored persons a disorderly one, and to arrest all who were participating in it. Nothing was more natural than that the negroes, with their social and even gregarious habits, should, in their new estate of freedom, be disposed to assemble for the purpose of considering their own interests and their

62

future prospects. It is eminently to the discredit of the state of Alabama and of the city of Mobile that so innocent a purpose should be thwarted, perverted, made criminal and punished.

"The fact will not escape attention that in these enactments the words ' master,' ' mistress,' and ' servant ' are constantly used, and that under the operation of the laws a form of servitude was re-established, more heartless and more cruel than the slavery which had been abolished. Under the institution of slavery a certain attachment would spring up between the master and his slave, and with it came a certain protection to the latter against want and against suffering in his old age. With all its wrongfulness and its many cruelties, there were ameliorations in the slave system which softened its asperities and enabled vast numbers of people possessing conscience and character to assume the relation of master. But in the treatment of the colored man now proposed, there was absolute heartlessness and rank injustice. It was proposed to punish him for no crime, to declare the laborer not worthy of his hire, to leave him friendless and forlorn, without sympathy, without rights under the law, socially an outcast and industrially a serf — a serf who had no connection with the land he tilled, and who had none of the protection which even the autocracy of Russia extended to the lowliest creature that acknowledged the sovereignty of the Czar.

"These laws were framed with malignant cunning so as not to be limited in specific form of words to the negro race, but they were exclusively confined to that race in their execution. It is barely possible that a white vagrant of exceptional depravity might, now and then, be arrested ; but the negro was arrested by wholesale on a charge of vagrancy which rested on no foundation except an arbitrary law specially enacted to fit his case. Loitering around tippling-shops, one of the offences enumerated, was in far larger proportion the habit of white men, but they were left untouched and the negro alone was arrested and punished. In the entire code this deceptive form, of apparently including all persons, was a signally dishonest feature. The makers of the law evidently intended that it should apply to the negro alone, for it was administered on that basis with rigorous severity. The general phrasing was to deceive people outside, and, perhaps, to lull the consciences of some objectors at home, but it made no difference whatever in the execution of the statutes. White men who had no more visible means of support than the negro were left undisturbed, while the negro, whose visible means of support were in his strong arms and his willingness to work, was prevented from using the resources conferred upon him by nature, and reduced not merely to the condition of a slave, but subjected to the demoralization of being adjudged a criminal.

"In Florida the laws resembled those of Alabama, but were perhaps more severe in their penalties. The 'vagrant' there might be hired out for full twelve months, and the money arising from his labor, in case the man had no wife and children, was directed to be applied for 'the benefit of the orphans and poor of the county,' although the negro had been declared a vagrant because he had no visible means of support, and was therefore quite as much in need of the avails of his labor as those to whom the law diverted them. Among the curious enactments of that state was one to establish and organize a criminal court for each county, empowered to exercise jurisdiction in the trial of all offences where the punisment did not affect the life of the offender. It is obvious that the law was originated mainly for the punishment of negroes; and to expedite its work it was enacted that 'in the proceedings of said court, no presentment, indictment, or written pleading shall be required, but it shall be sufficient to put the party accused upon his or her trial, that the offence and facts are plainly set forth with reasonable certainty in the warrant of arrest.' It was further provided that where fines were imposed and the party was unable to pay them, 'the county commissioner may hire out, at public outcry, the said party to any person who will take him or her for the shortest time, and pay the fine imposed and the cost of prosecution.' The fines thus paid went into the county treasury for the general expenses of the county. The law was thus cunningly contrived to hurry the negro into an odious form of slavery, and to make the earnings which came from his hard labor pay the public expenses, which were legitimately chargeable upon the property of the county.

" Accompanying the act establishing this court was a law prescribing additional penalties for the commission of offences against the state; and this, like the former, was framed especially for the negro. Its first section provided that where punishment of an offence had hitherto been limited to fine or imprisonment, there should be superadded, as an alternative, the punishment of standing in the pillory for one hour, or whipping, not exceeding thirty-nine lashes, on the bare back. The latter punishment was reserved expressly for the negro. It was provided further that it 'shall not be lawful for any negro, mulatto, or person of color to own, use, or keep any bowie-knife, dirk, sword, firearms, or ammunition of any kind, unless he first obtain a license to do so from the judge of probate for the county in which he is a resident.' The judge could issue the license to him only upon recommendation of two respectable white men. Any negro attempting to keep arms of any kind was to be deemed guilty of a misdemeanor, compelled to 'forfeit the arms for the use of the informer, stand in the pillory' (and be pelted by the mob) ' for one hour, and then whipped with thirty-nine lashes on the bare back.' The same penalty was prescribed for any person of color 'who shall intrude himself into any religious or other public assembly of white persons, or into any rail-road-car or other vehicle set apart for the accommodation of white persons;' and with a mock show of impartiality it was provided that a white man intruding himself into an assembly of negroes, or into a negro-car, might be subjected to a like punishment. This restriction upon the negro was far more severe than that imposed in the days of slavery, when, in many of the Southern states, the gallery of the church was permitted to be freely occupied by them. A peculiarly atrocious discrimination against the negro was included in the sixth section of the law from which these quotations are made. It was provided therein that 'if any person or persons shall assault a white female with intent to commit rape, or be accessory thereto, he or they, upon conviction, shall suffer death;' but there was no prohibition and no penalty prescribed for the same crime against a negro woman. She was left unprotected by law against the brutal lust and the violence of white men.

" In the laws of South Carolina the oppression and injustice towards the negro were conspicuously marked. The restriction as to firearms, which was general to all the states, was especially severe. A negro found with any kind of weapon in his possession was punished by 'a fine equal to twice the value of the weapon so unlawfully kept, and, if that be not immediately paid, by corporal punishment.' Perhaps the most radically unjust of all the statutes was reserved for this state. The legislature enacted that 'no person of color shall pursue the practice, art, trade, or business of an artisan, mechanic, or shopkeeper, or any other trade or employment besides that of husbandry, or that of a servant under contract for labor, until he shall have obtained a license from the judge of the district court, which license shall be good for one year only.' If the license was granted to the negro to be a shopkeeper or peddler, he was compelled to pay a hundred dollars a year for it; and if he wished to pursue the rudest mechanical calling he was compelled to pay a license-fee of ten dollars. No such fees were exacted of white men, and no such fees were exacted of the free black man during the era of slavery. Every avenue for improvement was closed against him; and in a state which boasted somewhat indelicately of its chivalric dignity, the negro was mercilessly excluded from all chances to better his condition individually, or to improve the character of his race.

"Mississippi followed in the general line of penal enactments prescribed in South Carolina, though her code was possibly somewhat less severe in the deprivations to which the negro was subjected. It was, however, bad enough to stir the indignation of every lover of justice. The legislalature had enacted a law that 'if the laborer shall quit the service of the employer before the expiration of his term of service without just cause, he shall forfeit his wages for that year up to the time of quitting.' Practically the negro was himself never permitted to judge whether the cause which drove him to seek employment elsewhere was just, the white man being the sole arbiter in the premises. It was provided that 'every civil officer shall, and every person may, arrest and carry back to his or her legal employer any freedman, free negro or mulatto, who shall have quit the service of his or her employer before the expiration of his term of service without good cause, and said officer shall be entitled to receive for arresting and carrying back every deserting employee aforesaid the sum of five dollars, and ten cents per mile from the place of arrest to the place of delivery, and these sums shall be held by the employer as a set-off for so much against the wages of said deserting employee; *provided* that said arrested party, after being so returned home, may appeal to a justice of the peace, or a member of the board of police, who shall summarily try whether said appellant is legally employed by the alleged employer.'

"It requires little familiarity with Southern administration of justice between a white man and a negro to know that such appeal was always worse than fruitless, and that its only effect, if attempted, would be to secure even harsher treatment than if the appeal had not been made. The provisions for enticing a negro from his employer, included in this act, were in the same spirit and almost in the same language as the provisions of the slave-code applicable to the negro before the era of emancipation. The person ' giving or selling to any deserting freedman, free negro, or mulatto, any food, raiment, or other things, shall be guilty of a misdemeanor,' and might be punished by a fine of two hundred dollars and costs, or he might be put into prison, and be also sued by the employer for damages. For attempting to entice any freedman or free negro beyond the limits of the state, the person offending might be fined five hundred dollars; and if not immediately paid, the court could sentence the delinquent to imprisonment in the county jail for six months. The entire code of Mississippi for freedmen was in the spirit of the laws quoted. Justice was defied, and injustice incorporated as the very spirit of the laws. It was altogether a shameless proclamation of indecent wrong on the part of the Legislature of Mississippi.

" Louisiana probably attained the worst eminence in this vicious legislation. At the very moment when the Thirty-ninth Congress was assembling to consider the condition of the Southern states and the whole subject of their Reconstruction, it was found that a bill was pending in the Legislature of Louisiana providing that ' every adult freed man or woman *shall furnish themselves with a comfortable home and visible means of support within twenty days after the passage of this act*,' and that ' any freed man or woman failing to obtain a home and support as thus provided shall be immediately arrested by any sheriff or constable in any parish, or by the police officer in any city or town in said parish where said freedman may be, and by them delivered to the Recorder of the parish, and by him hired out, by public advertisement, to some citizen, being the highest bidder, for the remainder of the year.' And in case the laborer should leave his employer's service without his consent, 'he shall be arrested and assigned to labor on some public works without compensation until his employer reclaims him.' The laborers were not to be allowed to keep any live-stock, and all time spent from home without leave was to be charged against them at the rate of two dollars per day, and worked out at that rate. Many more provisions of the same general character were contained within the bill, the whole character and scope of which were forcibly set before the Senate by Mr. Wilson of Massachusetts. It was not only a proof of cruelty enacted into law, but was such a defiance to the spirit of the Emancipation Amendment that it subjected the legislature which approved the amendment and enacted these laws to a charge of inconsistency so grave as to make the former act appear in the light of both a legal and moral fraud. It was declaring the negro to be free by one statute, and immediately proceeding to re-enslave him by another.

"By a previous law Louisiana had provided that all agricultural laborers should be compelled to 'make contracts for labor during the first ten days of January for the entire year.' With a demonstrative show of justice it was provided that 'wages due shall be a lien on the crop, one-half to be paid at times agreed by the parties, the other half to be retained until the completion of the contract; but in case of sickness of the laborer, wages for the time shall be deducted, and where the sickness is supposed to be feigned for the purpose of idleness, double the amount shall be deducted; and should the refusal to work extend beyond three days, the negro shall be forced to labor on roads, levees, and public works without pay.' The master was permitted to make deductions from the laborer's wages for 'injuries done to animals or agricultural implements committed to his care, or for bad or negligent work,' he, of course, being the judge.

'For every act of disobedience a fine of one dollar shall be imposed upon the laborer;' and among the cases deemed to be disobedience were 'impudence, swearing, or using indecent language in the presence of the employer, his family, or his agent, or quarrelling or fighting among one another.' It has been truthfully said of this provision that the master or his agent might assail the ear with profaneness aimed at the negro man, and outrage every sense of decency in foul language addressed to the negro woman ; but if one of the helpless creatures, goaded to resistance and crazed under tyranny, should answer back with impudence, or should relieve his mind with an oath, or retort indecency upon indecency, he did so at the cost to himself of one dollar for every outburst. The agent referred to in the statute was the well-known overseer of the cotton region, who was always coarse and often brutal, sure to be profane, and scarcely knowing the border-line between ribaldry and decency. The care with which the law-makers of Louisiana provided that his delicate ears and sensitive nerves should not be offended with an oath or with an indelicate word from a negro, will be appreciated by all who have heard the crack of the whip on a Southern plantation.

" The wrongs inflicted under the name of law, thus far recited, were still further aggravated in a majority of the rebellious states by the exaction of taxes from the colored men to an amount altogether disproportionate to their property. Indeed, of property they had none. Just emerging from a condition of slavery in which their labor had been constantly exacted without fee or reward of any kind, it was impossible that they could be the owners of anything except their own bodies. Notwithstanding this fact, the negroes, *en masse*, were held to be subjects of taxation in the state governments about to be reorganized. In Georgia, for example, a state tax of three hundred and fifty thousand dollars was levied in the first year of peace. The property of the state, even after all the ruin of the war, exceeded two hundred and fifty million dollars. This tax, therefore, amounted to less than one-seventh of one per cent upon the aggregate valuation of the state, — equal to the imposition of only a dollar and a half upon each thousand dollars of property. The legislature of the state decreed, however, that a large proportion of this small levy should be raised by a poll-tax of a dollar per head upon every man in the state between the ages of twenty-one and sixty years. There were in Georgia at the time from eighty-five thousand to ninety thousand colored men subject to the tax : perhaps, indeed, the number reached one hundred thousand. It was thus ordained that the negroes, who had no property at all, should pay one-third as much as the white men, who had two hundred and fifty millions of property in possession. This odious and unjust tax was stringently exacted from the negro. To make sure that not one should escape, the tax was held as a lien upon his labor, and the employer was under distraint to pay it. In Alabama they levied for the same purpose two dollars on every person between the ages of eighteen and fifty, causing a still larger proportion of the total tax to fall on the negro than the Georgia law-makers deemed expedient.

" Texas followed with a capitation tax of a dollar per head, while Florida levied upon every inhabitant between the ages of twenty-one and fifty-five years a capitation tax of three dollars, and upon failure or refusal to pay the same the tax-collector was 'authorized and required to seize the body of the delinquent, and hire him out, after five days' public notice before the door of the court house, to any person who will pay the said tax and the costs incident to the proceedings growing out of said arrest, for his services for the shortest period of time.' As the costs as well as the capitation tax were to be worked out by the negro, it is presumable that, in the spirit of this tax-law, they were enlarged to the utmost limit that decency, according to the standard set up

71

by this law, would permit. It is fair to presume that, in any event, the costs would not be less than the tax, and might, indeed, be double or treble that amount. As a negro could not, at that time, be hired out for more than seven dollars and a half per month, the plain inference is that for the support of the state of Florida the negro might be compelled to give one month's labor yearly. Even by the capitation tax alone, without the incident of the costs, every negro man was compelled to give the gains and profits of nearly two weeks' labor.

" A poll-tax, though not necessarily limited in this manner, has usually accompanied the right of suffrage in the different states of the Union, but in the late rebellious states it conferred no franchise. It might be supposed that ordinary generosity would have devoted it to the education of the ignorant class from which it was forcibly wrung, but no provision of the kind was even suggested. . . .

" It was at once seen that if the party which had insisted upon the emancipation of the slave as a final condition of peace should now abandon him to his fate, and turn him over to the anger and hate of the class from whose ownership he had been freed, it would countenance and commit an act of far greater wrong than was designed by the most malignant persecutor of the race in any one of the Southern states. When the Congress of the United States, acting independently of the executive power of the nation, decreed emancipation by amending the Constitution, it solemnly pledged itself, with all its power, to give protection to the emancipated at whatever cost and at whatever sacrifice. No man could read the laws which have been here briefly reviewed without seeing and realizing that, if the negro were to be deprived of the protecting power of the nation that had set him free, he had better at once be remanded to slavery, and to that form of protection which cupidity, if not humanity, would always inspire."

THE SOUTHERN "BLACK CODE"

" The objectionable and cruel legislation of the Southern states — examples of which might be indefinitely cited in addition to those already given " — fairly and forcefully illustrates the spirit and temper of the white people of the South, and their utter contempt for the unexampled generosity on the part of the nation which gave them commission, *carte blanche*, to reconstruct their states. They responded with a cruel and barbarous code which was an affront to Christian civilization.

CHAPTER III

SOUTHERN OPPOSITION TO RECONSTRUCTION

THE white people of the South thus took the whip hand in carrying out reconstruction, free and unhampered. They did not improve the opportunity; rather they shamefully abused it. In the same spirit they elected members, senators and representatives, to the Congress, every one of them former leaders in the Confederacy. These members presented themselves as early as December, 1865, but the Senate and the House of Representatives each refused to receive or admit the Southern delegations. Thus an issue was raised. A great struggle was on. Who can say that God was not leading a people? For out of this issue and struggle the ballot finally came to the negro. The ballot probably would not have been bestowed upon him, certainly not at the time nor in the way and manner it was, if the South had been lenient toward him and had shown a disposition to respect the Emancipation Proclamation and the Thirteenth Amendment as accomplished results; and protected him in life and property, the right of contract, marriage relations, locomotion, the privileges of schools, and other just and equitable relations, irrespective of the ballot, which make for the peace, prosperity, and well-being of the community.

But the determination of the Southerners to suppress the colored man and take vengeance on him for their defeat on the field of battle, and by Black Codes make his condition worse under emancipation than it was under slavery, depriving him of every protection, making him an outcast, with every man's hand against him, fired the hearts of the people of the North and aroused their keener sense of justice and deeper feelings of humanity as nothing else could have done.

It should be borne in mind that the Black Code of laws, partially outlined above, was only the first instalment of oppressive measures against the negro. Other and more cruel laws would certainly have followed the admission of the Southern delegates to seats in Congress. Besides, the admission of the Southern delegates at this time would have intrenched the doctrines of state rights in their most obnoxious and menacing forms. The ex-Confederates would have been masters of the situation. The solid South combined with a few scattering Northern votes would have ruled. The conquered would have dictated terms to the conqueror. The hands of the nation would have been tied hard and fast. The insistence on state rights would have prevented any legislation by the Congress which might have interfered with the Black Code. The Fourteenth and Fifteenth Amendments to the Constitution of the United States, would, obviously, have been impossible. The Black Code would have been enlarged, and the Thirteenth Amendment legislated out of existence. The cry would have been, " Slavery is dead! Long live slavery ! " The barren victory of crushing the rebellion would have gone to the North, the fruits of the victory to the South. The very extremity to which the arrogance of the South carried it in the enactment of the Black Code, its open defiance, saved the situation.

The rejection of the Southern delegations by Congress, and the universal condemnation of the Black Code throughout the North, and as well by the whole civilized world, were to the Southerners like the throwing of a lighted match into a powder magazine. They were enraged beyond expression. They inaugurated the reign of violence, terrorism, and blood-letting, which has continued under different guises, in full force and without lapse, until the present time. Their vengeance was visited without mercy on those white men who were known to be loyal to the Union, murdering or driving them from their homes ; and as for the colored people, they were nobody's property, so they were often killed for the sport of the killing. These two classes they blamed for their woes, and on them they heaped their wrath with ruthless and indiscriminate slaughter.

On September 3, 1866, just a little over a year after President Johnson's Amnesty Proclamation, the Southern loyalists, all whites, met in national convention at Philadelphia and issued an address to the nation, appealing for protection and denouncing the outrages and murders inflicted on the loyalists of the South. In this address they said: "Our last hope under God is in the unity and firmness of the states that elected Abraham Lincoln and defeated Jefferson Davis. . . . Every original Unionist in the South . . . has been ostracized. . . . More than one thousand devoted Union soldiers have been murdered in cold blood since the surrender of Lee, and in no case have their assassins been brought to judgment."

More than a thousand negroes also had been slaughtered.

On July 20, 1866, at New Orleans, the Union men were holding a state convention. This was raided and broken up by ex-Confederates, and over two hundred Union men were killed and wounded. It is very important to bear in mind that when these harrowing occurrences were taking place, when this unrestrained violence and blood-shedding was sweeping over the South like a "prairie fire," the Southern whites themselves, the ex-Confederates, had control of the government of every one of the Southern states. They had the state legislatures and all other offices; and their senators and Representatives, all ex-Confederates, were knocking at the doors of Congress. Not a single negro in the South was a voter; not a "carpet-bagger" was in office in all the land.

The South thus threw away its opportunity. By the enactment of the Black Code, the practical nullification of the Thirteenth Amendment, and the inauguration of the reign of terrorism, violence, and bloodshed, the South openly defied the nation, struck it a hard blow, spurned its magnanimity and clemency, and challenged the further assertion of its sovereignty. This introduces the third effort at reconstruction.

Events were moving rapidly. There was much heat and estrangement, — not only between the North and the South, but between President Johnson, who sided with the South, and Congress, backed by the great body of the people of the North. The great masses of the American people are humane, and have an innate love for justice and fair play, and in the long run are sure to assert these principles with irresistible force.

It was soon discovered that, as President Johnson upheld the contention of the ex-Confederates, any reconstructionary measures passed by Congress would have to run the gantlet of his veto. And as a matter of fact, all such measures of reconstruction were vetoed by him and had to be repassed over his veto by a two-thirds vote.

The Republican party that had brought the war to a successful termination saved the Union and freed the slave was in control of the government. Its line of duty was plain. It neither doubted nor faltered. It knew that " to doubt would be disloyalty, to falter would be sin." There were some internal dissensions, it is true, and some few members or followers dropped by the wayside ; but the party as a whole responded to the call of duty and faced the issues with firmness and determination. It was admirably led by Charles Sumner, William Pitt Fessenden, Benjamin F. Wade in the Senate, and Thaddeus Stevens, Lyman Trumbull, Henry Winter Davis, and Samuel Shellabarger in the House. They made haste slowly. Their measures of reconstruction were taken gradually by easy stages. No more was undertaken than the circumstances and necessities of the case actually required, and the public sentiment of the North

would approve and justify. A joint committee on reconstruction was appointed. The Freedmen's Bureau was established, and General O. O. Howard, who had lost an arm
in the Virginia campaign at Fair Oaks, and also had hurled
back the flower and chivalry of the South at Cemetery Ridge in
the battle of Gettysburg, and had rendered other distinguished services throughout the war, was placed at its head.
He was distinctively a Christian soldier, the Havelock of the
American army. The Bureau "was primarily designed as a
protection to the freedmen of the South, and to the class of
white men known as ' refugees,' driven from their homes by the
rebels on account of their loyalty to the Union." Its powers
were enlarged so as to not only enable it to protect these
two classes in life, but all property and civil rights.

The Congress now applied itself to the more serious question
of the reconstruction of the lately rebellious states. On the
30th of April, 1866, Mr. Thaddeus Stevens, in behalf of the
Committee on Reconstruction, reported a joint resolution
proposing an amendment to the Constitution of the United
States.

The amendment as finally adopted constitutes the Fourteenth Amendment to the Constitution, and is as follows:

SECTION 1. All persons born or naturalized in the United States,
and subject to the jurisdiction thereof, are citizens of the United
States, and of the State wherein they reside. No State shall
make or enforce any law which shall abridge the privileges or
immunities of citizens of the United States; nor shall any State
deprive any person of life, liberty, or property without due process of law; nor deny to any person within its jurisdiction the
equal protection of the laws.

SECT. 2. Representatives shall be apportioned among the several States according to their respective numbers, counting the
whole number of persons in each, excluding Indians not taxed.
But when the right to vote at any election for the choice of
electors for President and Vice-President of the United States,

representatives in Congress, the executive and judicial officers of a State, or members of the Legislature thereof, is denied to any of the male inhabitants of such State, being twenty-one years of age, and citizens of the United States, or in any way abridged, except for participation in rebellion or other crime, the basis of representation therein shall be reduced in the proportion which the number of such male citizens shall bear to the whole number of male citizens twenty-one years of age in such State. . . .

The Congress shall have power to enforce, by appropriate legislation, the provisions of this article.

The Fourteenth Amendment to the Constitution was passed by Congress on the 13th day of June, 1866. The principles of this amendment had been presented and debated in one form or another from the early part of this session until finally formulated and passed as it stands to-day and will stand forever.

The South had trampled the Thirteenth Amendment under its feet and treated with scorn the national good-will. The Fourteenth Amendment was the nation's answer to the Southern Black Code. Other legislation made it incumbent on each of the seceding states to accept and adopt this amendment before they would be recognized as assuming their practical and proper relations with the Union. But neither this amendment nor any other legislation of Congress disfranchised the masses of ex-Confederates. Amnesty was open to all.

It is the chief complaint of leading Southerners that "the white people of the South were suppressed and that the ballot was given to the negro over their heads and for the purpose of perpetuating the Republican party in power." This charge is not tenable. He who says that the Republican party "was playing politics" and gave the negro the ballot with sinister motives speaks without knowledge of the facts in the case, or states what he knows to be untrue. The Fourteenth Amendment simply assured to the negro the ordinary natural rights of citizenship which belong to every member of the state, such, for instance, as belong to women and children, but it did not bestow the ballot.

The ballot, the exercise of the election franchise, still rested with the state. Each Southern state could give it or withhold it as it might please. But no Southern state withholding the ballot from the colored people could count the colored population in the matter of representation in Congress or for presidential electors.

The Fourteenth Amendment did destroy the Southern Black Code and gave the colored people a legal status, and it made the ballot possible. It did not actually make a single negro voter in all the South. Was this " playing politics " ? How could this in any way tend " to perpetuate the Republican party in power " ?

At this time neither Congress nor the people of the North contemplated bestowing suffrage on the negro. But the minds of both were fully made up to preserve the fruits of emancipation and protect the colored people in all their civil and natural rights and prevent all discrimination against them on account of " race, color, or previous condition of servitude," " at any sacrifice." And on this issue they held that there was no ground for compromise.

The white people of the South received the Fourteenth Amendment with a wild tempest of rage. Every Southern state still in the hands of ex-Confederates, except Tennessee, rejected it. Outrages, murders, and violence on Unionists and especially on the colored people, increased.

In the rejection of the Fourteenth Amendment the South threw away its *second* opportunity to reconstruct the seceding states in harmony with the changed conditions and yet without bestowing the ballot on the colored people. Its acceptance of the Fourteenth Amendment would have made unnecessary the Fifteenth Amendment.

The Congress, however, was imperturbable. It knew its power. It dared to do. It met the defiance, hostility, and violence of the South with the mailed hand of martial law. It promptly accepted the gage of battle laid down by the South. It divided the ten seceding States into five military districts and General Grant by direction appointed for each district a commander of the rank above a brigadier-general. These commanders were empowered to arrange for the registration of citizens above the age of twenty-one "without regard to race or color," and without prejudice to the masses of ex-Confederates, who should vote for a constitutional convention. This convention should adopt a state constitution, prohibiting slavery and recognizing the results of the war, and it should establish a complete machinery of state and local government and provide for the election of senators and representatives to Congress. The course of events in the South in the meanwhile, the indecent haste in enacting the Black Code, with its barbarous inflictions, the reign of violence and murder on helpless colored people and " refugee " Unionists, the defiant rejection of the Fourteenth Amendment by every Southern state except Tennessee, the general scorn of the nation's good-will and clemency, and the open hostility to national authority, had the effect of ripening public sentiment in every Northern state in favor of negro suffrage. The South had shown its hand. It was perfectly apparent that it could not be trusted to do justly or even act humanely towards the colored people or the white "refugees " who were loyal to the Union. The critical point was reached, the hour had struck when the nation must look to others than the ex-Confederates and their sympathizers to reconstruct the lately rebellious states " with reference to the emancipation of slaves" and bring them into harmonious relations with the Union.

Mr. Blaine, touching this point, said : " The South had its choice, and it deliberately and after fair warning decided to reject the magnanimous offer of the North and to insist upon an advantage in representation against which a common sense of justice revolted. The North, foiled in its original design of reconstruction by the perverse course of the South, was compelled, under the providence of the Ruler of nations, to deal honestly and justly with the colored people. . . . A higher than human power controlled these great events. The wrath of man was made to praise the righteous works of God. Whatever were the deficiencies of the negro race in education for the duties and responsibilities of citizenship, they had exhibited the one vital qualification of an instinctive loyalty and, as far as lay in their power, a steadfast helpfulness to the cause of the national Union, — . . . his race contributing nearly a quarter of a million troops to the national service."

The famous Reconstruction Act, placing the South under martial law, was passed on March 2, 1867. It embodied negro suffrage. Under God, justice had come. The ex-Confederates had been exercising full control over the government of every Southern state for two years after the war, and had defied the national laws and authority, and had persistently thwarted the work of reconstruction.

In debating this act in Congress, placing the South under military law, Mr. Garfield, afterwards President of the United States, said: "I call attention to the fact that from the collapse of the Rebellion to the present hour, Congress has undertaken to restore the States lately in rebellion by co-operation with their people, and that our efforts in that direction have proven a complete and disastrous failure. . . . The constitutional amendment (the Fourteenth Amendment) did not come up to the full height of the great occasion. It did not meet all I desired in the way of guarantees to liberty, but if the rebel States had adopted it as Tennessee did, I should have felt bound to let them in on the same terms prescribed for Tennessee. I have been in favor of waiting to give them full time to deliberate and act. They deliberated. They have acted. The last one of the sinful ten has at last, with contempt and scorn, flung back in our teeth the magnanimous offer of a generous nation. It is now our turn to act. They would not co-operate with us in building what they destroyed. We must remove the rubbish and build from the bottom."

Mr. Brandegee of Connecticut said: "The American people demand that we shall do something, and quickly. Already fifteen hundred Union men have been massacred in cold blood (more than the entire population of some of the towns in my district), whose only crime has been loyalty to your flag. . . . In all the revolted states, upon the testimony of your ablest generals, there is no safety to property or lives of loyal men. Is this what the loyal North has been fighting for? Thousands of loyal white men, driven like partridges over the mountains, homeless, houseless, penniless, to-day throng this capital. They fill the hotels, they crowd the avenues, they gather in these marble corridors, they look down from these galleries, and with supplicating eye ask protection from the flag that hangs above the Speaker's chair,— a flag which thus far has unfurled its stripes, but concealed the promise of its stars."

Mr. Lawrence of Ohio said: "For myself, I am ready to set aside by law all these illegal governments. They have rejected all fair terms of reconstruction. They have rejected the constitutional amendments we have tendered them. They are engines of oppression against all loyal men."

Mr. Boutwell of Massachusetts said: "To-day there are eight millions or more of people, occupying six hundred and thirty thousand square miles of territory in this country, who are writhing under cruelties nameless in their character, and injustices such as have not been permitted to exist in any other country of modern times. . . . It is the vainest delusion, the wildest of hopes, the most dangerous of aspirations,

83

to contemplate the reconstruction of civil government until the rebel despotisms enthroned in power in these ten States shall be broken up."

Mr. Kelly of Pennsylvania said: "The passage of this bill or its equivalent is required by the manhood of this Congress, to save it from the hissing scorn and reproach of every Southern man who has been compelled to seek a home in the by-ways of the North, of every homeless widow and orphan of a Union soldier in the South, who should have been protected by the government."

Mr. Allison of Iowa, now United States Senator, said: "Believing as I do that this measure is essential to the preservation of the Union men of the South, believing that their lives, property, and liberty cannot be secured except through military law, I am for this bill."

Mr. Blaine's amendment to the bill provided that "the elective franchise shall be enjoyed equally and impartially by all male citizens of the United States twenty-one years of age and upwards, without regard to race, color, or previous condition of servitude." He said: "I believe the true interpretation of the election of 1866 was that, in addition to the proposed constitutional amendment, impartial suffrage should be the basis of reconstruction. Why not declare it so? Why not, when you send out this military police through the lately rebellious States, send with it that impressive declaration?"

It was even so. The declaration was sent. Under these circumstances the ballot came to the negro. The Congress and the nation now had to look to others than ex-Confederates to do the work of reconstruction. The negro was commanded to share in it. How otherwise could these states have been reconstructed in accordance with the national sentiment and the emancipation laws? It was plain that the ex-Confederates would not do it. It was equally clear that the colored people composed the only possible large constituency in the South to be depended on ; and that by giving them the ballot, and enlisting the support of the loyalist and of the more conservative Southerners, and the assistance of the Union soldiers who had settled in the South, the work of reconstruction could be carried out ; but even then only under the protection of martial law.

These three elements — the large colored populations, the Union soldiers who had settled in the South after the close of the war, more than two years before, and the loyalists and conservative Southerners who accepted the new situation — constituted the agency through which the Southern states were reconstructed and brought back into their practical and proper relations with the Union. They gave the Southern states constitutions in harmony with the changed conditions and the emancipation laws. They established orderly governments, and because of their necessary participation in these governments, there arose the cry of " negro domination," " carpet-baggers," and " scalawags."

It is quite pertinent to remark here that, notwithstanding all the protest of the Southern whites, no one has yet shown — not even Senator Tillman or Senator Money — how the seceding Southern states could have been brought back into their normal and proper relation with the Union by the formal acceptance of the Thirteenth and Fourteenth Amendments to the Constitution of the United States and the guaranties for the protection of life, liberty, and property, " without regard to race, color, or previous condition of servitude," otherwise than through this very agency which they and others so heatedly and intemperately denounce.

The reconstruction which proceeded under martial law was a necessity. It was an unusual as well as undesirable resort, but there was no alternative ; the attitude of the ex-Confederates made it necessary — it is a full justification.

The business and financial interests of the country and

every other interest demanded a settlement of the questions growing out of the war. The nation, righteously, would not have the Black Code and its accompaniments ; the South, unrighteously, would have nothing else. And yet reconstruction must be accomplished. To put the whole South under martial law indefinitely or until its passions were cooled down was far more objectionable and dangerous than to put it under martial law for a limited period and until the states could be reconstructed with the assistance of the colored vote and the conservative and loyal elements. The American people will not tolerate martial law save as a temporary necessity. Suppose the ex-Confederates had said to Congress and the nation, "Put us under martial law, if you choose. We will stay under your martial law forever before we will strike one line from the Black Code, before we will accept your Fourteenth Amendment or any other law objectionable to us. Do your worst. We defy you." And that was the real position taken by the South, declared in its press and by its leaders on the rostrum, — that they " would never submit to the Fourteenth Amendment." What then? A little child can lead a horse to the water, but a giant can't make it drink. There was no power by which the Congress could coerce the ex-Confederates to reconstruct the Southern states against their will.

Let it be observed here that, as in the course of the war the Emancipation Proclamation, as a war measure, was necessary to save the Union, increasing as it did its material and moral forces at home and abroad, and correspondingly decreasing the material and moral forces of the Confederacy and destroying with a few strokes of the pen its mightiest pillar of support, just so, in the course of reconstruction, the bestowal of the ballot on the negro, as a reconstruction measure, was absolutely necessary to restore the seceding states to their former relations in the Union. The enforcement of martial law for an indefinite period would have proved most injurious to the national cause, and increasingly so every day after the South had been normally pacified.

For the Southern leaders would have temporarily desisted from acts of violence and murder, until they gained their point, the recognition of their states and the admission of their members into Congress. Then, fortified by the heresies of state rights, they would have "turned loose the dogs of war" on the helpless colored people, and the fugitive white Unionists, and the lives of these people would have been made intolerable. The cruelty and brutalism inflicted on the colored people to-day when they are equal citizens show what might have been expected without the protection of the constitutional amendments; and are likewise an ample, a complete vindication of the wisdom, justice, and humanity of reconstruction legislation.

The Southern people could have appealed to the nation and to the Supreme Court of the United States for autonomy, declaring that disorder had ceased in their states, that there was no resistance to any national law, that the Black Code rested upon the rights of the states to regulate domestic affairs, and that rejection of the Fourteenth Amendment was not resisting the national authority, as that amendment was not a law of the land until approved by three-fourths of all the states. What then? The Southerners, finally, would have won. The waiting policy would have acted tremendously in their favor. They could have forced a compromise, demanding pay for the slaves; reimbursement for certain losses by the war; refused to pension Union soldiers unless Confederates were also pensioned; declined to accept the national debt unless certain debts of the Confederacy were also accepted; legislated as to the colored people according to their own capricious will; and, intrenched behind the doctrines of state rights in their most objectionable and dangerous forms, they could have hampered and harassed the national government without limit; and the world would have beheld the amazing and bewildering spectacle of a great and powerful nation, triumphant in the greatest war of history, standing utterly limp and helpless in the presence of the conquered, and meekly yielding to their dictation. For the Fourteenth Amendment not only gave the negro a legal status, but its fourth section made inviolable the public debt, provided for pensions, prohibited payment for slaves, and made void all debts of the Confederacy. Without negro suffrage, these would remain open questions.

It was the ballot in the hands of the negro that saved the nation from unspeakable humiliations, established beyond question its supremacy and sovereignty, destroyed forever the menacing and dangerous forms of state rights, and preserved "the jewel of liberty in the family of freedom," thus fulfilling in a most signal, unexpected, and remarkable manner Lincoln's prophecy that "they would probably help in some trying time in the future to keep the jewel of liberty in the family of freedom."

Under the desperate and chaotic conditions existent in the South at this time, it is not surprising that in the selection and election of men to carry out the work of reconstruction serious blunders were made ; that some thieves and plunderers forged to the front and filled some of the offices. It is the universal experience in governmental affairs that under normal conditions, in times of profound peace, bad men and thieves have been elected to offices and have betrayed their trusts. It was unavoidable, it could not have been otherwise during the Reconstruction era. The circumstances were propitious for this. The South had gone far beyond her financial ability in the prosecution of a disastrous and wasteful war. She had no public moneys, and her private fortunes were wrecked ; a billion dollars in slave property had evaporated. Money was needed to operate state and local government. Taxes were assessed. Bonds were issued. From 25 to 75 per cent of the par value of these bonds remained in the safes and lockers of the bondholders in the North; in fact, the Northern bondholders got a larger proportion of money which should have been used to run these state governments than it was possible for the " carpet-baggers " to steal.

Those Southern leaders who attribute the poverty of the South following the war to the stealings of " carpet-baggers " are unwise in their utterances. This poverty was due more to the waste of war, the unsettled conditions, and the low price of Southern bonds than to the stealings of the " carpet-baggers." Much stealing has been done since the passing of these conditions; millions have been stolen in later years by defaulters, embezzlers, grafts, and boodlers.

But after all that may be charged against the blundering and plundering of the carpet-bag governments in the South, it is probably true that the Tweed ring in New York City actually stole and squandered more of the people's money than all the " carpet-baggers " in the South combined.

It is also noteworthy that some of the seceding states were never under the so-called carpet-bag government; such were Georgia, Tennessee, and Texas; others were so controlled for only a short time, as, for instance, Louisiana, Mississippi, Virginia, Alabama, and Arkansas, for three or four years; North Carolina for about six years : and only Florida and South Carolina for about eight years. So it will be seen at a glance that the so-called carpet-bag government of the South was neither so general nor so extended in time as Southern leaders pretend.

But the rank and file of the Northern men who settled in the South after the close of the war were not unworthy men, nor were they thieves; nor were the rank and file of the loyalists, and those conservative Southerners who accepted the changed conditions, unworthy men or thieves; and as to the colored people, they were far too inflated with the ideas of freedom, too happy in their new life of liberty,

THE AFTERMATH OF SLAVERY

too deeply impressed and concerned about the "sovereignty under the hat," too busily engaged in trying to trace the members of their families — husband, wife, daughter, son, sister, brother, father, mother, and other kindred — who had been scattered to the four corners of the earth by the inhuman and brutal system of the slave-pen and the slave auction-block — to give even a thought about money making in politics.

These Northern men who had settled in the South, and whom the ex-Confederates called "carpet-baggers," responded to the call of their country to assist in reconstructing the Southern states in the same spirit of patriotism which they displayed when Sumter was fired on. The loyalists of the South, who had borne contumacy and outrage during the four years of the war and the two years following it, and whom the ex-Confederates called "scalawags," applying this term also to those Southerners who accepted the situation, responded to the call to assist in reconstructing the Southern states, because they rejoiced that the day of judgment had come to the South, and with their help Old Glory would flutter over a restored Union.

And the colored people! They bubbled over with rejoicings; there was nothing that they would not have done for "the Lincoln government" and to sustain the North. There was not a colored man in the South who would not have borne arms in defence of the nation. If the South had tried "guerilla warfare" after General Lee's surrender, then the very last guerilla would have been driven to cover, simply by arming the 700,000 colored men.

These three classes rendered the nation services of inestimable value in a most critical and perilous hour, — services for which the nation owes a lasting and incalculable debt of gratitude. There has been entirely too much random abuse of "carpet-baggers" and "scalawags." It is time to call a halt to these indiscriminate denunciations. Vilification and abuse are not arguments. The services which they rendered at a grave crisis were as necessary and indispensable in reconstructing the Southern states as were the march of Sherman to the sea, the triumphs of Grant at Vicksburg, Banks at Port Hudson, Meade at Gettysburg, Farragut at New Orleans and Mobile Bay, the "Monitor" over the "Merrimac" in Hampton Roads, and Sheridan's famous ride down the valley of the Shenandoah, in strangling and stamping out the Rebellion. The perplexing problem of reconstruction was as threatening to the nation's sovereignty as the war to the nation's life. The white people of the South themselves are responsible for the so-called negro domination and carpet-bag governments. They threw away two opportunities to reconstruct, and for a third time refused even to share in the work of reconstruction. If some stealing and plundering accompanied the performance, theirs was the blame.

Among the so-called "carpet-baggers" and "scalawags" there were men as pure in purpose, as lofty in patriotism, as bright in intellect, as unselfish in the discharge of public duties, and as honest, courageous, and noble in spirit as America has ever produced. Because the Southerners could not rule, or because they were not permitted to work ruin, they sulked ; and their sulking brought about the very evils of which they so loudly and bitterly complain. For it should always be borne in mind that, while there was a sufficiently numerous constituency in the large colored population of the Southern states, augmented and supported by the strong and important body of Northern settlers and reinforced by the large number of loyalists and pacified Southerners, to achieve their reconstruction, yet there was no inhibition against the great mass of white Southerners participating in the reconstruction of their respective states. The great masses of the ex-Confederates could freely register and vote under the provisions of the same act which bestowed the ballot on the colored people. In deliberately choosing to sulk and defy the nation, and in large measure allow the elections to pass by default so far as they were concerned, they became even more responsible for all the evils which followed.

In the meantime, nevertheless, the work of reconstructing the Southern states proceeded under the law authorized by the Congress. The " voters of twenty-one years of age and upward " were registered " without regard to race or color," and without prejudice to the great masses of ex-Confederates, who for a third time spurned and rejected the nation's good-will. Elections were held ; constitutional conventions assembled ; constitutions were framed and submitted to the electorate as registered in the several states for their approval ; complete machinery for state and local governments was put in operation; senators and representatives were elected to the Congress. Tennessee had already abolished slavery, ratified the Thirteenth and Fourteenth Amendments, and had resumed her place in the Union, July 23, 1866 ; Arkansas was restored to her place in the Union June 22, 1868 ; North Carolina, South Carolina, Alabama, Florida, Louisiana, and Georgia, June 25, 1868 ; Virginia, January 26 ; Mississippi, February 23 ; and Texas, March 30, 1870, the delay being due to non-fulfilment of requirements. The state of Georgia expelled the colored men elected to her legislature, and this raised the question of the right to hold office. Whereupon Congress took action and passed a bill December 16, 1869, declaring that " the exclusion of persons from the legislature upon the ground of race, color, or previous condition of servitude would be illegal and revolutionary and is hereby prohibited." Georgia's senators and representatives were denied admission to Congress until the colored members were reinstated. Thus the question of the right of colored men to hold office was promptly met and settled.

The reconstruction of the Southern states was now completed, all the seceding states being restored to their autonomy in the Union, under a bill providing in each case that the said state "is entitled and admitted to representation in Congress, as one of the states of the Union upon the following fundamental condition: that the Constitution of [naming the state] shall never be so amended or changed as to deprive any citizen or class of citizens of the United States of the right to vote, who are entitled to vote by the Constitution herein recognized, except as a punishment for such crimes as are now felonies at the common law, whereof they shall have been duly convicted."

It was under this solemn compact that the lately rebellious states were declared admitted to the Union. The question pertinently arises: Has not each of those Southern states, adopting new constitutions with the "grandfather clause" or other device to deprive the colored people of their right to vote, violated, both in letter and spirit, this solemn compact, and broken faith with the nation? And again, if South Carolina and Louisiana can violate the "fundamental condition" in relation to the ballot, upon which they were admitted to the Union, what is to prevent Utah and other states that may choose to do so, from violating their solemn compact with the nation in relation to polygamy? A state is in honor bound to respect and observe its compact with the nation. The violation of such a compact is an act of bad faith which the people of a state cannot afford to uphold; and in case the compact is violated the nation, through Congress or the courts, may make intervention. The nation may sometime wake up to realize that what is "sauce" for the South Carolina "goose" to-day will be "sauce" for the Utah "gander" to-morrow.

The success attained in organizing these governments did not have the effect of softening the animosities or allaying the bitter resentment and hostility of the white people. It greatly aggravated them. The South had now suffered two defeats, and in each the negro was an important factor. In the war, the negro as a soldier was potent. In reconstruction, the negro as a voter was indispensable.

In suffering and blood, the white people of the South have exacted a staggering price from the colored people for their loyalty and service to the nation. And the end is not yet.

The Confederate army was practically reorganized into a secret, oath-bound society — the Ku Klux Klans — covering all the Southern states. They made onslaughts on the governments established, and war on their supporters. They killed and murdered, by day and by night, loyalists, pacified Southerners, and negroes without discrimination and without mercy. Mr. Blaine said : "In prosecuting their purposes these clans and organizations hesitated at no cruelty, were deterred by no considerations of law or humanity. They rode by night, were disguised with masks, were armed as freebooters. They whipped, maimed, or murdered the victims of their wrath. White men who were co-operating with the colored population politically were visited with punishments of excessive cruelty." "Over two thousand persons were killed, wounded, and otherwise injured in" Louisiana "within a few weeks of the presidential election of 1868 ;" . . . the state "was overrun by violence, midnight raids, secret murders, and open riots." In one parish "the Ku Klux killed and wounded over two hundred Republicans, hunting and chasing them for two days through fields and swamps." "Over twenty-five bodies were found at one place in the woods."

The horrors and cruelties of the Ku Klux Klans in Louisiana were fully rivalled in Mississippi, and more or less largely sustained in each of the Southern states. It is estimated by persons well acquainted with the situation that from forty to fifty thousand colored people, white loyalists, and Northern men were murdered in cold blood during this era. The blood of these martyrs to liberty and the Union cries out from the ground!

Some of the members of the Ku Klux Klan were captured, indicted, and put on trial. A number were arraigned before the United States Court in South Carolina. The white people of the state engaged the most eminent counsel for their defence. Their leading lawyer was the noted and learned Reverdy Johnson of Maryland, who, after hearing the evidence, much of it confessions by the Ku Klux themselves, his honest nature revolting, refused to make a plea for his clients, but left them to the mercy of the Court, saying: " I have listened with unmixed horror to some of the testimony which has been brought before you. The outrages proved are shocking to humanity; they admit of neither excuse nor justification; they violate every obligation which law and nature impose upon man; they show that the parties engaged were brutes, insensible to the obligations of humanity and religion. The day will come, however, if it has not already arrived, when they will deeply lament it. Even if justice shall not overtake them, there is one tribunal from which there is no hope. It is their own judgment; that tribunal which sits in the breast of every living man; that small, still voice that thrills through the heart, the soul, and the mind, and as it speaks gives happiness or torture; the voice of the conscience, the voice of God. If it has not already spoken to them in tones which have startled them to the enormity of their conduct, I trust, in the mercy of Heaven, that that voice will speak before they shall be called above to account for the transactions of this world; that it will so speak as to make them penitent, and that trusting in the dispensations of Heaven, whose justice is dispensed with mercy, when they shall be brought before the bar of their great tribunal, so to speak, that incomprehensible tribunal, there will be found in the fact of their penitence or their previous lives some grounds upon which God may say, ' Pardon.'"

When it is considered that Reverdy Johnson was a Southerner by birth and education, that his sympathies were with the Southern people in their contentions, and that he strongly opposed the Fourteenth Amendment and denounced the great Reconstruction Act, his language constitutes as strong an indictment as can be brought against a civilized people.

Governor Daniel H. Chamberlain of South Carolina, one of the ablest of the so-called "carpet-baggers," in appealing to President Grant for military assistance to guarantee a fair and peaceful election in South Carolina, after detailing the ruthless slaughter of colored citizens in the Hamburg riot, said : " My first duty is to seek to restore and preserve public peace and order, to the end that every man in South Carolina may freely and safely enjoy all his civil rights and privileges, including the right to vote. . . . But I deem it my solemn duty to do my utmost to secure a fair and free election in this State, to protect every man in the free enjoyment of his political rights, and to see to it, that no man or combination of men of any political party, shall overawe, or put in fear or danger, any citizen of South Carolina, in the exercise of his civil rights. . . . I understand that an American citizen has a right to vote as he pleases ; to vote one ticket as freely and as safely as another ; . . . and I know that whenever, upon whatsoever pretext, large bodies of citizens can be coerced by force or fear into absenting themselves from the polls, or voting in a way contrary to their judgment or inclination, the foundations of every man's civil freedom is deeply, if not fatally, shaken."

Replying to this letter, President Grant wrote to Governor Chamberlain to go on in the discharge of his duties, and that he would have the full sympathy and co-operation of the national government. Commenting on the general conditions prevailing in the South, General Grant used these strong and forceful words : " The scene at Hamburg, as cruel, bloodthirsty, wanton, unprovoked, and as uncalled for as it was, is only a repetition of the same that has been pursued in other Southern states within the last few years, notably in Mississippi and Louisiana. Mississippi is governed to-day by officials chosen through fraud and violence, such as would scarcely be accredited to savages, much less to a civilized and Christian people. . . . How long these things are to continue, or what is to be the final remedy, the Great Ruler of the Universe only knows. . . . Nothing is claimed for one state that is not freely accorded to all the others, unless it may be the right to kill negroes and Republicans without fear of punishment, and without the loss of caste or reputation. This has seemed to be a privilege claimed by a few states."

Concerning the Ku Klux Klan, it may be said that " murder with them was an occupation, and perjury was a pastime." Many of their bloodiest and blackest crimes on the colored people have been sealed in the stillness of the death of their victims.

The Southland in some respects and at many points had now become a charnel-house and chamber of horrors. The foul and bloody work so relentlessly carried on by the whites, and the general demoralization consequent thereto caused the Congress to divine that additional guarantees to preserve the civil and political liberties of the colored people were necessary. There was no ground for hope of just or humane treatment for them on the part of the whites. Up to this time suffrage rested in the states, but the adoption of the Fifteenth Amendment to the Constitution of the United States, which was ratified March 30, 1870, made suffrage national and impartial.

So far as the organic law of the land is concerned, the civil and political rights of the colored people are safe and secure forevermore. The right of suffrage in this republic is now and forever national. It is now and forever impartial. Its abrogation is morally inconceivable, practically

7 97

impossible. The words of this great charter of liberty are:

" The right of citizens of the United States to vote shall not be denied or abridged by the United States, or by any State, on account of race, color, or previous condition of servitude."

The leaders of the South have been protesting so loud and long about the " crime " committed in this Reconstruction era that the great masses of its people have probably fully persuaded themselves that a crime really was committed. And because of the bitter and continuous denunciation of " carpet-baggers," " scalawags " and " negro domination "— some good people in the North, who have not taken the trouble to investigate the facts in the case, have been almost persuaded that a serious blunder was made in the bestowal of the ballot on the negro.

The Reverend Dr. C. H. Parkhurst, a most distinguished divine and the pastor of a wealthy and influential church in the city of New York, representing this class, in a public address says: " The instance of the convict is in principle exactly what occurred in the case of the blacks. Emancipation pushed the bolt for them. There was a great deal of heroism in the course of the war, North and South, but there was not much statesmanship in the construction of the peace, and one of the radical mistakes made was in supposing that altering the colored man's condition altered the colored man ; that letting a wolf out of a cage domesticates the wolf ; that substituting coat and trousers for swaddling clothes makes an infant a man, and that emancipation not only relieved the slave of his fetters, but qualified him to be a citizen." Dr. Parkhurst also says through the public press : " Since my return from the South, I have been informed that some of my critics have accused me of expressing regrets that slavery days are over. That is not true. I have merely said that most of the ' niggers ' are unfit for the responsibilities of citizenship.

" The 'niggers' will never be assimilated by the nation. They never, never will contribute, in any part, toward forming the national type of the Americans of the future. They grow blacker and blacker every day. Their color forms a physical barrier which even time, the great leveller, cannot sweep away.

"Persons who talk of assimilation in connection with the race problem do not understand what they speak of. Future generations of our race will be very much as we are. The physical barrier that separates the blacks from the whites to-day will be just as broad and as high throughout all the centuries to come."

Aside from the unparliamentary and unchristian language of this minister of the Gospel of the Lord Jesus Christ — the decisive answer is forthcoming that the Proclamation of Amnesty, pardoning the ex-Confederates, had quite as little effect in altering their condition, or lessening in the least degree their animosities, or transforming them into law-abiding, liberty-loving, patriotic American citizens ; and that moreover the ex-Confederates had actually demonstrated their unfitness to legislate with wisdom, to deal justly or even humanely with either the freedmen or with white men who were loyal to the Union, or to accept in good faith the clemency of a magnanimous nation. And the further argument is conclusive, that the people of " the North believed, and believed wisely, that a poor man, an ignorant man, and a black man who was thoroughly loyal, was a safer and a better voter than a rich man, an educated man, and a white man who in his heart was disloyal to the Union."

The Honorable Carl Schurz, who was appointed by President Johnson after the close of the war as a Commissioner to visit the South and examine into and report upon the condition of things there, in his report says : The loyalty of the Southern people " consists in submitting to necessity." There was generally " an entire absence of that national spirit which forms the basis of true loyalty. . . . It will hardly be possible to secure the freedmen against oppressive legislation and private persecution unless he be endowed with a certain measure of political power. . . . The extension of the franchise to the colored people, upon the development of free labor, and upon the security of human rights in the South, being the principal object in view, the objection raised upon the ground of the ignorance of the freedmen becomes unimportant. . . . The only manner in which the Southern people can be induced to grant to the freedmen some measure of self-protecting power, in the form of suffrage, is to make it a condition precedent to readmission."

Contemplate this report, made in 1866, in the light of the attitude of the South to-day, with all the wrongs imposed on the colored people, and Carl Schurz will at once take rank as a wise seer with the gift of a prophet.

Some of Dr. Parkhurst's friends might do well to inform him that assimilation is not necessarily of blood ; that a people may thoroughly, through the course of the years, assimilate the civilization of another people and become a most pronounced type of that civilization, and yet not be of the same blood. As a matter of fact, the assimilation of a civilization is far more important than the assimilation of blood. It is the former, and not the latter that makes the type. There are many thousands of colored people in the South who have already assimilated American civilization ; who are thorough-going, patriotic, law-abiding Americans in every tissue and fibre of their being. There are also in the South many thousands of whites who are unassimilated and are as alien to the standards and ideals of American civilization as if they had not been born and raised in a land where the gospel of the Christ is preached from every hill-top and in every valley, and where the chief glory of the people is their dedication to the principle that all men are equal before the law. The color of a man's skin can no more affect " the national type of the American of the future " than will the color of his hair, the heaviness of his eyebrows, or the size of his feet; but, rather, he will be marked by the quality and achievement of his intellect, the purity and goodness of his heart, the nobility of his soul and purpose, the strength and breadth of his patriotism, his loyalty to the truth and to his God, and his love and services for man — not white man, not black man, but *Man*. Race barrier or no race barrier, he will best represent the type who best represents the civilization, whether he be as white as the driven snow or as black as the ace of spades.

As to " the national type of the American of the future," the colored people can well afford to leave that in the hands of Almighty God, whom Dr. Parkhurst may perhaps regard as being abundantly able to rule over it wisely, beneficently, to the well-being of the human family and to His own glory and honor. Dr. Parkhurst's ungracious insult, unprovoked and unwarranted, to the colored people who have served their country nobly in war and faithfully and well in peace, by stigmatizing and applying to the whole race the offensive and degrading epithet, the " niggers," and comparing them with " convicts " and " wolves," belittles him and impeaches his own right to be regarded as a consistent disciple of the Christ, or a faithful preacher of righteousness. Much learning, great eloquence, and a pure white skin, good and helpful as they are, yet are not the only nor the chief requisites of a Christian minister. These, without the spirit and mind of the Christ, are " as sounding brass and a tinkling cymbal." Would it not be a happy event for Dr. Parkhurst to go into his closet and wrestle with his God, and himself " assimilate " the mind and teachings of Jesus, the Christ ; giving heed to the injunction of the Apostle Paul, the great apostle to the Gentiles : " Let this mind be in you, which was also in Christ Jesus." Without this spirit all preaching is in vain.

Would Dr. Parkhurst dare to apply offensive and degrading epithets to all the white people of the South ? Why did he gratuitously and grossly insult every self-respecting colored man and woman in the United States ? He knew that the negro is prostrate and helpless, and he felt that he might "dance a jig " on the negro's chest with entire safety to himself. He may continue his jig dancing on the chest of the prostrate negro, but it may yet come to him that he owes the colored people — who have never done him aught of harm and against whom he has no grievance — an apology for thus stigmatizing them ; and as long as that apology is withheld considerate thinking people not only in the North and South but the world over will regard him as unmanly, and as not comporting himself with the dignity and honor of the scrupulous citizen, the punctilious man, or an ambassador of the Christ.

No one would, perhaps, challenge the correctness of the principle that wars are unusual occurrences and therefore they call for the exercise of unusual powers, not only in conducting them but also in the settlement of complex and perplexing questions growing out of them. A nation's life or sovereignty is paramount.

So it was with the Civil War, and so it was with reconstruction. And with reference to negro suffrage, it is all-important to consider the fundamental truths connected therewith.

The giving of the ballot to the negro became the necessary means for the accomplishment of the rehabilitation of the Southern states ; and the use of the ballot in the hands of the negro was effective in achieving the following results : —

First : It established the sovereignty of the nation.

Second : It utterly destroyed all that was vicious, mischievous, and menacing in the doctrines of state rights.

Third : It made effective the Thirteenth Amendment, and enacted the Fourteenth and Fifteenth Amendments to the Constitution of the United States — giving rise to the strange paradox, unique in the history of the world, that the ballot of the ex-slave had become necessary to save the face of a conquering nation, preserve the fruits of victory, and assist in the enactment of laws which made his own freedom secure ; and it wrote his own citizenship ineffaceably into the Constitution, the organic law of the land.

Fourth : It was effective in causing the adoption of free constitutions for the Southern states, the establishment of orderly government in them, and, in a word, rehabilitating them and restoring them to practical and proper relations with the Union.

Fifth : It gave the South its first system of Free Public Schools, a benefaction and blessing of incalculable value.

It is not, therefore, too much to say that the glory and the power of the republic to-day — the foremost and most powerful nation in the world — may be traced to the effective use of the negro as a soldier and as a voter in the most stormy and perilous hour of its existence. He was unquestionably the deciding factor. " The truth is delight," and in the light of the truth these facts blaze forth.

It must, therefore, appear evident to every serious, patriotic American who has more regard for liberty and Union than for race hatred and caste prejudice, that the bestowal of the ballot on the colored people, under the circumstances, and at the time, and in the manner that it was bestowed, was not only not a crime, but, on the contrary, was perhaps the sublimest act of enlightened statesmanship.

All the specious pleas, vituperation, and misrepresentations on the part of Southern leaders and their Northern sympathizers cannot efface or darken the light of this blazing truth, which shines forth, and will shine with increasing and resplendent glory —

> " Until seas shall waste,
> And the sky in smoke decay."

CHAPTER IV

THE WAR ON NEGRO SUFFRAGE

THE ballot in the hands of the colored man — this is the crux of the Southern problem.

The ballot is the citadel of the colored man's safety; the guarantor of his liberty; the protector of his rights; the defender of his immunities and privileges; the savior of the fruits of his toil; his weapon of offence and defence; his peace maker; his Nemesis that watches and guards over him with sleepless eye by day and by night.

With the ballot the negro is a man; an American among Americans.

Without the ballot he is a serf, less than a slave; a thing.

It is not at all singular, therefore, that his ballot, this fortress of his power, should be beleaguered and stormed by all who would oppress, or degrade, or out-law him, or alienate him from human society.

The negrophobists of the South thoroughly understand that, in order to annul him as a factor to be reckoned with in American life and civilization, his ballot, which keeps open " the door of hope, the door of opportunity," must first be demolished.

For this reason the dominant Southern leaders, from the reconstruction day to the present time, have been discharging their heaviest artillery, oratorically speaking, at negro suffrage; their Maxim, machine, and Gatling guns have kept up an incessant roar, through the public press, against negro suffrage; their repeating rifles and small arms, through stump-speakers and otherwise, have been turned upon it without intermission. All this has been accompanied by the ruthless murder of many thousands of innocent colored people as a bloody feint and demonstration. So common has the killing of colored people become that the murder of half a dozen or more, or the driving out of a score, an hundred, or even a thousand, from their homes, and the looting and burning of their property provokes scarcely more than a perfunctory protest here and there and fails to arouse public attention in any part of the country.

It is one of the most serious aspects of the Southern question that the determination to destroy the negro's ballot by violence and keep the colored people in subjection is encouraged by many of its "best citizens." Senator Tillman of South Carolina has recently advocated the killing of thirty thousand colored men in that state. Is there not "a better way" to secure good government in South Carolina? Is not Senator Tillman himself a greater menace to all that is decent in politics, orderly in government, laudable in citizenship, praiseworthy in manhood, pure in Christianity, and humane in society than the worst negro in his state? It is not a difficult matter in the South to deal with a negro, man, woman, or child, whether there are any evidences of crime or not. In public lectures Senator Tillman has repeatedly boasted of the part he took in shooting down "niggers." For instance, in a lecture in Detroit, Michigan, he said : " On one occasion we killed seven niggers; I don't know how many I killed personally, but I shot to kill and I know I got my share." Not one of these unfortunate colored people had committed, or had even been charged with any offence. They simply attempted to exercise their rights as American citizens and cast their ballots. For this they were shot to death.

The desideratum of any nation is good government and the preservation of liberty. Sometimes this may be secured by a government of the few; sometimes by a government of the many ; and sometimes by a government of the whole people.

The special value of republican institutions is that good government can be more safely fostered and assured and liberty made impregnable by a government of the whole people.

This does not mean government by the ignorant and vicious, or by revolutionists, or by those who believe in killing negroes to get rid of their votes, any more than by anarchists who believe in assassinating rulers to get rid of established governments. It does mean the rule of the people; the sway of their opinion, expressed through the ballot-box, in the establishment and enforcement of laws under which all the people shall find equal protection of life, liberty, and property and in the pursuit of happiness, and all who measure up to a fixed standard, and that a reasonable one, shall have a common share in the government.

It does not follow that the whole people, or even most of them will always vote wisely; no, not even in the best governed communities. On the contrary, experience has shown that they have often made serious mistakes. But the redeeming element in republican government is that, despite all defects, more of good comes to the people, and liberty is better safe-guarded, when they are collectively their own master and can elect rulers and enact laws at regular intervals, than by other methods; and that although unscrupulous leaders may fool the people some of the time, they can't fool them all the time. It is not conceivable that the body of the white people of the 'South will stay fooled all the time, for this would mean the failure of civilization.

The nobler and more Christian manhood and womanhood of the South must surely arouse themselves and cast out the evil spirits which have possessed the corporate body dominating Southern life and have produced the present intolerable conditions. Never among any civilized people has there existed a condition wherein oppression was so heartless and wide-spread; the denial of liberty and the simplest of human rights so general; justice such a mockery; humiliations and gross injustices so atrocious; withering wrongs so multiplied, and human life held so cheap. The leaders aim at the destruction of the ballot in the hands of the colored man, and, as a necessary sequence, his elimination as an entity in American life, his relegation to serfdom.

To compass this end the most reprehensible methods have been employed. Notwithstanding the two hundred and fifty years of patient and profitable labor which the negro race gave to the South; notwithstanding the four years of splendid service which they gave to the whites in guarding their families and protecting their property during the war, the Southern leaders have done their utmost to prejudice mankind against this race. They press with great vigor and malevolence against the race three specific charges: first, Poverty; second, Ignorance; third, Immorality.

If it were strictly true that the negro is poor, and ignorant, and immoral, this certainly is not a sufficient reason for his further debasement; it ought rather to elicit sympathy for his misfortune. For these are not inherent qualities; they are incidental conditions in the evolution of a people. Outlawry is not a remedial agent.

If the white people would respect and protect the black man's home, and set a worthy example for him, reinforce the school facilities, and encourage the Church to do its holy work unfettered, these evils would largely disappear.

If the white people of the South will go back far enough in history they can behold their race in a far worse condition than the negro is to-day. But would that have constituted a just ground for their oppression, and denial of the right to rise to the full height of manhood? Even at the present time are there not many thousands of whites in the South, who are actually as poor, as ignorant, as immoral as are some negroes, and without the excuse of the latter? On the other hand, are there not many thousands of negroes, possessors of property, who are educated and clean in character?

Not all the unfortunates and the degraded are on the negro side of the race lines. The Southerners cannot afford to impeach the negro race on these grounds. After despoiling the negro race absolutely of all the fruits of its toil for two hundred and fifty years, it is not becoming for these people to taunt the negro with his poverty.

After enforcing ignorance on the negro race for two and a half centuries, making it a punishable offence for a negro even to be caught with a spelling-book in his possession, these people are not in a position to sneer at the negro because of his ignorance.

After claiming complete ownership of the negro for *eight* long generations and after enforcing on him day by day object lessons of immorality of the most debasing kind, as the enormous amount of Anglo-Saxon blood in negro veins abundantly testifies, it is the height of inconsistency for these people to reproach the negro race on the ground of immorality. All that is true in these charges makes for the greater misfortune of the colored people, and for the shame of the whites.

Colonel Thomas Wentworth Higginson, in an article in the *Atlantic Monthly*, says : " Supposing, for the sake of argument, that there is to be found in the colored race, especially in the former slave states, a lower standard of chastity than among whites, it is hard to imagine any reasoning more grotesque than that which often comes from those who claim to represent the white race there.

" For my own part, I have been for many years in the position to know the truth, even on its worst side, upon this subject. Apart from the knowledge derived in college days from Southern students, then very numerous at Harvard, with whom I happened to be much thrown through a Southern relative, my classmate, I have evidence much beyond this. I have in my hands written evidence, unfit for publication, but discovered in a captured town during the Civil War, —

evidence to show that Rome in its decline was not more utterly degraded, as to the relation between the sexes, than was the intercourse often existing between white men and colored women on American slave plantations. How could it be otherwise where one sex had all the power and the other had no means of escape?

"It may be assumed, therefore, that there is no charge more unfounded than that frequently made, to the effect that the negro was best understood by his former masters. This principle may be justly borne in mind in forming an opinion upon the very severest charges still brought against him.

"It was only the Abolitionists who saw him as he was. They never doubted that he would have human temptations — to idleness, folly, wastefulness, even sensuality. They knew that he would need, like any abused and neglected race, education, moral instruction, and, above all, high example. They knew, in short, all that we know about him now. They could have predicted the outcome of such half-freedom as has been given him, — a freedom tempered by chain-gangs, lynching, and the lash."

Colonel Higginson also refers to Rufus Choate as among the most conservative men of his time and quotes him as saying that, "for the colored woman, the condition of slavery was 'simply hell.'"

It is instructive to note certain stock phrases in use in the South, phrases that are used with the purpose of increasing race animosities. Among these are "social equality," "white man's country," "negro inferiority," "negro domination," "race prejudice." Such phrases are "the bloody shirt" of the South. Their effect has been to nullify, for the time being, the benefits guaranteed by the Constitution of the United States.

Since these are weapons aimed at the ballot of the negro they invite close examination. Race prejudice is the most elastic of them. It can and does cover a multitude of sins.

109

The leaders depend much upon it. Senator Money of Mississippi, in a speech in the United States Senate, declared with great bravado, "I am glad we have race prejudice, I rejoice in it, I thank God for it." But the Holy Scriptures tell of a Pharisee who lived some centuries before him who was also glad and thanked God that he was not as other men. The Saviour of the world, however, did not send him away justified.

Race prejudice is variously designated, and is thus made into a handy five-chamber weapon. Sometimes it is called *inborn* race prejudice, and then again it is labelled *inbred ;* and some declare it is taken in with the *mother's milk*, while others heatedly contend that it is an *instinct ;* but all agree that it is *ineradicable* and must therefore control in Southern life.

This inborn, inbred, mother's-milk, instinctive, ineradicable race prejudice is set forth as the chief, and sometimes as the sufficient cause for the mistreatment of the colored people, and the denial to them of civil and political rights and the protection of the law.

The New York *World* says : " Deeper than the question of suffrage, of education, or of political privilege is this question of " racial instinct " or prejudice. If it is to prevail and dominate our land, where is it to stop? Is it compatible with the precepts of a religion based upon ' the fatherhood of God and the brotherhood of man ' ? Can it be reconciled with the principles of a government founded upon the ' inalienable rights ' of all men, and ordaining in its Constitution equal rights and equal privileges for equal citizens ? If, for example, Booker Washington, with his heart and brain and capacity for elevating his race, cannot enter the front door of the White House without arousing a clamor of unreasonable protest, or hold any public office, simply and solely because he is black, is not the republic a mockery to nine millions of its citizens ?

" There was something more than rhetoric or sentiment in President Roosevelt's pregnant phrase, ' the door of hope' for the negro. When this door leads to education, to industry, thrift, and the patriotism that inspires men to fight and die for their country, as our negroes did in Cuba, must the usual rewards of such character and conduct be denied to them because they are black ? This is the real 'negro question.' "

The contention for inborn, inbred, mother's-milk, instinctive, ineradicable race prejudice is itself not only dangerous to the social organism, but it is also fallacious. It lacks the saving grace of even a half-truth. It is a Gibraltar of straw to be destroyed by the first volley from the battery of Common-Sense.

In the darkest day of slavery, the colored children of household and other servants played and romped freely with the children of the masters ; they as freely took " bites " in turn from the same apple, and sometimes from the same cherry. They never knew the difference in station except as they were taught. The colored nurse would shower her kisses on the white child, cool its food with her breath, and taste it with her tongue. The important question with the parents was not the race or color, but the health of the nurse. Nurses frequently slept with the children, and cared for them with a tenderness and devotion which won their affections forevermore. Many were the instances in which the white child showed preference for the attendance and companionship of the colored nurse to that of the white mother. And this is not unusual even to-day.

Kindness wins, and always will win the hearts and confidence of children without regard to race prejudice of which they know nothing and care less. Many of the very best white women in the South never failed to bestow praises and kisses on their black " mammies " who had fondled them in childhood, and whom they loved and venerated.

More significant still, many of the children of the leading Southern families drank the milk of their black "mammies" alone ; and many in maturity, like the late Henry W. Grady of Atlanta, Georgia, never ceased to express their love and veneration for these black "mammies" who nursed them with a mother's solicitude and guided their early footsteps. If race prejudice is an instinct, inborn, and inbred, how could the whites drink and thrive on the milk of these black "mammies" in childhood, and in the maturity of manhood and womanhood lavishly display such glowing respect and devotion to these black "mammies"?

There are numbers of authenticated cases of white children being raised entirely by colored families, who never recognized any difference between themselves and the colored children, notwithstanding, "inborn, inbred" race prejudice. For obvious reasons they had been given over to colored "mammies" to be raised, and they were most happy in these relations during childhood ; and in maturity, when apprised of their identity and offered privileges, some of them indignantly refused to give up their colored "mammies" who had always shown them a mother's care, fidelity, and love. Some such continued to live, and married, among the colored people, and became to all intents members of that race.

The case is too plain for cavil that *any* white child raised entirely in a colored family may grow to old age without recognizing its race identity. And the prejudice would be against the whites, and not the colored. How is it to be explained that this "inborn, inbred, mother's-milk, instinctive, ineradicable" race prejudice does not reveal itself to its own possessor? And it may be pertinently asked, of what value is it if it cannot reveal itself?

Conductors of railway trains and street cars in the South are of course supposed to have this race prejudice, and they are paid to enforce it. But they have repeatedly caused awkward and sometimes ugly situations by mistaking white persons for colored persons and colored persons for white persons — producing a " comedy of errors."

Race or color does not necessarily affect the peace or happiness of a child, or of an adult. Men and women of different races have mutually reciprocated good offices and enjoyed friendly relations, cherishing the highest respect for each other; while men and women of the same race, sometimes of the same family, have despised one another. The white child smiles as radiantly with the colored coachman or gardener as with its father. It will coo alike to its father, the colored nurse, the cat, or rubber doll.

Race prejudice is largely a matter of teaching and training. Any people can teach their children to hate or despise another people, or even to hate and despise a branch of the family of their own blood relations. Also parents can indoctrinate the young in the principles of the Sermon on the Mount and the teachings of the lowly Nazarene, and the result will be as different as day from night.

Again, there are other cases, fully authenticated, of persons possessing African blood and yet passing for white. Some are doing so to-day in the North as well as in the South.

It is a great pity — a lamentable evil — that race prejudice should so operate as to compel a man to conceal his race identity, and pose as a member of another race in order to secure fair or decent treatment or a chance to make an honest living. In this particular race prejudice not only harms the negro, but it injures the entire social organism. It is most creditable to the negro race, to their growing self-respect and race pride that only a few of their numbers in sheer desperation resort to the trick of passing for what they are not. It should be noted in this connection that in South Carolina and other Southern states there are certain settlements of persons possessing African blood who, nevertheless, are not treated as a part of the black race, but as whites. When they remove away from their homes, passing for whites, they live and move among whites and even marry among them. And no one is the wiser.

Senator Tillman on the floor of the Constitutional Convention of South Carolina, more specifically called for the purpose of disfranchising the colored people, made a special plea for these particular settlements of people with African blood in that state, but who were passing for and accepted as white people, saying : " Some of them owned slaves before the war, all of them sympathized with the Confederacy, and many of them fought in its army ; therefore they should be regarded and treated as whites." Is this not a cruel blow to " inborn, inbred, mother's-milk, instinctive, ineradicable " race prejudice ? Does not the logic of it expose the fallacy of the contention ?

The whole case falls to the ground ; for here the " ineradicable " is eradicated. But Senator Tillman's specious plea is worthy of more than a casual glance. Those for whom and in whose interest he made it were admittedly colored people, possessing African blood. But they in most instances were set free by their white fathers before the war of the Rebellion ; and some of them inherited their father's slaves and thus became slave owners. They intermarried among white and colored ; and because some of them were slave owners, and because all of them sympathized with the Southern Confederacy, and because many of them fought in the Confederate army, — therefore all of them were transformed from "niggers" into white folks.

Here is the plain enunciation of the doctrine that loyalty to the late Confederacy shall count as paramount in fixing the status of citizenship in the South, and can even metamorphose a " nigger " into a white man.

But there were four millions of other colored people who were " true-hearted, whole-hearted, faithful, and loyal " to the Union and responsive to its martial music. None of these

114

owned slaves ; all of these sympathized with the Union ; and, momentous fact, 200,000 of these rushed to the national defence and faced the chivalry of the South.

Shall not the republic show as much concern in the protection of the lives and liberty of those who freely offered themselves on its altar as the ex-Confederates and their sons show in protecting the handful of mixed-bloods who joined with them in the effort to " shoot the government to death ? "

The " mother's-milk, instinct," argument to bolster up race prejudice is worthless.   Instinct acts spontaneously, and not by promptings ; naturally, and not by moral force or suasion ; independently, uniformly ; it peremptorily rejects the incompatible.   But there has been no uniformity of race prejudice in the South against the colored people.   On the contrary, there have been many relations, in some cases of the closest kind.

The deplorable conditions existing in the South are not natural or spontaneous, but artificial.   They are the direct result of the vicious and mischievous teachings of the leaders. As to the " mother's-milk " end of the argument, this is sure to put some very good Southerners into a very bad dilemma.   For if " logic is logic," the prejudice should trend in favor of the source of the milk.   Natural-mother's-milk prejudice should be in favor of the natural mother.

" Black-mammy's "-milk prejudice should be in favor of the " black mammy."

Cow's-milk prejudice should be in favor of the cow.

Goat's-milk prejudice should be in favor of the goat.

No milk, then no prejudice.

And as to " Prepared Food," " that is the question " which will command all the acumen and store of legal lore of the proverbial Philadelphia lawyer to solve, as to whether prejudice should run in favor of some one manufacturer, or what particular component element of his " Food."

" Logic is logic," — that is all.

115

It is plain, however, that the milk or other food which nourishes the child has no more to do in creating race prejudice in the child than corned beef and cabbage, the juicy bivalves, Boston baked beans, or Chinese " Chop Suey " have in producing race prejudice in the full-grown man.

Ineradicable race prejudice ! What hypocrisy ! A greater proportion than three out of every five negroes met casually in the street or seen in public gatherings will show traces of Anglo-Saxon blood.

A matter of very great importance and one not to be overlooked herewith is that the negro race in the United States is practically a new race. The race in America is far removed from the ancestral African — in language, in method of thought, in religion and civilization. Its basic element is in the strong and virile blood of the fatherland, but built upon by the blood of all the great races. It is sure to become a strong and powerful people in the future. It will not seek close affiliations with the white race, for the reason that it will have all the colors and blendings of every race within itself, from the fairest Caucasian to the darkest ebony — making it truly the Colored Race. As a rule, the law of race pride and clan allegiance will be the law of natural selection. To the simple question of prejudice no great importance is to be attached. The history of ages record its existence. There is abundant prejudice between white and white ; colored and colored ; white and colored ; English and Irish ; French and German ; English and French ; Irish and German ; and the Jews and the rest of the world.

But it should be borne in mind that there is prejudice and prejudice. Every man has prejudices ; and these may control his personal habits, his recreations, his associations, his friendships, his politics, his religion, and all his relations of life. He may wear shoes without socks, or go barefoot if his prejudices lead him to do so ; but he would not be tolerated if he tried to compel a neighbor to become a " Sockless Simpson." The white people of the South are at liberty to have and to hold their prejudices against the colored people or against Yankees; and against this liberty it is not for public opinion to protest nor for the government to make objection.

To eliminate prejudice from the hearts of men and emancipate the people from its evil effects is a work generally delegated to the doctrinaires of religion. But when the white people of the South convert their prejudice into an engine of hostility, a force of oppression and destruction to others, it then becomes the imperative duty of public opinion to protest, and the obligation of the government to intervene.

The Honorable Carl Schurz, writing in *McClure's Magazine*, referring to this attempt to subjugate the negro race, says: " And now the reactionists are striving again to burden the Southern people with another 'peculiar institution,' closely akin to its predecessor in character, as it will be in its inevitable effects if fully adopted by the Southern people, — that is, if the bulk of the laboring class is again to be kept in stupid subjection, without the hope of advancement and without the ambition of progress. For, as the old pro-slavery man was on principle hostile to general negro education, so the present advocate of semi-slavery is perfectly logical in his contempt for the general education of the colored people, and in his desire to do away with the negro school. What the reactionist really wants is a negro just fit for the task of a plantation hand and for little, if anything, beyond.

"Therefore, quite logically, the reactionist abhors the educated negro. In fact the political or social recognition of the educated negro is especially objectionable to him for the simple reason that it would be an encouragement of higher aspirations among the colored people generally.

"The reactionist wishes to keep the colored people, that is, the great mass of the laboring force in the South as ignorant as possible, to the end of keeping it as submissive and obedient as possible. . . . And now imagine the moral, intellectual, and economic condition of a community whose principal and most anxious — I might say historic — care is the solution of the paramount problem 'how to keep the nigger down,' — that is, to reduce a large part of its laboring population to stolid brutishness. . . . That is not all. The reactionist fiercely insists that the South 'must be let alone' in dealing with the negro.

"This was the cry of the pro-slavery men of the old antebellum time. But the American people outside of the South took a lively interest in the matter, and finally the South was not let alone, . . . they can hardly hope to be 'let alone.' Thus it may be said without exaggeration that by striving to keep up in the Southern States a condition of things which cannot fail to bring forth constant irritation and unrest, which threatens to burden the South with another 'peculiar institution' by making the bulk of its laboring force again a clog to progressive development, — and to put the South once more in a position provokingly offensive to the moral sense and the enlightened spirit of the world outside, — the reactionists are the worst enemies the Southern people have to fear."

The white people of the South would hotly resent any suggestion of their incapacity for self-government. But their policy is their own condemnation. For if they cannot rise above the low level of race prejudice and vulgar assumptions in the making and the enforcement of the law, is it not self-evident that they fail in the vital requisites and capacity for self-government? A people who cannot, or will not, maintain orderly government in their local affairs invite distrust in broader or national affairs. The law of the spiritual life prevails here, — he who is faithful over a few things shall be made ruler over " many things."

The republic is governed by law, and not by race prejudice. Race prejudice is not law. Its operation is akin to anarchy. To give it the sanction, prestige, and force of law is to subvert American institutions and to destroy liberty and civilization. The result is certain. If once justified as law, where and when is it to end? If the colored people are to be the victims of it to-day, who are to feel its fell and ruinous blow to-morrow? Shall liberty, truth, and righteousness be sacrificed to race prejudice? Is race prejudice everything, and the Constitution of the United States and the laws of God nothing?

Good citizenship measures up to the Constitution. The Constitution does not and cannot contract to the narrow confines of local prejudices, " inborn, inbred," or otherwise ; for this would mean the ruin of all that has been gained, as well as all that is hoped for in the evolution of man and the march of civilization.

When the white people of the South set themselves deliberately and with the purpose aforethought to the work of reducing the colored race, as Mr. Schurz says, " to stolid brutishness," and keep them " in stupid subjection without the hope of advancement and the ambition of progress," and plead as a justification therefor " inborn, inbred, mother's-milk, instinctive, ineradicable " race prejudice, they transgress against the moral sentiment of Christendom.

That they should demand that the strong arm of the Federal government shall be brought into requisition to aid them in consummating so diabolical a work by turning every colored person out of every Federal office, and discharging every colored man from the army and navy, and forcing every colored person into inferior relations in every walk of life and into serfdom, — this but accentuates the folly and frenzy which has possessed the head and heart of the South. That the white people of the South are practically united in this reactionary, anti-Christian policy does not lessen its heinousness.

That some well-meaning men in the North look upon it with sympathy or approval does not add one glimmer of virtue to

119

it. By condoning oppression and outlawry, such apologists encourage further disorders and violence. The policy of the South is wrong. No number of adherents and advocates for it can make it right. Its consummation in the dawn of the twentieth century and after forty years of heroic struggle against the most tremendous odds, and in the light of the wonderful, unsurpassed progress and achievements of the negro race in civilization,— would be the crime of these centuries.

God Almighty did not grant to the white people of the South a perpetual lien on the labor and toils of the colored people, nor the right to rule, oppress, and outrage them to their hearts' content. If the whole South approves, then the whole South is wrong. But the evidence is not conclusive that the whole South does approve. There are more than murmurs of emphatic dissent from many noble-hearted Southerners, who see the blistering disgrace and burning shame which overshadow their fair land and discredit its civilization. But, at any rate, even the whole South should not be permitted to commit the republic to the nefarious policy of destroying the hope of millions of its own citizens. Many people who approved of slavery, endorsed the hanging of John Brown whose "soul goes marching on," and acclaimed secession with joy and enthusiasm, now regret with pangs indescribable the existence of one and the occurrence of the others.

Some good men have gone wrong on every great moral issue of the past, and some good men are sure to go wrong on every great moral question of the future. This seems to be inevitable. But in the end the Right will win. The Right leads the trek of humanity, and God leads the Right. Furthermore, the white people of the South themselves display grave suspicions of the durability of this race prejudice. If this prejudice is all that they claim, why is it necessary to hedge it about, buttress it around, prop it up, shield it over, and bastile it over with proscriptive, oppressive, and unlawful laws? Why inaugurate a reign of terror and bloodshed to cultivate it?

After all, to every serious American it will be manifest that all the smoke and noise and deadly work of this five-barrel weapon — this "inborn, inbred, mother's-milk, instinctive, ineradicable" race prejudice — are intended to cover the enactment of a tragedy in the Southland : the overthrow of the ballot of the colored man, the despoiling and subjugation of a people.

The Reverend Dr. Newell Dwight Hillis, who fills the Plymouth pulpit at Brooklyn, New York, made famous by Henry Ward Beecher, in a recent sermon said : "Just now the whole country is suffering from a reaction on the negro question, and the colored race have known a month of such depression and sorrow and heartache as they have not known in forty years — and there is reason for the depression. Consider the Presbyterian preacher in New York who last week said that the emancipation of the slaves was like the release of criminals from the penitentiary, and that the future of the 'nigger' was blacker and blacker and more hopeless. Consider that editorial in the Richmond paper that, commenting on the speech of a Southerner and of a great religious editor in New York, said that the two men evidently might have exchanged addresses. Think of the Southern soldier who insists in his article that the negro is an animal ; that, like the dog and horse, he has by association borrowed some of man's characteristics, but that he is without soul, and that he fears like the animal and never can have a home.

"In 1866 Mr. Beecher said here that we must insist on suffrage for the negro; that races, like children, are trained by responsibility ; that the poorest government of an ignorant man who governs himself is better than the best government that is imposed upon him from without. Mr. Beecher also said that in view of two centuries of injustice and slavery it might take a century before we would see the outcropping of an occasional orator, an occasional colored educator. What if Mr. Beecher could return to-day? He would find that the greatest orator, from many points of view, in the country is a negro, and a black man to-day receives $150 to $300 a night, and there is only one other man in the country who receives as much.

"The colored people are needlessly alarmed. The reaction is an eddy from the South itself. All the enemies of liberty, whether they want to or not, have to help the forces of liberty."

True words these! "All the enemies of liberty, whether they want to or not, have to help the forces of liberty." The violent outburst of Southern wrath on the colored people and the extreme and cruel persecution of them "will help the forces of liberty." Intended for evil, they "will work together for good." These things will not be without value as an object lesson exposing the mind and purpose of the South,— an object lesson of which the nation will not fail to take note; an object lesson which will serve to rally "the forces of liberty," and assure the decisive defeat of the conspiring "enemies of liberty."

A white man's country! This phrase is often pressed into service, and it has the effect chiefly of exciting race intolerance. It has been used with great detriment to the colored people, causing many of them to be driven from their homes ; and some to be killed because they stood on the principle that "a man's home is his castle."

It would deny them the right of domicile on American soil. And if they have not the right of domicile, it would follow that they have not the right of citizenship nor the ballot, nor the protection of the law. It would place the race in the position of interlopers, subject to expulsion at the whim of any party, at any place or at any time, or to be driven helter-skelter by the blind fury of the mob.

A little incident, indeed a very little one, occurred recently at Washington City, which throws a flood of light on this pretension and dissolves its logic. It happened in this wise : A prominent Indian chief went from the Western prairies to visit the President at the White House. He was received and entertained in the cordial and hearty manner characteristic of Mr. Roosevelt. The Indian chief was greatly delighted. After the conference with the Great Father, he left the White House and soon after this encountered a leading Southerner. In the conversation which followed, the Southerner inquired of the Indian chief if he did not think it would be a good thing to send all the negroes back to Africa. Without a moment's hesitation the great chief bluntly replied, " Yes, all the negroes ought to be sent back to Africa," and added with true Indian sternness, " and all the Chinese to China, and all the Germans to Germany, and all the French to France, and all the English to England, and all the Italians to Italy ; and all the other people too should be sent back to their own countries, and America should be given back to the Indians to whom it rightfully belongs."

This was truly a rebuff to the Southerner. He got his answer, and with it a corollary which he had not expected. He found that the Indian chief was no respecter of persons. The rugged common-sense, the innate honesty, and the irresistible logic of the answer of this noble son of the plains will be applauded by every one. And the probability is that the Southern leaders will attain as little success in proving at the bar of public opinion that the colored people have no right to a domicile in this country as this particular Southerner had in demonstrating it to the satisfaction of the Indian chief.

As a matter of history the white Southerners have barely eight years of priority on American soil over the colored

Southerners. So that if the colored people were obliged to make their departure in this year of grace, or at any other time, the white Southerners, to be chronologically consistent, would have to pack their "carpet-bags" and vacate the country just eight years later.

As a matter of history also, the negroes were here even before the ever memorable and historic settlement at Plymouth Rock which has crowned this country with honor and glory.

A country rightfully belongs to its inhabitants. All in common, whatever their race, have vested interests in the soil. If the colored people have no such rights, then none of the heterogeneous peoples inhabiting the country possess them.

If long and continued residence establishes the right, the colored people possess it, for they have been here practically as long as the whites. If an entrance which was not an intrusion or a trespass would give the right, the colored people have a much stronger claim than the whites, for they were not only the unwilling, but the forcefully entreated and detained occupant guests.

If centuries of hard and faithful toil, the toil which develops the natural resources of a country, and which causes " the wilderness to bloom as the rose," would make perfect such a right, the colored people would have a claim superior to that of Southern whites.

If the loyalty and patriotism which move men to offer their services, spill their blood, and fight and die in defence of their country, would seal the right of inheritance and vested interests in the soil, here too the colored people would have peculiar advantages over many of their white neighbors and would take at least equal rank with any class of the population.

The blood of Crispus Attucks, a negro, was the first blood that was shed in the Revolutionary War. He was the first to fall from the volley of the " red coats " in the " Boston massacre." Thus a negro's blood actually sealed American Independence.

The City of Boston has erected on her Common, a monument to the first martyrs of American liberty, and at the head of the list is a negro, the selfsame Crispus Attucks. Peter Salem, a negro, fought side by side with Warren and his comrades in the battle of Bunker Hill.

Colored men fought under Washington in several of his campaigns. General Greene, in writing to Alexander Hamilton, the 10th of January, 1781, from the vicinity of Camden, South Carolina, said : "There is a great spirit of enterprise among the black people, and those that have come out as volunteers are not a little formidable to the enemy."

The negro was with Perry in his great victory on Lake Erie.

Andrew Jackson, whom the South has delighted to honor, fought with negroes at the battle of New Orleans, and praised their heroism in his official report. The colored soldiers held the extreme right of the American lines and drove back the British at the point of the bayonet.

There is certainly no room for equivocation or doubt as to the meaning of these words which General Jackson, in his proclamation to the negroes dated September 21, 1814, used : " To every noble-hearted, generous freeman of color volunteering to serve during the present contest with Great Britain and no longer, there will be paid the same bounty, in money and lands, now received by the white soldiers of the United States, namely, one hundred and twenty-four dollars in money, and one hundred and sixty acres of land. The non-commissioned officers and privates will also be entitled to the same monthly pay and daily rations and clothes furnished to any American soldier. To assure you of the sincerity of my intentions, and my anxiety to engage your invaluable services to our country, I have communicated my wish to the Governor of Louisiana, who is fully informed as to the manner of enrolment, and will give you every necessary information on the subject of this address."

Furthermore, on December 18, 1814, General Jackson, in an address to his colored soldiers, said: "To the men of color. Soldiers! From the shores of Mobile I collected you to arms; I invited you to share in the perils and to divide the glory of your white countrymen. I expected much from you; for I was not uninformed of those qualities which render you so formidable to an invading foe. I knew that you could endure hunger and thirst and all the hardships of war. But you surpassed my hopes. I have found in you, united to these qualities, that noble enthusiasm which impels to great deeds. Soldiers! The President of the United States shall be informed of your conduct on the present occasion; and the voice of Representatives of the American nation shall applaud your valor, as your General now praises your ardor."

That foremost patriot and expounder of the Constitution, Alexander Hamilton, in a letter to John Jay, March 14, 1779, said: "I have not the least doubt that the negroes will make very excellent soldiers with proper management; and I will venture to pronounce that they cannot be put into better hands than those of Mr. Laurens [Colonel Laurens of South Carolina]. . . .

"An essential part of the plan is to give them their freedom with their muskets."

The Honorable Henry Laurens, father of Colonel John Laurens of South Carolina, a great figure in the Revolutionary War, writing to General Washington, March 16, 1779, says: "Had we arms for three thousand such black men as I could select in Carolina, I should have no doubt of success in driving the British out of Georgia and subduing East Florida before the end of July."

A fact of transcendent interest may be recorded here, to wit: that the Congress of the United States on March 29,

1779, passed a series of resolutions (see " Secret Journals of Congress," pages 107–110) in part as follows :

" *Resolved*, That it be recommended to the States of South Carolina and Georgia, if they shall think the same expedient, to take measures immediately for raising three thousand able-bodied negroes." . . . And further " *Resolved*, That Congress will make provision for paying the proprietors of such negroes as shall be enlisted for the service of the United States during the war a full compensation for the property at a rate not exceeding one thousand dollars for each active, able-bodied negro man of standard size, not exceeding thirty-five years of age, who shall be so enlisted and pass muster."

Congress also passed on the same day the following resolution : " Whereas John Laurens, Esq., who has heretofore acted as aid-de-camp to the Commander-in-Chief, is desirous of repairing to South Carolina, with a design to assist in defence of the Southern States : —

" *Resolved*, That a commission of Lieutenant-Colonel be granted to the said John Laurens, Esq."

Thus Colonel Laurens of South Carolina, who was commissioned by special resolution of the Congress, was foremost in " carrying the plan of the black levees into execution."

The Honorable William Eustis of Massachusetts, who was a soldier through the Revolutionary War and afterwards Governor of Massachusetts and member of Congress, in a speech in the Congress, Dec. 12, 1820, said : " At the commencement of the Revolutionary War, there were found in the Middle and Northern states many blacks, and other people of color, capable of bearing arms ; a part of them free, the greater part slaves. The freemen entered our ranks with the whites. The time of those who were slaves was purchased by the states ; and they were induced to enter the service in consequence of a law by which, on condition of their serving in the ranks during the war, they were made freemen.

" In Rhode Island, where their numbers were more considerable, they were formed under the same considerations into a regiment commanded by white officers; and it is required, in justice to them, to add that they discharged their duty with zeal and fidelity. The gallant defence of Red Bank, in which this black regiment bore a part, is among the proofs of their valor.

" Among the traits which distinguished this regiment was their devotion to their officers; when their brave Colonel Greene was afterwards cut down and mortally wounded, the sabres of the enemy reached his body only through the limbs of his faithful guard of blacks, who hovered over him and protected him, every one of whom was killed and whom he was not ashamed to call his children.

" The services of this description of men in the navy are also well known. I should not have mentioned either, but for the information of the gentleman from Delaware, whom I understood to say that he did not know that they had served in any considerable numbers.

" The war over and peace restored, these men returned to their respective states; and who could have said to them, on their return to civil life, after having shed their blood in common with the whites in the defence of the liberties of the country, ' You are not to participate in the rights secured by the struggle, or the liberty for which you have been fighting '?

" Certainly no white man in Massachusetts."

Straight to the point are the positive utterances of the Honorable Charles Pinckney of South Carolina, who, in a speech in the Congress, December, 1820, said: " They [the negroes] were, as they still are, as valuable a part of our population to the Union as any other equal number of inhabitants. They were in numerous instances the pioneers, and, in all, the laborers, of your armies. To their hands were owing the erection of the greatest part of the fortifications raised for the protection of our country; some of which, particularly

Fort Moultrie, gave, at that early period of the inexperience and untried valor of our citizens, immortality to American arms; and in the Northern states numerous bodies of them were enrolled into, and fought by the sides of the whites, the battles of the Revolution."

The conclusion is unavoidable that these brave and much praised black patriots, whose "invaluable services" were ungrudgingly acknowledged by leading men North and South, were, with their descendants, gradually forced back into slavery. And as the institution grew and flourished they were lost in it and their identity and services forgotten.

The great services of the negroes on land and at sea in the War of the Rebellion are well known. Admiral Porter, in his *Naval History of the Civil War*, says: "A remarkable instance of patriotism on the part of the colored people was evinced in the bringing out of the armed steamer 'Planter' from Charleston and delivering her over to the naval officers blockading that port. . . . [This act] would have done credit to any one, but the cleverness with which the whole affair was conducted deserves more than a passing notice." Robert Smalls, a mulatto, was the pilot of the Confederate steamer "Planter." Seizing the vessel while the white officers were on shore, with the assistance of the negro crew he cast off the hawser under the very eyes of a sentinel, steamed down the bay performing the proper salutes, passed Fort Sumter, and proceeded to sea before the Confederates realized that the vessel was bound for the blockading fleet. Smalls' heroic services were recognized by Congress, and he afterwards became a member of Congress from South Carolina.

Colonel Le Grand B. Cannon, in a volume entitled "Personal Reminiscences of the Rebellion," makes this most interesting recital: "Some little time after the duel in Hampton Roads, early in the month of April, four big steamships — the "Vanderbilt," the "Arago," the "Ericsson," and the "Illinois" — came down to Fort Monroe, to be in the harbor in readiness to attack the "Merrimac" if she came out, and to destroy her by running her down. Captain Gadsden of the "Arago," a merchant ship chartered for this service, on reaching Fort Monroe and opening his orders, found that his ship was to be a ram. His crew in some way got to know the nature of the mission their ship was in, and the dangerous character of the work in which they were to engage, and promptly deserted in a body.

"The next morning Captain Gadsden found he had not a man aboard his ship except his officers. He went to the admiral of the fleet and stated his dilemma. The admiral said he had not a man to spare. General Wool (of the land forces) brought Captain Gadsden to me, and the latter related to me the condition of affairs. He said negroes would do for his purposes quite as well as white men, and asked me if I would give him fifty negroes.

" 'Yes,' I answered, 'I will let you have all the negroes you want under certain conditions.'

" 'What are they?' asked Captain Gadsden.

" 'They must be volunteers,' I said.

" 'What will be the pay,' I asked.

" 'Thirteen dollars a month and rations,' he answered.

" 'All right,' I said, 'you come to me at 12 o'clock.'

"At 12 o'clock Captain Wilder had three hundred and fifty sturdy negro stevedores drawn up in double lines. I addressed them saying: 'I do not know what the result of this war will be in regard to your condition. I hope it will result in your freedom. Some have got to shed their blood, and others to lay down their lives. You have seen the battle which has been fought between the "Merrimac" and our vessels of war. We have brought down four big ships to destroy the "Merrimac" by ramming her. The enterprise is a hazardous one, but it is one of glory. From on board one ship the white sailors have deserted because of the hazard of the service. It is my privilege to offer to fifty of you the opportunity to volunteer to go on that ship. Every man who survives will be a hero, and those who fall will be martyrs. Now, those boys who will volunteer to go on board this fighting ship will move three paces to the front.'

"And the whole line moved up in a solid column, as though actuated by a single impulse. It was a thrilling response, and the most remarkable and impressive scene I ever witnessed. We picked out fifty of the most likely men, and they were sent at once on board the "Arago." They were escorted down to the boats by all the negroes round about, with shouting, singing, and praying, and every demonstration of exultant joy. It was a most exciting and inspiring sight.

"The volunteers put aboard the "Arago" proved themselves most apt and willing workers, and soon proved their value and justified our confidence. A week or two after this incident Captain Fox, First Assistant Secretary of the Navy, came down to Fort Monroe. I told him what we had done, and he was greatly pleased and interested and saw the men, and inquired fully as to their capabilities and value. Shortly afterward he issued an order that the fleets should be recruited entirely from negroes. Thus were negroes, fugitives, slaves, enlisted in the naval service of the United States, as free men and free agents, on the same footing as the white volunteers, nine months before the Proclamation of Emancipation by President Lincoln."

Colonel Thomas Wentworth Higginson, of Boston, who in turn commanded both white and colored soldiers, in a recent issue of the *Atlantic Monthly*, of the colored soldiers says: "As to the general facts of courage and reliability, I think that no officer in our camp ever thought of there being any essential difference between black and white; and surely the judgment of these officers, who were risking their lives at every moment, month after month, on the fidelity of their men, was worth more than the opinion of the world besides.

As the negroes were intensely human at these points, they were equally so in pointing out that they had more to fight for than the white soldier. They loved the United States flag, and I remember one zealous corporal, a man of natural eloquence, pointing to it during a meeting on the Fourth of July, and saying with more zeal than statistical accuracy, 'Dar's dat flag, we hab lib under it for eighteen hundred and sixty-two years, and we'll lib and die for it now.' But they could never forget that, besides the flag and the Union, they had home and wife and child to fight for. War was a very serious matter to them. They took a grim satisfaction when orders were issued that the officers of colored troops should be put to death on capture. It helped their *esprit de corps* immensely. Their officers, like themselves, were henceforward to fight with ropes around their necks. Even when the new black regiments began to come down from the North, the Southern blacks pointed out this difference, that in case of ultimate defeat, the Northern troops, black or white, must sooner or later be exchanged and returned to their homes, whereas, they themselves must fight it out or be re-enslaved. All this was absolutely correct reasoning and showed them human. And further, no matter how reckless in bearing they might be, those negroes were almost fatalists in their confidence that God would watch over them ; and if they died it would be because their time had come. 'If each one of us was a praying man,' said one of my corporals in a speech, 'it appears to me that we could fight as well with prayers as with bullets, for the Lord has said that if you have faith even as a grain of mustard seed cut into four parts, you can say to the sycamore tree "Arise," and it will come up.' And though Corporal Long's botany may have got a little confused, his faith proved itself by works, for he volunteered to go many miles on a solitary scouting expedition into the enemy's country in Florida, and got back safe after he had been given up for lost."

THE WAR ON NEGRO SUFFRAGE

The Reverend Dr. Joseph E. Roy, now residing at Oak Park, Illinois, in an article in *The New Englander and Yale Review,* on "Our Indebtedness to the Negroes for their Conduct during the War," speaks of Wagner, Port Hudson, the "Tragedy of the Crater" at Petersburg, and Fort Pillow as giving the severest test of these black soldiers and as winning the favor and the admiration of the army and of the country.

He quotes the opinions of General Grant, General Burnside, Captain Jewett, Colonel Bassett, General Hunter, Captain Pease, Governor Rush of Wisconsin, and others, who were in touch with colored soldiers and knew their value. He then proceeds: "It would be edifying to our patriotism to follow them through the two hundred and forty-nine battles and engagements in which they participated, down the Atlantic coast, down the Mississippi, and along with the armies of the Potomac, the James, and Cumberland. In such a tour we would find them at Ship Island successfully resisting the assault of Confederate veterans twice their number; we would find them at Milliken's Bend, whipping the enemy that came yelling, 'No quarter!' at Fort Powhatan, where the ex-slaves met three charges from the Virginia masters under Fitzhugh Lee and held out for a five hours' fight, carrying the day; at Bermuda Hundred, where they took six redoubts with their connecting rifle-pits and captured seven pieces of artillery; at Decatur, capturing a battery with a loss of six officers and sixty men; at Dalton, where an inspecting captain reported to General Steedman, 'The regiment over there is holding dress parade under fire'; at Honey Hill, where in a battle that had twenty-three hundred union soldiers killed or wounded, as Captain Jewett tells me, his men, lying down to protect a battery, would beg permission and go out, a few at a time, to join in the fight, only a part of them coming back; and at Nashville, where a negro division was put forward to open the battle, and where, as Captain Lyman told me, his colored regiment, in making the sixty rods to capture a bastion, had fifty-six men killed and one hundred and twenty-eight wounded.

"Captain H. V. Freeman, of Chicago, addressing the students of Hampton upon the bravery of the colored troops, said: 'It was the second day of the battle of Nashville that the charge on Overton Hill occurred. Three regiments of General Thomas's brigade — the 12th, 13th, and 100th —, were colored troops. These were put in with a division of colored troops — General Wood's 4th Army Corps — for the charge on Overton Hill. The first charge was not successful, owing to the wounding of General Post of the 4th Army Corps, and also to the difficulty of crossing the ploughed ground. You know what Tennessee clay soil is when it gets wet — there seems no bottom to it. Going through that corn field, it seemed as if there was no bottom to it, and as we pulled our feet out — all the while the cannons playing on us from the hill — each foot seemed to weigh a ton. At the bottom of the hill we got over a rail fence — all that were left of us — and found ourselves on good turf. It seemed then as if we could fly; but there were tree tops cut down and as I saw my men struggling through them, they seemed to be sticking to them like flies in a spider's web, the rebel cannon sending in grape shot and canister upon them. The result was that the only men who reached the ramparts were men of the colored regiments. They scaled the ramparts, and every man who did was shot down. The first charge, as I said, was not a success, but the regiments did not retreat. Those left lay down at the foot of the hill, and at the next order to charge, with the whole line they swept over the ramparts.'"

Dr. Roy also quotes General S. C. Armstrong, as follows: "At the siege of Richmond, I received an order to push my regiment — the 9th U. S. Colored Infantry — to the flank of General Terry's division, which was being hard pressed. Standing there in line we were harassed by an unseen foe hidden in the bushes. It was impossible to hold the position and I ordered my men to fall back, and, to avoid a panic and stampede, I ordered them to walk ; and they did so the whole distance — shot at by the unseen enemy as they went, and having to climb over fallen trees and go through rough ground. They got back panting with fatigue and lay down exhausted. As they lay there the order came from our brigade commander to go back over the same ground and retake the position. I knew that meant death for every one of us, but a soldier has only to obey, so I gave the order and we started. But General Terry saw us going, and understanding the position, ordered us back and saved us. What struck me was that every man went forward. Exhausted as they were, knowing as they did the difficulty of the way and the certainty of death before them, not one man faltered."

At Fort Harrison, within five miles of Richmond, where the rebel garrison cried out, " Come on, darkies, we want your muskets!" they did come on, shouting, " Remember Fort Pillow!" to capture those taunting cavaliers and their stronghold; of which exploit General Butler, on the floor of Congress, said: " It became my painful duty, sir, to follow in the track of that charging column, and there, in a space not wider than the clerk's desk, and three hundred yards long, lay the dead bodies of five hundred and forty-three ebony-colored comrades, slain in the defence of their country, who had laid down their lives to uphold its flag and its honor as a willing sacrifice.

" Our indebtedness to these people for their conduct during the war — who can reckon it up ? We early set about discharging a part of that obligation. We gave them their freedom. We clothed them with citizenship. We conferred upon them the suffrage. The Government is in covenant, before God and the nations, with these allies, whose late coming was like that of Blucher to our Waterloo. It maintains the rights of only an intended citizen everywhere around the globe. Will it keep faith with ten millions of native Americans, whose citizenship has been sealed in blood?

"They are Americans, baptized as such by the sprinkling of blood. We must honor their rights of inheritance and of baptism."

The testimony of two other important witnesses may be inserted here.

General George H. Thomas, the hero of the battle at Nashville, Tennessee, after riding over the field and viewing the bodies of white and colored soldiers mingled together, said: "This day proves the manhood of the negro."

And President Lincoln said: "I was, in my best judgment, driven to the alternative of either surrendering the Union and with it the Constitution, or of laying strong hands upon the colored element. I chose the latter."

He also said: "Take 200,000 [black soldiers] from our side and put them in the battlefield or cornfield against us and we would be compelled to abandon the war in three weeks." And again: "Then there will be some black men who can remember that, with silent tongue, with clinched teeth, with steady eye, and with well poised bayonet, they have helped mankind on to this great consummation [the preservation of free institutions], while I fear that there will be some white men unable to forget that with malignant heart and deceitful speech they have striven to hinder it."

In the Spanish-American war the negro soldier won renown for American arms.

Mr. James Creelman, the war correspondent, reported in the New York *Journal* as follows: "A perfect storm of shot and shell swept the hillside. There was a moment of hesitation along the line. Then the order was, Forward, charge! Roosevelt was in the lead waving his sword. Out into the open and up the hill where death seemed certain, in the face of the continuous crackle of the Mauser, came the Rough

Riders with the Tenth (colored) Cavalry alongside. Not a man flinched, all continuing to fire as they ran. Roosevelt was a hundred feet ahead of his troops, yelling like a Sioux, while his own men and the colored cavalry cheered him as they charged up the hill. There was no stopping as men's neighbors fell, but on they went faster and faster.

"It was something terrible to watch these men race up that hill with death. Fast as they were going it seemed that they would never reach the crest. . . . We could clearly see the wonderful work the dusky veterans of the Tenth were doing. Such splendid shooting was probably never done under these conditions. As fast as the Spanish fire thinned their ranks the gaps were closed up, and after an eternity they gained the top of the hill and rushed the few remaining yards to the Spanish trenches. The position was won. Across the gulch the soldiers wildly cheered the gallant Tenth. The Tenth gave tongue with an answering cheer and rush on to drive the enemy further. Over the Spanish trenches they tore, passing the Spanish dead."

Associate Justice Curtis, of the Supreme Court of the United States, in his dissenting opinion from Chief Justice Taney in the celebrated Dred Scott case, says : " At the time of the ratification of the Articles of Confederation, all free native-born inhabitants of the states of New Hampshire, Massachusetts, New York, New Jersey, and North Carolina, though descendants from African slaves, were not only citizens of those states, but such of them as had the other qualifications possessed the franchise of electors, on equal terms with other citizens. It has already been shown that, in five of the thirteen original states, colored persons then possessed the elective franchise, and were among those by whom the Constitution was ordained and established. If so, it is not true, in point of fact, that the Constitution was made exclusively by the white race. And that it was made exclusively for the white race is, in my opinion, not only an assumption not warranted by anything in the Constitution, but contradicted by its opening declaration, that it was ordained and established by the people of the United States for themselves and their posterity. And as free colored persons were then citizens of at least five states, and so in every sense, part of the people of the United States, they were among those for whom and whose posterity the Constitution was ordained and established."

Thus it is absolutely indisputable that the colored man not only fought for American independence but also assisted as a voter in ordaining and establishing the Constitution of the United States.

In view of these and many other things, it may appear, after all, that the negro can establish a very clear title to his rights and domicile on American soil — a title as clean and as perfect in every respect as that of his persecutors and oppressors.

A white man's country forsooth! There is but one step further for these Southern leaders to take, and that is to claim that the God of the universe is a white man's God; the Redeemer of the world is a white man's Redeemer; the sun, moon, and stars are the white man's possession ; the cooling zephyr, the air that is breathed, the mighty deep, and all the waters which bear the traffic and commerce of the world on their bosom, and all the bountiful gifts of nature belong to the white man. After this these leaders can wrap themselves in the mantle of their vast and superb superiority and wait and watch and even weep for other claims to stake.

It will seem, however, to rational people, and there are a great many such in the South, that this "white-man's-country" argument is so monstrously stupid, so silly and inane, that the mere statement of its logical inferences is sufficient to destroy it.

Social equality! This is the bogy-man of the South. And it appears that he is nowadays frightening, not the children, but the old folks ; and doubtless many are in a state of perturbation bordering on hysteria.

Some twenty years or so ago, when the white people of the South first displayed this bogy-man, Mr. George W. Cable, himself a Southerner, a man gifted with the courage of his convictions, killed the bogy-man with this simple short, piercing sentence, " Social equality is the dream of a fool."

The nation instantly accepted this declaration as a verity. The poor old bogy-man was laid away in his grave and had almost gone "out of the memory of man." But lo, and behold, the leaders of the South have dug him up, taken off his grave clothes, put strange robes on him, electrified him, and made him all over into a most "horrible fright," and now present him once more like an automaton to the public. By the deft touch of the Southern magicians, he is made to pose first this way, and then that way, and still other ways, creating wild and violent excitement among the whites and carrying violence and death to the colored people.

The gyrations of the galvanically manipulated old bogy-man have been so industriously and effectually worked by the Southern leaders that the white people of the South have themselves been thrown into a strange panic ; while the people of the nation at large, self-possessed, are either hot with indignation, or are grimly humorous over the excitement of the leaders of this movement, with their ravings and comical and crazy antics, regarding it as a free show by the hysterical, frenzied social-equality Southern leaders.

Social equality ! It is fitful, transient, elusive. Shall this visionary, fleeting, intangible thing, with its many-sidedness, dominate the life of the republic? Is it to be a new test of American manhood and citizenship? If so, then who is to act as judge in regard to it? The social-equality man of to-day is the convict in the prison cell on the to-morrow. Shall not character, good citizenship, competency, talent, honest manhood, faithful service, and patriotism outweigh the fool's dream of social equality? What matters it, whether the prime virtues and graces of life are found under the white or the ebony skin? Did not the same God make both? Does He not plant His divinity in both alike? Can the color of the skin lessen the character and merit of the man?

Is it not true that

"All men are equal in God's sight;
There is no black, there is no white"?

In the constitution of human society social equality has never existed anywhere, it does not exist anywhere, and it never can exist anywhere. There are circles, and circles within circles; there are sets and grades and cliques and clans within sets and grades and cliqués and clans. Which, then, is the real thing?

What are the lines of differentiation which would shut out every colored person — for this is the plain purpose of the Southern leaders — from consideration as a member of the social organism which would not be an impeachment of common-sense, Christianity, and civilization? Members of the same family and household are not necessarily social equals; one member may be good, and another bad; one talented and refined, and another ignorant and coarse; one magnificent and glorious in usefulness to the world, and another a curse to humanity.

What of social equality? Human life does not move smoothly on a dead level. Its course is up, down; down, up. Many born to station, luxury, and wealth have died in poverty, in the slums, and in the gutter.

What of social equality? Many have risen from the ranks of the lowliest, the most destitute, and even from the abandoned classes, to the highest walks of life, and some such have been crowned with a people's respect, love, and homage.

What of social equality? The lowly born do not always remain lowly. The high born do not always stay on top. Each rank is continuously recruiting the other. What of social equality?

Alexandre Dumas with his strain of negro blood is counted an honor to France. There are thousands of colored people in the South who in every one of the essentials of life — in intelligence, education, refinement, culture, industry, as holders of property and tax-payers, as good citizens living orderly and decent lives, as public-spirited and useful members of the community, in moral worth — are superior to some thousands of whites. Why should these people be crushed and offered as a sacrifice to the social-equality bogy?

Are free institutions, "government of the people, for the people, and by the people" to give place to government of social equality, for social equality, and by social equality? The glory of the republic is that it has been governed by the people. No social-equality set has ever ruled it. It is a presumption for these leaders to mark dividing lines and say that an American citizen shall not rise beyond them in life, in honor, in the respect of his fellows, in usefulness, in the service of the nation. The idea is alien, extremely vicious, pernicious, mischievous, hideous.

If this cry of social equality at one time destroys the liberty and rights of the colored people, what is to prevent it at another time from crushing out the liberty and rights of the Jews, or the Irish, or the Italians, or the Poles, or the Swedes, or any other people? Tyranny or oppression grows by what it feeds on. It ever seeks a victim. This nation is cosmopolitan, embracing representatives of all the peoples of the world. At many places or localities these representatives may be few, or may not be influential. What is to save their liberties and rights from destruction? Just and equal laws for all the people are the only safety of all the people.

If the republic were in peril, and called on its citizens for its defence, who would dare to raise social equality as a test or standard for service? All who are competent to bear arms and face the enemy would be welcomed. Many were the loyal and patriotic citizens who responded to the call of their country in 1861, and who never so much as heard of such a thing as social equality. They went in with muskets on their shoulders, and as unknown quantities. Many came out rich in the affection, and amid the glare of trumpets and the cheers and shouts, of a great and free people, who will never forget their deeds of valor, nor allow the fruitage of their sacrifices to be destroyed.

When the republic is at peace it savors of effrontery for any one to presume to make social equality a passport to the public service. Are there not men of high social standing who are absolutely unfit for the duties of the public service? And on the other hand, are there not men without such standing who are qualified to discharge the most delicate and arduous duties of the official life?

The question naturally arises, Are all the white Southern office-holders men of the equality type? If they are, then some facts generally known bespeak a condition of social order among them which cannot be regarded as encouraging.

Fresh in the minds of the public are these happenings: A lieutenant-governor of South Carolina presided over the Senate with a brace of revolvers in his hip pockets, and went straight from the Senate chamber to the streets and shot down an unarmed and highly respected citizen; a lieutenant-governor of Louisiana was shot to death in a street brawl; a lieutenant-governor of Missouri was forced to resign from his office, admitting under oath that he was a bribe taker and bribe giver; a United States senator and a congressman battered each other in a curbstone fight in Arkansas; two United States senators from South Carolina tried conclusions in a pugilistic encounter on the floor of the United States

Senate and in open session; a United States senator from Texas demonstrated his ability as an all-round "scrapper" by the manner in which he "punched" a most reputable member of that body; a mayor of the leading city in Georgia was repeatedly haled to court for intoxication; a congressman from Missouri assaulted and attempted to stab a street-car conductor in the city of Washington rather than pay a five-cent fare; a governor of Alabama and a judge of a court in that state argued their difference with the strenuosity of fisticuffs; a son of a governor of Kentucky who was also his private secretary was shot to death for dishonoring a home, and his victim with him; grave senators and members of a state legislature have confessed under oath to receiving bribes and giving bribes for votes on matters of legislation; city aldermen and leading citizens more than a score have been charged and convicted of betraying their trusts, receiving and disbursing bribe money; feuds have flourished, thirty-eight citizens having been assassinated in one Kentucky county in a brief period of time; defalcations and embezzlements have been frequent — Tennessee lost $500,000 by the defalcation of its state treasurer; Alabama lost $400,000; three other Southern states also suffered heavy losses; and as to county treasurers, a long list of them have embezzled the people's money and voluntarily exiled themselves from their homes between the setting and rising of the sun.

And this is not the half that might be said along these lines; but it is enough to prick the bubble of Southern nonsense that social equality shall be the test for holding public office. The question is asked again, Do these men — for some of them are still in office — represent the ideal of Southern social equality?

It is a false pretext to claim that the possession of a public office establishes social equality. If it were true, the Bowery and Fifth Avenue would fraternize; and there would be no difference socially between the typical east-side politician and

Grover Cleveland, Judge Parker, or Mayor Low; and the dive-keeping alderman might lead the " Grand March " at the most fashionable event of the season. Public office does not and cannot establish social equality. The governor of a state cannot go into a citizen's home and enjoy his social board unless the citizen invites him to come.

If the appointment or election of a white man to office does not make him the social equal of every other white person, by what species of logic can it be demonstrated that the holding of office would make the colored people social equals of the white people? It is a travesty on common-sense to say that a man cannot transact any public, or even private business with another man without offering his daughter in marriage to him, or tendering him the hospitality of his home.

Outside of the South, the world over, men have learned how to treat a public official with becoming decency and dignity without raising the question of social privileges or proffering their daughters in marriage to such officials; and they have also learned how " to break bread " with a cultured or reputable man of any race without suggesting a marriage during or at the close of the meal. Truly, as Mr. Schurz says, these leaders " are the worst enemies the Southern people have to fear."

Again, is Southern social equality in public affairs so elastic that it can take under its protecting wings murderers, brawlers, moral lepers, amateur pugilists, bribe givers, bribe takers, drunkards, embezzlers, defaulters, and what not, since they are white? And is it yet so lofty in its own self-esteem that it can afford to assassinate the liberty of a people, and deny to such men as Lyons, Crum, Dancy, Allgood, and Washington, the lawful rights of American citizenship because of their color?

It is of interest to note the attitude of the influential Northern press in this matter.

THE WAR ON NEGRO SUFFRAGE

The New York *World* asks these pointed questions: "But why is the question of 'social equality' never raised by the appointment of white men to office or by their attendance upon any public meeting — no matter how ignorant, depraved, or even dirty they may be? When a man is appointed Collector of the Port of New York does any body think of his 'social equality'? Does any one feel obliged to invite a white official to dinner, or does such a man consider that his commission affects his social status?"

The Boston *Herald* declares: "Americans are fond of quoting Robert Burns' immortal line, 'A man's a man for a' that, for a' that.' His 'a' that' meant more than poverty and weakness. It was a noble soul's protest against all the ignoble prejudices based on conditions of fortune. 'For a' that' means notwithstanding color as much as notwithstanding ignorance and humbleness. Manliness is a matter of character, and does not depend on the color of the skin nor on the strain of race. God has not made any race forever incapable of it, nor any race forever incapable of recognizing and honoring it. The habit of distributing humanity in fixed castes according to the accident of birth, from which there is no escape, is a trait of immaturity and unreason. Christianity wars against it, enlightenment wars against it, democracy wars against it. The tendency of civilization is to break the arbitrary fetters of manhood, whether of fortune, race, or color, and acknowledge and honor the virtues, in whomsoever they are found."

And the Detroit (Michigan) *Free Press* uses the following language: "This Southern childishness in relation to the social side of the race question can hardly be treated with patience. People of the North, who are quite as good as the people of the South, sometimes meet negroes at receptions without having the bloom rubbed off their social prestige. The social standing of Theodore Roosevelt is, we think, quite as good as that of any Southern congressmen, but Mr.

Roosevelt is not constantly tormented by the fear that he will be thought no better than a 'blue-gummed nigger' if a respectable negro happens to cross the sill of the White House."

This alarm over social equality is a part of the stock in trade of the Southern leaders, by which the whites are inflamed and the colored people oppressed. That it should scare so many good people in the South is amazing, in view of the fact that for forty years colored men have been holding offices and white men have repeatedly petitioned for their appointment and have repeatedly voted for colored men in local elections and have signed their bonds.

But the ascendency of the Tillmans, the Vardamans, the Graves, the Walkers, the Aycocks, the Candlers, the Baileys, Carmacks, Richardsons, and other reactionists has broken the bonds of mutual regard between the races, and by their wicked harangues they have confused the minds of the white people on the race question.

These men are "the worst enemies the Southern people have to fear." It would be a day of jubilee to the Southland and to the whole country if these fire-eaters could be deported to some distant, uninhabited island in the Pacific; there to end their days. They would be alive but a short time; for in the absence of negroes to oppress and lynch and burn, they would soon be oppressing and lynching and burning each other, and it would not be long before the last of the brood would be reaping what they have sown. But as this cannot be done, the country will have to bear their shame, and the negroes their violence, for some time to come, and until returning reason — "the moral sense and the enlightened spirit" — shall assert the true manhood of the South.

"Negro inferiority" is a phrase which appeals more to the great masses than to the classes among the Southern whites, and the lower the social strata, the more effective is the appeal. One can readily see how it ministers to the pride and vanity of the lowest element, "no matter how ignorant, depraved, or even dirty they may be," to feel and be assured that they are better than any negro.

Under other circumstances, the negro of character, education, and property would receive a degree of consideration and respect from the whites who are less prosperous.

The better class of whites have always held in high esteem character, education, and property; and they would not have gone to extremes in refusing all recognition to colored people possessing these. Indeed, many among this class have given public expression of their surprise and gratification at the progress made by the colored people since their emancipation. There are notable instances of true and hearty friendship and ungrudging appreciation between some of the whites and colored people.

The former slave has in a number of instances provided for the support of the family of the former master which was in indigent circumstances. Some have willed their property to the former master. And in many cases the former master has been sympathetic and helpful to the former slave.

To destroy respect for the negro among the masses, and all interest in the negro among the classes, the leaders boldly proclaim the doctrine that the negro is necessarily an inferior to the white man and that there can be no common interest between them; that the lowest white man is the superior of the best negro, and should therefore receive greater consideration.

This means that the white criminal or degenerate is above the colored man of probity and standing. Is it true that the mere tint of a man's skin makes him either superior or inferior to another man? The leaders know better, but it serves their purpose to declare it. And such teaching has brought incredible woes upon the negro.

There are many well known cases of white criminals and degenerates who have been pardoned from the penitentiaries, and yet who have the freedom of the ballot, a privilege denied to colored men of moral and material value to the community.

And these white criminals and degenerates have also other privileges of a white man, while the same are denied to colored persons. Even in the state prisons white criminals are placed on an entirely different footing from colored criminals.

The idea of negro inferiority enters into the framing and the execution of the law. It has been molded into custom and unwritten law. It is enforced with fierceness and cruelty unspeakably shocking. It permeates every phase of Southern life, and the visible proofs of it are to be seen in every direction in which one may cast the eye.

It has resulted in the passage of " Jim Crow " laws which can be fitly described only when called barbarous ; and the appropriate apellation for the makers of such laws would be the " Jim Crow" politicians. These " Jim Crow " politicians have "Jim-Crowed" all railway trains, stations, lunch-counters, dining-rooms, waiting-rooms ; they have " Jim-Crowed " all libraries, theatres, museums, art galleries, public parks, and places of public resort and amusements ; they have " Jim-Crowed " the street cars; they have " Jim-Crowed " all ferry-boats and steamboats; they have " Jim-Crowed " some of the trades and callings ; they have " Jim-Crowed " the churches and schools and colleges and other institutions of learning ; they have "Jim-Crowed " the elevators in stores, office buildings, public buildings, and other places ; they have " Jim-Crowed " restaurants, cafés, ice-cream parlors, hotels, saloons, and even the soda-water fountains ; they have " Jim-Crowed " the courts, the making and the administration of the law ; they have " Jim-Crowed" all offices, municipal, county, and state ; they have " Jim-Crowed " the jury-box ; they have " Jim-Crowed " the ballot-box. In short, they have " Jim-Crowed " everything. They have " Jim-Crowed " the beautiful "Sunny South " into the " Jim Crow South."

And controlled by a perverted moral sense and a diseased mind, a mania on the questions affecting the negro, some of these leaders are now making a bold, desperate, even reckless effort to "Jim-Crow" the President of the United States and to "Jim-Crow" the government of the United States and to "Jim-Crow" this great Christian nation of eighty millions of free people into a "Jim Crow nation." Surely the cup of iniquity of the "Jim Crow" politicans is not only full, but is running over. Is it not time for the decent public sentiment of the South to crystallize itself and, reinforced by the irresistible public opinion of the nation, call a halt to "Jim Crow" politicians, and strangle Jim Crowism?

This "Jim-Crowing" of the South by unequal laws, or by statutes which contravene the spirit of the Constitution of the United States, and by barbarous customs, is intended to place all colored persons on a different footing from the whites before the law and in every other relation of life, and thus force the race into hopeless degradation. It means the revival of the *ante bellum* doctrine that negroes have no rights which white men are bound to respect.

Governor Aycock of North Carolina said: "We will force every negro in the South to hold an inferior relation to every white man!" Perhaps so, perhaps not. For this work of compulsion may encounter opposing forces which Mr. Aycock has not taken into consideration, — the opposition of honest men; the antagonism of Christian men; the overruling power of a just God "who loveth righteousness and hateth iniquity."

Who would pretend to say that this frenzy for "Jim-Crowing" promotes good government? It is destructive to every incentive to good government. It is intended to keep the whites inflamed against the colored. His eminence Cardinal Gibbons writes to a leading citizen, saying: "In reply to your letter of yesterday, I hasten to say that the introduction of the 'Jim Crow' bill into the Maryland legislature is very distressing to me. Such a measure must of necessity engender very bitter feelings in the colored people against the whites.

"Peace and harmony can never exist when there is unjust discrimination, and what the members of every community must constantly strive for is peace."

It may also be noted that the advocates of negro subjugation have invaded the North and have been propagating their principles in lecture tours, newspaper interviews, and in the endless writing of letters to the press. Some have obtained positions in newspaper offices, in pulpits, and elsewhere, and have used these as opportunities of injuring the negro. This statement does not include the many excellent Southerners in the North, men of high character and who stand for liberty and fair play for the negro.

Some of these emissaries have visited the annual and other meetings of great organizations held under Northern skies and have attempted to "Jim-Crow" them. And the members of some of these great organizations have sat as if in a trance and meekly permitted themselves to be bulldozed into taking the "Jim Crow" *cure*. It is a wonder that the spirits of their fathers did not rise up before them!

The Boston *Evening Record*, referring to the meeting of an important organization held in that city, says: "Boston was a curious place in the world for the stationary engineers to meet in, if they expected endorsement or sympathy for their action in barring the negro from membership.

"But that is what the association has just done. The question was decided almost unanimously against the negro, but not until after the delegates of the North, and especially those from Massachusetts, had expressed themselves in a most passionate manner.

"Grant of New Orleans made the demand to have the word 'white' prefixed to the word 'engineers' in one of the articles of the constitution. Mr. Grant said that the business men in the South look upon the engineers' association as one of standing; and should the negro be allowed the social equality which he does not deserve, the association would be ruined in the South and the Southern branches would drop out. 'This is the white man's country. Africa is where the negro belongs,' he said. Grant was loudly applauded.

"Mr. Optenberg of Wisconsin upheld the negro. Mr. Babbit of Worcester declared he would stand for the colored man at all times. C. S. Howarth of Fall River, speaking for the negro, was hissed for at least a full minute, and cries of 'Put him out!' were heard all over the convention floor. The speaker, after exalting the negro, said, 'Why, there are men in this room whom I would rather discard than the negro.'"

So the "Jim Crowites" of the South are using the free men of the North to strike down the negroes on the ground of color alone; and deny them the right to use their talents to make an honest living. Such organizations control in large measure the employment of workmen.

It is not a little amazing that great educational institutions in the North should invite to their lecture platform the worst specimens, the most rabid and frenzied "Jim Crow" leaders — well knowing their reputation for abusive and intemperate attacks on the negro; and each attack creates race antagonism. There were colored students in these universities, young men and women of character, scholarship, and promise. These students were compelled to sit quietly and hear their race denounced in bitter and violent language. This is not in keeping with the fitness of things. The efforts of these emissaries are designed to break the bond of peace between the negro and the Northern white man and stir up race strife and Southernize the North.

The policy and methods of the reactionists are a direct challenge to the Church. They are incompatible with the essentials of Christianity. The Church will not assent to the teaching that the color of the skin is superior to character, intelligence, thrift, godliness; that the tint of a man's skin is sufficient reason to deny him the rights of citizenship in a free republic, for the creation and preservation of which his blood was spilled; that this tint is a justifiable ground to deny him manhood right and to bar every place against him in the public service. "God moves in a mysterious way his wonders to perform," and it may be that the very madness of the policy and acts of the Southern politicians who are bent on destroying the suffrage of the negro, and alienating him from membership in human society, may be God's way of bringing discomfiture to them, safety to the negro, and peace and honor to the republic.

CHAPTER V

THE FALSE ALARM OF NEGRO DOMINATION

ALTHOUGH, owing to the entailments of slavery, a majority of the white people of the South may, at the present time, be opposed to negro suffrage, and although a few people of the North may sneer at it, nevertheless, facts and figures will show that the ballot in the hands of the negro has been of priceless value to the republic. It is a national asset to be depended upon in emergencies. By its service to the republic in trying ordeals it has demonstrated its right to exist. No element of the population is so broadly and intensely national in character as the negro. The Reverend E. F. Williams, D. D., of Chicago, recently said: "We need the negro as much as he needs us. In war he shouldered the musket and knew how to shoot straight. His ballot has been cast, when allowed to be cast, for the good of the nation. As we have needed him in the past, we shall certainly need him in the future."

There is no danger in negro suffrage. It is rather a safety-valve. The cry of negro domination is a false alarm.

In the following table are given the states which may come under the general designation of Southern states; also the total white and the total colored population of each, as well as the total white and the total colored vote of each, according to the census of 1900. A glance at this table will show the absurdity of the alarm of negro domination. It will be seen that in the South as a whole there are more than two white men to every colored man. So that the frightful apparition of negro domination does not loom up with such hideousness on the political horizon as the alarmists would make one believe.

States	Total White Population	Total Colored Population	Total White Vote	Total Colored Vote
Alabama	1,001,152.	827,307	232,294	181,471
Arkansas	944,580	366,866	226,597	87,157
Florida	297,333	230,730	77,962	61,417
Georgia	1,181,294	1,034,813	277,496	223,073
Kentucky	1,862,309	284,706	469,206	74,728
Louisiana	769,612	650,804	177,878	147,348
Maryland	952,424	235,064	260,979	60,406
Mississippi	641,200	907,630	150,530	197,936
Missouri	2,944,843	161,234	809,797	46,418
North Carolina	1,263,603	624,469	289,263	127,114
South Carolina	557,807	782,321	130,375	152,860
Tennessee	1,540,186	480,243	375,046	112,236
Texas	2,426,669	620,722	599,961	136,875
Virginia	1,192,855	660,722	301,379	146,122
West Virginia	915,233	43,499	233,129	14,786

Special note should be made of the important fact that in only two of the Southern states does the colored population exceed that of the whites; that is in South Carolina and Mississippi. In all the other Southern states, the white population predominates over the colored. So that the cry of negro domination is insincere. If the matter were, however, reduced to the simple question of the procurement of good government in the Southern states, no patriotic citizen in the republic would utter a single protest against any law treating all races alike.

Every intelligent colored man would allow that the race can work out its destiny under equal laws, but would be cruelly handicapped if they are made unequal and oppressive.

Under normal conditions Collector Crum, Register Lyons, Recorder Dancy, Principal Washington, and the army of negro school-teachers, preachers, professional men, mechanics, and hardy toilers would all line up on the side of good government. This has occurred repeatedly, in local elections: as in Atlanta, Nashville, and other places, when the more reputable whites, men and women, were freely admitted to address meetings in colored churches for the purpose of rallying the colored voters to aid them in overthrowing "ring government." This met with success in every case.

When the liberty of the colored man has not been at stake, he has never failed to respond to the kindly entreaties of the better class of whites. He wants good and just government: it is his salvation. But when the Southern leaders set themselves to the work of disfranchising by the wholesale the colored race without regard to their merit, and grant the franchise to every white man regardless of his demerit, — the immorality and unrighteousness of the act is without question; and a definite, a direct issue is joined between justice and injustice, humanity and inhumanity, the friends of liberty and the enemies of liberty.

Let us briefly analyze the statistics regarding the voters in the states which have passed or are contemplating the enactment of wholesale disfranchisement.

In Alabama there are 232,294 white voters against 181,471 colored voters: the whites having a clear majority over the negroes of 50,823. Any kind of a fair education or property qualification, or both, would probably reduce the colored vote not far from fifty per cent, while the white vote would not be largely affected. What, then, becomes of the apparition of negro domination? Why resort under false pretences to wholesale disfranchisement?

In Louisiana the white vote is 177,878; against 147,348 colored voters: the whites having a clear majority of 30,530. Here again, any kind of a fair education or property qualification, or both, would operate to cut the colored vote in half, making the white vote at the ballot-box twice as large as the the colored vote. What chance would one colored man in Louisiana have in outvoting two white men? Wholesale disfranchisement is a subterfuge.

In North Carolina the white vote is 289,263 against 127,114 colored voters: the whites having a clear majority over the negroes of 162,149; this majority itself being 35,035 more than the total colored vote. And under a fair educational or property qualification, or both, the whites would be impregnable, — having at the ballot-box probably not less than three white men to one colored man. In this instance the cry of negro domination is a hollow mockery, and wholesale disfranchisement is the perpetration of a fraud.

In Virginia the white vote is 301,379 against 146,122 colored voters: the whites having a clear majority over the negroes of 155,257; this majority by itself being nearly 10,000 larger than the total colored vote. In this case too, a fair educational or property qualification, or both, would intrench the whites in power, — giving them three white men to one colored man, with some thousands to spare. The evidence is cumulative that the alarm of negro domination is a sham, and that wholesale disfranchisement is an outrage.

In Maryland, where the Southern " bloody shirt " is being waved so vigorously by Senator Gorman, and where he is making the effort of his life to destroy the liberties of the colored people — the total white vote is 260,979 against barely 60,406 colored voters; the whites having a clear majority of 200,573 over the negroes. There are actually more than four white men in the state to every colored man. Here disfranchisement is a crime. Senator Gorman is fastening a foul blot on the good name and honor of Maryland.

In Kentucky the Southern " bloody shirt " is also being flaunted with even greater recklessness, and the liberty of the negroes hangs in the balance. There are in this state 469,206 white voters against but 74,728 colored voters: the whites having a clear majority of 394,478 over the negroes, and there being about six white men in the state to every colored man. In these latter two cases, the cry of negro domination is too ridiculous for consideration, and the disfranchisement of the race is a proceeding of which a civilized people ought to be incapable. May the nobler spirit of "Old Kentucky" keep this stain from her proud escutcheon!

As before mentioned, South Carolina and Mississippi are the two exceptions where the colored population are in the majority.

In South Carolina the total white vote is 130,375 against 152,860 colored voters: the colored having a clear majority over the whites of 22,485. But a fair educational or property qualification, or both, would probably reduce the colored vote below 75,000; thus giving the whites a safe margin.

In Mississippi the total white vote is 150,530 against 197,936 colored voters: the colored having a clear majority over the whites of 47,406 voters. But here again, a fair educational or property qualification, or both, would probably cut the total colored vote in half, giving the whites above 50,000 majority at the ballot-box. If the "district system" which already applies to Mississippi should also be adopted in South Carolina, white control would be absolutely certain without the demoralizing evils and the deadly effects on Southern conscience and public morality of wholesale disfranchisement. Under this "district system" the "black" counties are consolidated or formed into one "district," with a limited number of representatives and senators in the legislature, while the great bulk of representatives and senators are elected from a number of other "districts." The more important local officers, as the conditions require for the good of all, are made appointive by the governor.

If in an honest effort it shall seem necessary in the case of South Carolina and Mississippi to take precautionary measures to secure good government, and laws are made which are reasonable, and humane, and life and property are protected, and the civil and political rights are respected of all, without regard to race, who measure up to the fixed qualification, —

then there can be no reasonable ground of complaint from any person. As we have seen, in not one of the other Southern states does the colored vote portend negro domination. In most of them, it is but a minor fraction of the whole vote. In all of them, under just and equal laws, good government could be assured.

But wholesale disfranchisement has bearing on others besides the negro.

The New York *World* speaks most advisedly when it says : " If the Southern Democrats who are forcing these measures do not perceive their ultimate inevitable cousequence they are lacking in political understanding. The preponderating vote of the Northern states will not consent permanently to representation, in Congress and in the electoral college, of millions of disfranchised inhabitants in the Southern states. Especially is this true when the disfranchising qualifications apply and are intended to operate, not against illiteracy or shiftlessness or unworthiness, but solely against color.

" In the few states of the ' dark belt ' where the colored population outnumbers the white, precautions against ' negro rule ' are justified, even by residents from the North living there, by the ' higher law ' of necessity. But in border states like Maryland and Kentucky, where white preponderance is overpowering, no such excuse can be urged. Nor do the Democrats who are pushing these measures seem to have calculated the possible effect upon their party in doubtful Northern states of arraying solidly against it the very considerable negro vote. This issue may make the South solid, but it has another side.

" Back, however, of the questions of political expediency and of the inequality growing out of the representation of non-voters, is the deeper question of constitutional guaranties and of the anomaly and danger in a republic of an enormous number of citizens disfranchised for their color alone."

"Disfranchised for their color alone" is the burning shame, the condemning truth in this whole wretched affair. And it is clap-trap to urge in justification that the negroes pay but a very small fraction of the taxes.

The state of South Carolina has a total colored population of 782,321. To say that these negroes are not the tax-payers of that state is the merest twaddle. They are more than the tax-payers; they are pre-eminently the *tax-makers*. And the makers of the taxes are quite as important to the well-being and prosperity of the state as the payers of the taxes.

The negroes are the producing element, the backbone of every department of labor and industry. To still their hands would bring about the paralysis and ruin of every business interest in the state. For they represent the productive and the industrial life. What would the Custom House in Charleston amount to without the patronage of negro productivity? How could the city of Charleston itself flourish without the toil of the thousands of negroes within her gates, and the hundreds of thousands of them in the state, — the fruits of whose labor, like a never ending stream, are poured into her lap? Without the negro productivity in this state, the commercial and other great interests would drop to *nil*. Further, the great educational system, and all the charitable and benevolent institutions of the state are dependent on negro productivity. It is not to be inferred from this that there are no white toilers, for there are many; but neither in numbers, nor in the variety of work, nor in the total fruitfulness of toil, do they approach unto the colored people. If the resources of the state were limited to the fruits of white labor, South Carolina would be in hopeless, irretrievable bankruptcy.

The denial, then, of the colored man's liberty, the refusal to allow him any share in the government under which he lives and of which he is a copartner and to the support of which he is not only the largest, but the indispensable contributor, is a wrong which must invoke the condemnation of honest men and the frowning displeasure of a righteous God.

What has been related herewith in reference to South Carolina would hold true also as regards Mississippi, with her total colored population of 907,630. The negroes are the mainstay of her productivity, — the tillers of her soil, the makers of her taxes, the guarantors of her prosperity, the supporters of her institutions. Without the fruitfulness of the negroes' toil Mississippi would be in stagnation as a commonwealth, helpless, beggared.

In the several other Southern states, while the proportion of the negroes is not so large, yet their vast productivity and their varied labors, especially as the tillers of the soil, are generally regarded as the factors of paramount importance in the development and prosperity of the South. Agriculture is the life of the South, and negro labor is the life of agriculture.

But in the wholesale disfranchisement of the colored race, a question of greater gravity and far wider scope is involved than that of cheating the Constitution of the United States in order to destroy the liberty of the negro. This other issue affects the constitutional rights of great states and all their people. It destroys representative government. For the wholesale disfranchisement of the colored race in the South necessarily results in the 'partial disfranchisement of every state in the North, by lessening the propor- tional share of every Northern man in the government of his country.

Concerning this, the New York *Press* says : "The fraudu- lent misrepresentation, in Congress and the electoral college, of the 10,000,000 American blacks, chiefly resident in the Southern states, is no more a question to be hushed up and put. off than was that of the felonious servitude of their 4,000,000 predecessors. Northern manhood revolted then at the spectacle of a great party paltering with a national sin because it was the darling of a powerful section. Northern manhood will revolt again if the spectacle is repeated.

"It has stood for a good while the glaring violation of its rights by which one vote between the Potomac and the Gulf counts for two between the Potomac and the Lakes. But it will not stand much longer, we verily believe, the gag that chokes in the old Calhoun fashion all utterance upon a peculiar institution of the South in the halls of Congress."

The *Wisconsin Evening Journal*, of Milwaukee, speaks to the point in saying: "Henry Watterson, of Louisville, . . . addressed the Hamilton Club of Chicago, last night. . . .

"Watterson's whole speech was directed to the point that the negro should be disfranchised in the Southern states as unfit for the privilege of suffrage. There are many white men throughout the country who are unfit for the ballot, and they are permitted to vote merely because they have a white skin. While Watterson was urging the disfranchisement of the Southern blacks he did not say a word in favor of reducing the Southern representation in Congress on account of the diminished vote in the Southern states. Watterson ignored the paramount principle, which is this: The disfranchisement of the negro is a gross injustice to white people in the North, for one white vote in South Carolina or Virginia is equal to five white votes in Wisconsin. This establishes a permanent Southern aristocracy to rule the Union. Watterson affects to be a Democrat, but he is certainly a false one, because such inequality of suffrage cannot be permitted in a republic.

"The South will find before it gets through with this matter that it will be sorely punished by the reduction of its representation in Congress. The North begins to wake up on this question. The Union League Club of New York, one of the strongest and most influential organizations in the United States, perceives that by the disfranchisement of the negro the nation is drifting into the condition which brought on the great Civil War. Cornelius N. Bliss, one of the first

11   161

citizens in the great metropolis, and Secretary of the Interior under President McKinley, has taken hold of the matter and has issued a thousand circulars to the leading political organizations in the United States pointing out the dangers that will inure to our country if the Southern blacks are disfranchised. This disfranchisement will not only be a gross violation of the Fourteenth Amendment to the Constitution, but will establish an aristocracy of white voters in the Southern states which will rule the nation as despotically as did the slaveholders before the Civil War."

When the South disfranchises the negro, and at the same time appropriates to itself the full quota of representatives in the Congress and members in the electoral college based on negro citizenship, it does by this act unduly increase its power in the government and destroys the equality of representation which should exist among the people of all the states.

But more significant still: when the South denies the negro his rights as a citizen, and at the same time counts the very last one of them to increase its representation — thus offsetting the entire negro population against an equal number of Northern white people — is this not equivalent to saying that, while the negro shall not be the equal of the Southern white man at the ballot-box, he shall be the equal of the Northern white man and shall offset his vote?

The South is thus using the negro to increase her proportional representation in the national council, in order ultimately to accomplish the Southern domination of the republic and intrench the traditions of a barbarous system of slavery. For instance, the state of Connecticut has a white population of 892,424; the state of Mississippi has a colored population of 907,630; thus Mississippi, by playing its colored population against the white population of Connecticut, completely offsets and neutralizes the power of this great

162

state in the House of Representatives and in the electoral college.

The state of Maine has a white population of 692,226; the state of Virginia has a colored population of 660,722; thus Virginia, by playing its colored population against the white population of Maine, puts the quietus on every white man in that state, and makes the voice of that state of non-effect in the House and in the electoral college.

The state of Minnesota has a white population of 1,737,036; the states of Alabama, Louisiana, and Florida have a combined colored population of 1,708,841; thus Alabama, Louisiana, and Florida, by playing their colored population against the white population of Minnesota, neutralize the voice and power of this great state in the House of Representatives and in the electoral college. It is hardly necessary to continue these comparisons further, as it must be apparent that the wholesale disfranchisement of the negro in the South, in its practical effects, may be the wholesale disfranchisement of great states in the North. It is beyond question the partial disfranchisement of every Northern state.

The colored people are either citizens or they are not citizens. If they are not citizens, the South has no ground in law or morals to claim representation for them. If they are citizens, their disfranchisement is a crime against citizenship. For the colored people, who are denied citizenship *en masse* in the South, are nevertheless counted and used as equal citizens *en masse* to neutralize the effectiveness of citizenship in the North; thus bringing about the curious anomaly that the colored man is not a citizen to cast his own vote, or share in the government, but he is a citizen, an equal citizen, to offset or nullify a Northern citizen's vote and promote Southern domination of the government.

But this condition must be regarded from still another point of view. South Carolina has a white population of 557,807, while Colorado has a white population of about the

163

same size, being 529,046; and yet the white men of South Carolina elect seven members of the House of Representatives, while the same number of white men in Colorado elect only three members.

North Carolina and Virginia have a combined white population of 2,456,458; Indiana has a white population of 2,458,502; and yet the white men of North Carolina and Virginia jointly elect twenty members of the House, while the same number of white men in Indiana elect only thirteen members.

Alabama, Louisiana, and Florida have a combined white population of 2,068,097; Wisconsin has a white population of 2,057,911; and yet the white men of Alabama, Louisiana, and Florida jointly elect nineteen members of the House, while the same number of white men in Wisconsin elect only eleven members. Georgia, Mississippi, and Arkansas have a combined white population of 2,767,074; Massachusetts has a white population of 2,769,074; and yet the white men of Georgia, Mississippi, and Arkansas jointly elect twenty-six members of the House, while the same number of white men in Massachusetts elect only fourteen members.

Again, Louisiana with a white population of 769,612 elects seven members of the House, while Connecticut with a white population of 892,424 elects only five members, and Nebraska with a white population of 1,056,529 elects only six members.

Mississippi with a white population of 641,200 elects eight members of the House, while Kansas with a white population of 1,416,319 elects only eight members. Georgia with a white population of 1,181,294 elects eleven members of the House, while Iowa with a white population of 2,218,667 elects only eleven members. South Carolina with a white population of 557,807 elects seven members of the House, while Maine, New Hampshire, and Delaware with a combined white population of 1,255,994 elect only seven members. Florida with a white population of 297,333 elects three members of the House, while Rhode Island with a white population of 419,050 elects only two members.

Expressed in the popular vernacular, it may be said that the Southern leaders are playing their game with loaded dice. Furthermore, as recounted, through the disfranchisement of the colored race, the white people of the South elect about fifty members of the House and about fifty members in the electoral college which are based on the count of the negro population.

The power thus gained and wielded is a standing peril to republican government. It has happened in the memory, not of "the oldest inhabitant," but of a majority of the people now living, that a single vote in the electoral college decided the election of a president of the United States. Mr. Hayes was elected by a bare majority of one vote : receiving 185 votes, to 184 for Mr. Tilden.

Not once but many times in the history of the government a single vote, or a small number of votes, has decided the fate of a measure of greatest national importance in Congress.

In a close and exciting campaign, or even in calm deliberation, these fifty votes unrighteously and unlawfully seized and cast by the white people of the South may not only determine the election of a president of the United States, but may also revolutionize the great national policies of the government. As we have seen, some of the great states of the North would be practically disfranchised or deprived of an equal share in the election of a president, and an equal voice in matters of legislation. Such a miscarriage of justice might occur at any time as would bring ruin to the great financial, commercial, and industrial life of the nation. A condition of affairs so manifestly unequal and unjust, and so perilous, would seem to demand the application of a drastic treatment.

Another feature of this matter which should command the serious attention of the American people is the decadence of popular government in the South under the ascendency of the present leadership. It is no longer the government of the people, but the government of the "Jim Crow" leaders, for the "Jim Crow" leaders, and by the "Jim Crow" leaders.

The Honorable John S. Wise, a descendant of a former governor of Virginia, in a public address said : "No republican form of government exists in Virginia to-day. The Czar of Russia does not hold more absolute sway than is held by the fractional oligarchy of whites in the Southern states. By the present system of registration in Virginia, 100,000 names have been stricken from the lists in the last twelve months.

"The government of the United States should say that such a practice is either right or wrong. It must be one or the other. The government has the right and the power to stop it if it will but enforce that power. The indifference of the government is forcing the colored men of the South to become law-breakers. A crisis is surely approaching."

The New York *World* says : "The *World* has noted the travesty on popular government in South Carolina, where at the recent election less than 40,000 votes were cast in a state having more than 280,000 men of voting age.

"The showing in Louisiana was even worse. This Gulf state has 325,000 citizens of voting age, yet the total vote cast on November 4 was only 26,265, of which 22,218 were Democratic and 4,047 Republican. The *Times-Democrat* puts it in another way in saying that 'about one out of six of the persons who can vote under the constitutional provisions took the trouble to pay their poll-tax, get registered, go to the polls, and cast their ballots.' The negroes, something less than half the population, are, of course, for the most part disfranchised.

166

FALSE ALARM OF NEGRO DOMINATION

"Here is a state having six representatives in Congress elected by 22,218 voters — the republican candidates getting on an average only 578 votes each. There are several separate Congressional districts in this city that cast more votes than were polled in the entire state of Louisiana. This is a state government neither republican in form nor democratic in fact."

The following table will show the votes cast in the eight congressional districts in Mississippi, as compared with the first eight districts of Indiana: —

	INDIANA	MISSISSIPPI
First District	41,397	8,245
Second District	42,788	2,528
Third District	38,007	1,146
Fourth District	41,793	2,834
Fifth District	47,333	3,081
Sixth District	44,705	1,774
Seventh District	48,456	2,022
Eighth District	49,693	1,433
Total	354,172	23,063

Such wholesale disfranchisement of the negroes has reacted on the whites. They have ceased to go to the ballot-box. And this gives the "Jim Crow" leaders their opportunity to establish a corrupt oligarchy which rules with a rod of iron.

Fair and just election laws would result in bringing practically every colored voter to the polls at every election; for the negro, whenever the opportunity is given him, takes pride in the exercise of sovereignty. And the knowledge that the colored vote would be cast at any election would arouse and bring forth the white vote. Thus a healthy political condition would result. Nothing would do so much to promote good government in the South as the expectation that large bodies of colored voters were sure to be at the polls. It would rally the whites and secure the nomination of the best men for offices. But this, the "Jim Crowites" do not want, for their occupation would be gone.

167

These states are in the control of an imperious and unscrupulous oligarchy, and, when the people fail to vote, it fraudulently counts and makes such returns of votes as it pleases.

For instance: the new disfranchising Constitution of Alabama received a total of 108,613 votes; but there are 232,294 white voters, and 181,471 colored voters in that state — making 413,765 of both races. So that only about one-fourth of the voters gave approval to the new constitution.

In the counting of these votes, numbering 108,613, glaring frauds were committed. In Chambers county 4,604 votes were returned for the Constitution; yet the total white vote of the county is only 3,457. Dallas county returned 8,125 votes for the Constitution; yet Dallas county has but 2,525 white voters. Hale county returned 4,696 votes for the Constitution; yet this county has only 1,385 white voters. Perry county returned 3,209 votes for the Constitution; yet this county has only 1,559 white voters. Wilcox county returned 4,652 votes for the Constitution; yet this county has only 1,704 white voters.

This is the way officers are elected and laws and constitutions are made in the South. Palpable fraud is plainly written on the face of these returns.

The plan is to use repeaters, or to keep the colored voters from the ballot-box, and still count their votes to swell the returns. County after county in Alabama show frauds in the election returns.

Mr. Joseph C. Manning, a leading white citizen of Alabama, in a speech before the Middlesex Club of Boston, Massachusetts, says: " The registered vote of about 181,000 voters in Alabama, out of a population of the voting age of 413,765, is notice to the country upon the part of the governing power of this state that a majority of the voting population is without a republican form of government, for

232,765 citizens of voting age in Alabama have, with but scant exception, been illegally, unjustly, and outrageously deprived of suffrage. Of the number of registered colored voters there are not 3,000.

"Out of the total colored male population of over 21 years of age in the State of Alabama there are 73,533 literate citizens. There are 11,123 colored citizens who own farms in Alabama, 2,871 part owners, 116 owners and tenants, 72 managers, 56,202 cash tenants, 23,689 share tenants. The report of the department of education of Alabama states that 940 colored male teachers drew money from the public funds in 1902. A stringent examination as to character and education is required of applicants for license to teach in the public schools of Alabama. There are fully 1,000 colored male teachers engaged in the public and private schools of the state. In Alabama there are also colored merchants, colored bankers, colored artisans, colored physicians, colored lawyers, colored editors, colored ministers, all of these numbering not less than 5,000 citizens. Surely the 5,000 citizens engaged in these various callings, surely the 1,000 colored male teachers and the many thousand colored owners of their own farm homes — I declare that surely these citizens should come up to the requirements of good citizenship and of character at least under which test no white citizen whatever was excluded by the board of registrars in 1902. Had the registration been impartial no negro applying for a certificate would have been refused registration, for certainly no white man who applied was denied this privilege. Only one negro was allowed to vote in my county, Tallapoosa, with a colored population of 2,055. The negro principal of the colored public school in the town in which I live was denied registration. He was repeatedly told that the registrars were not registering negroes at that day. It was never his day. This man was fully qualified to register. Negroes of property and good standing were humiliated by the same treatment.

"Fellow-countrymen, there is a God of nations and of men; there is a standard of honor for governments and individuals; there is justice and there is injustice. Not in all the history of the conduct of Christian governments and acts of civilized men can there be found a parallel to the depravity to which this Alabama autocracy, the progeny of the former slave-holding Democracy, has come."

In South Carolina, Mississippi, North Carolina, Virginia, and other states where disfranchising constitutions and laws have been put in force, not a third of the voters of the states have sanctioned with their ballots these constitutions. In some cases the constitution was promulgated without being submitted to the voters. The leaders were afraid of the condemnation of the people. Many Southerners are opposed to laws which can only be made and sustained through fraud and force. Ex-Governor MacCorkle of West Virginia, at the Montgomery conference, said:

"The franchise system, as it is at present constituted in many of the states of the South, is, to say the least, practically the policy of repression. Repression has been tried at every stage of the world's history, and always with the same unvarying result, utter and tremendous failure. It leads nowhere. It raises no man. It demands no education. It holds ignorance as dense as ever. It drives away intelligence. It breeds discontent. It represses any rising inspiration of the heart. It leaves the land at the end of the cycle just as it found it at the beginning. It is the policy of deadly inaction overridden by discontent."

The objective of such laws is not good government, but to build up an office-holding oligarchy by keeping the races at strife.

Another matter of importance connected with this subject is the manner in which the colored man has used his ballot. Has that ballot been cast on the side of good government and for the national weal? Have the larger interests of the whole people been promoted by negro suffrage?

In the Reconstruction era, and in the years immediately following, the negro's vote was cast strictly in accordance with good sense, the dictates of humanity, and the highest welfare of the republic. Even the temporary "carpet-bag" rule established by the negro's vote was demanded by national exigency, and was preferable to the infamous Black Code, which nullified the Proclamation of Emancipation and the Thirteenth Amendment, and practically re-established slavery. There was no middle ground; it was a choice between the Black Code and all it meant, and the temporary evils in such free government as could be organized.

And the negro voted for free government. In so doing he rendered an inestimable service to the nation. Let every serious American reflect on this, — that it was the negro vote which elected General Grant as President of the United States in 1868. That is to say, if the negro vote had been suppressed in 1868 as it is to-day — the votes of the solid South added to the eighty scattering votes which Mr. Seymour received in the North would have elected him President over General Grant the hero of Appomattox. So that in the very first presidential election following the war, it was the negro's vote which saved from humiliating defeat the greatest military genius of the age,— the man above all others then living to whom the nation owes its life. If Mr. Seymour had been elected and the South had come back into the Union, and by its solidity had gained the ascendency in the government in 1868, the gravity of the complications which would have ensued cannot be exaggerated.

In 1876 the negro vote again decided the presidential election, giving the electoral vote of South Carolina, Florida, and Louisiana to Mr. Hayes, whom a single vote would have defeated.

Mr. Roosevelt, in his canvass for the governorship of New York, was elected by about 17,000 majority ; and no one doubts that it was 31,425 colored voters of the state of New York who sealed his election. Governor Odell was elected by about 9,000 majority, and without the colored vote his canvass would have been hopeless.

At many points in the North the negro's vote has effected the election of members of Congress and has been decisive in local elections; and it has been cast on the side of good government.

Probably the best demonstration of the safety and value of the negro as a voter, of late years, is revealed in the election returns for the year 1896. An examination of those returns will prove beyond a doubt that the negro vote defeated Mr. Bryan and elected Mr. McKinley as President of the United States.

There are the facts : California gave Mr. McKinley eight electoral votes by 2,797 majority ; but California has 3,711 colored voters. Delaware gave Mr. McKinley three electoral votes by 3,630 majority; but Delaware has 8,374 colored voters. Indiana gave Mr. McKinley fifteen electoral votes by 18,181 majority ; but Indiana has 18,186 colored voters. Kentucky gave Mr. McKinley twelve electoral votes by 281 majority; but Kentucky has 74,728 colored voters. Maryland gave Mr. McKinley eight electoral votes by 32,264 majority; but Maryland has 60,406 colored voters. West Virginia gave Mr. McKinley six electoral votes by 11,487 majority ; but West Virginia has 14,726 colored voters. These six states gave Mr. McKinley 52 electoral votes.

There can be no doubt of the colored vote being the deciding factor in each of these states, as that vote outnumbered the majority in each state, and the colored vote is practically wholly republican. If this vote were suppressed in these states, Mr. McKinley's majorities would be wiped out in each case. If these 52 votes are subtracted from the 271 electoral votes which Mr. McKinley received, it would leave him 219. If these 52 votes be added to the 176 electoral votes cast for Mr. Bryan, it would give him 228 electoral votes, a majority of nine over Mr. McKinley, and he would have been made president.

The evidence seems thus conclusive that, in the most exciting campaign of a generation, a campaign involving directly the vast financial interest of the nation, and with it every business enterprise of whatsoever nature, and the direct and immediate interest and welfare of every man, woman, and child, — that in this momentous campaign the negro vote was the saving factor. It prevented a result which would have ruinously affected every class of population. The negro vote saved the country from the follies and crime of free silver, free trade, and free riot.

An examination of the election returns of 1880 in Connecticut, Colorado, Indiana, New York, Oregon, and Rhode Island will also show that it was the negro vote in these states which elected General Garfield to the presidency.

The returns of the election of 1888 also disclose the fact that the negro vote in Illinois, Indiana, New York, Ohio, and Rhode Island determined the election of General Benjamin Harrison as president.

The credit is given to the negro vote because it is the only vote that is contested, and gigantic efforts have been made and are being made to destroy it. If it had been fully suppressed throughout the country, then, as we have seen, the solid South would have defeated Grant in 1868, Hayes in 1876, Garfield in 1880, Harrison in 1888, and McKinley in 1896. Besides, neither the McKinley nor the Dingley tariff measures would have been possible if the negro vote had been suppressed throughout the country as it is in South Carolina and Mississippi to-day.

It has so happened that in each instance the majority in the House of Representatives which has enacted the great national policies of the government from the time of reconstruction, 1868, to the present has been due to the ballot in the hands of the colored man. It thus becomes evident that if by defamation and persecution of the colored man, his ballot can be destroyed, the autocrats of the solid South would have a clear chance to gain control of the government, shape its destiny, and intrench the barbarous traditions of slavery. The majority in the 58th Congress which passed the Panama Canal bill and other important legislation is due to the negro ballot.

Senator Blair of New Hampshire, in a recent address at Washington, said : " The colored people are the only ones in the South that have sense enough to vote the Republican ticket, and disfranchisement is not only unwise, and unjust, but a crime."

Here is the kernel of a great truth. The white people of the South have voted persistently and solidly against every measure of great national benefit for forty years. The colored people have voted as persistently and as solidly, wherever permitted to do so, in favor of such measures ; so that while the white vote of the South has been inimical to the great interests of the country, these have been saved by the colored vote.

Thus the colored vote has proved a veritable godsend to the nation. Without this vote the most important and fruitful national policies would have been impossible of inauguration. The negro vote is a failure only when it is suppressed by the intimidation, fraud, and shot-guns of the whites.

The Union League Club of the city of New York, one of the most influential of all political organizations aside from the two great parties, has recently taken action which will have important bearings on the whole question. This club rendered the republic invaluable services in the dark days of the rebellion, and it has proved a tower of strength in the emergencies of subsequent years. At a recent meeting, it unanimously adopted the following resolutions : —

"*Resolved*, That the Government be requested to instruct the district attorneys in the various states where an illegal suppression of votes is alleged, to prosecute every case where there has been a violation of the laws of the United States in respect of the suffrage, if adequate evidence can be obtained to justify a submission of such case to the grand jury.

"*Resolved, First*, That Congress be requested and respectfully urged to investigate with thoroughness and impartiality the charges of a suppression of votes contrary to the Fourteenth and Fifteenth Amendments to the Constitution of the United States, and in every case where such reduction is accomplished by a limitation of the franchise for any reason, and that in proportion to the number of votes so disfranchised, the representation of such state in Congress be reduced ; and also to see that the Fifteenth Amendment be in no way violated, either directly or by subterfuge ; and,

"*Second*, That where the decisions of the courts or the practices at elections disclose the fact that the present statutes are inadequate, amendatory acts be passed remedying the defects disclosed."

These resolutions were based on a report of a committee which had thoroughly investigated every phase of the question, and which was summarized as follows : —

"The demoralizing effect of such a condition as this every one must admit. The idea that the people of this country, great and small, old and young, of every nation, kindred, and tongue, are to be educated upon the theory that a continued and wholesale violation of the fundamental law of the nation can go unpunished must produce a frightful effect ; and there has never been a time in the history of the country, when, if it be true that these violations exist, there was a condition at all like the present.

175

"If the facts asserted in regard to this matter be true, there is a deliberate nullification of the Constitution of the United States, — a thing which no country can or ought to permit while it cherishes the idea that it is governed by law. If this condition exists, we are far from our great ideal, for we are a government of some of the people, by some of the people, and for some of the people."

Here is a moderate, conservative, dignified petition to the Government of the United States to investigate certain evils, wrongs, and crimes against a whole class of American citizens ; evils, wrongs, and crimes which every man in the republic knows to exist, and which are repugnant to civilization, inimical to good order, and in open violation of the Constitution of the United States.

The Government is petitioned to use its lawful authority to ameliorate these conditions. How is this calm, dispassionate, and dignified petition received?

The "Jim Crowites" were greatly stirred up. Mr. Robert C. Ogden, a prominent business man of New York, practically voicing Southern sentiment, declared that the influence of the petition would be as follows : —

First. To injure the material, political, and educational interest of the negro in the Southern states.

Second. To discourage the growth of academic freedom in the South. The recent action of the board of trustees of one of the most important of Southern colleges was a notable victory for intellectual independence. The movement toward academic freedom will be hindered just in proportion to Northern use of the negro in party politics.

Third. A prominent representative of the opposition party is seeking the Democratic nomination for the presidency upon the negro issue. If the proposed action is taken it will contribute powerfully toward securing that nomination.

Fourth. The Northern introduction of the color question into Republican politics will make doubly sure the continuity of the Democratic solidity of the South, and supply the very weapons that Democracy needs in the fight against Republicanism, thus adding to the difficulty of electing our national candidate.

Fifth. It will retard and hinder the further progress of the sober public opinion of the best South in the effort to secure justice for the negro.

Mr. Ogden also affirms that he believes in the Fourteenth and Fifteenth Amendments. He is like unto the old deacon in Maine, who "believed in prohibition, but was agin its enforcement."

Let us examine in detail Mr. Ogden's specific statements. His first reason is the same old argument so vigorously employed by the Southern leaders — that if the nation shall dare to interfere with them in their work of subjugating a people they will take reprisals on the negro, cut down his school privileges, deny him protection of the law, make life hard for him, and otherwise maltreat him, or even lynch him. They can at will foment race slaughter, like that at Kishineff, and dignify such acts as race riots, but the whole world will know that there was a race massacre.

But the Government should not be moved by such consideration ; it should go straight ahead and do what is right and proper in the premises. When these leaders stir up race riots, the Government and the great legions of law-abiding people in the South can take care of that matter. There is a large and increasing element among the Southern people who believe that the leaders have gone entirely too far and have brought nothing but disgrace on the South.

Mr. Ogden's second reason is an insult to the Southern people. "Academic freedom?" Is not the South civilized? Is it not a Christian people? Do they need "academic freedom" to decide whether law and order should be observed ; whether an equal citizen should be outlawed and forced into servitude, and the laws of the land and the laws of God set at nought; whether the Constitutional guaranties of American citizenship and manhood are myths; and whether a man living in South Carolina should be three times as potential in Congress and in the electoral college as a man in New Hampshire or Colorado?

Does Mr. Ogden not know that while " academic freedom " is incubating the Southern leaders are going straight ahead fastening the chains of serfdom around the neck of a whole race? Will he kindly inform the public just how long it will be necessary to suspend the Constitution of the United States in order to achieve this " academic freedom "?

His third reason is childish. He is afraid that, if the proposed action is taken, the South will "get mad," and through the Democratic party nominate a man like Mr. Gorman or Mr. Tillman for the presidency. Everybody knows that the Democratic party has done rash things, but it has done nothing so foolhardy as this. And if it should make such a nomination, the day of election would disclose that the Democratic party in the North was not only " out of business," but stiff in the grasp of rigor *mortis*. Mr. Ogden may rest contented. His fears will not materialize. The Democratic party will not commit suicide.

His fourth reason would seem to indicate, if we did not have good evidence to the contrary, that he had been asleep forty years, twice as long as good old Rip Van Winkle. He says, "The Northern introduction of the color question into Republican politics will make doubly sure the continuity of the Democratic solidity of the South."

If Mr. Ogden should jog his memory just a little, it would tell him that the color question was in Republican politics at the birth of the party, and it has been very much alive in Republican politics ever since. The one thing that has distinguished that party and has made it " the party of grand moral ideas," that has caused it to represent before the world the conscience of the American people, and brought to it its greatest victories, is the color question in its politics. Its highest glory and most magnificent achievements in peace and in war are inseparably associated with the color question in its politics.

If, because the Republican party upholds the Constitution of the United States and demands that the vital issues settled by the War of the Rebellion shall stay settled, and that serf-dom shall not take the place of slavery, and that all American citizens shall have equal rights before the law, without regard to race or color — if these things shall "make doubly sure the continuity of the Democratic solidity of the South," then may the good Lord have mercy on the South.

Mr. Ogden's fifth reason is a flagrant impeachment of the "best South." If this petition "will retard and hinder the further progress of the sober public opinion of the best South," then indeed the conditions of the social organism in the South are worse than the average American would like to believe. This would seem to prove that the barbarism of slavery is a greater handicap on the whites than on the colored people.

The "best South" ought to welcome most heartily any lawful steps by the Government which will promote law and order, and bring about an honest and righteous settlement of the race question, guaranteeing the equal protection of the rights and liberty of all classes and restoring the equality of representation among the states.

Alexander Hamilton, the trusted supporter of George Washington, and exponent of the Constitution, said: "There can be no truer principle than this, that every individual of the community has an equal right to the protection of Government. Can this be a righteous government if partial distinctions are maintained?"

The French Constitution of 1793 holds aloft this torch for the illumination of the world: "Government is instituted to insure to man the free use of his natural and inalienable rights. These rights are equality, liberty, security, property. All men are equal by nature and before the law. Law is the same for all, be it protective or penal. Freedom is the power by which men can do what does not interfere with the rights of another; its basis is nature; its standard is justice; its protection is law; its moral boundary is the maxim, 'Do not unto others what you do not wish they should do unto you.'"

Inequalities before the law lead surely to abuses, wrongs, oppression, and inhumanities. Unsettled questions exist regardless of the peace of a nation. There can be no peace until South Carolina and Mississippi shall be as just in government as Massachusetts and Minnesota; until liberty and law, for one and for all, shall be respected by all, even as it is written in the Constitution of the republic.

The Supreme Court of the United States has rendered a decision covering the vital questions of the Thirteenth, Fourteenth, and Fifteenth Amendments to the Constitution of the United States. Let that decision (see Wallace's Reports, 16th volume) speak for itself.

Associate-Justice Miller, speaking for the court, said: "The process of restoring to their proper relations with the Federal Government and with other states those which had sided with the Rebellion, undertaken under the proclamation of President Johnson in 1865, and before the assembling of Congress, developed the fact that, notwithstanding the formal recognition by those states of the abolition of slavery, the condition of the slave race would, without further protection of the Federal Government, be almost as bad as it was before. Among the first acts of legislation adopted by several of the states in the legislative bodies which claimed to be in their normal relations with the Federal Government, were laws which imposed upon the colored race onerous disabilities and burdens, and curtailed their rights in the pursuit of life, liberty, and property to such an extent that their freedom was of little value, while they had lost the protection which they had received from their former owners from motives both of interest and humanity.

"They were in some states forbidden to appear in the towns in any other character than menial servants.

"They were required to reside on and cultivate the soil, without the right to own it or purchase it. They were excluded from any occupation or gain, and were not permitted to give testimony in the courts in any case where a white man was a party. It was said that their lives were at the mercy of bad men, either because the laws for their protection were insufficient or were not enforced.

"These circumstances, whatever of falsehood or misconception may have been mingled with their presentation, forced upon the statesmen who had conducted the Federal Government in safety through the crisis of the Rebellion, and who supposed that by the Thirteenth Article of Amendment they had secured the results of their labors, the conviction that something more was necessary in the way of Constitutional protection to the unfortunate race who had suffered so much. They accordingly passed through Congress the proposition for the Fourteenth Amendment, and they declined to treat as restored to their full participation in the government of the Union the states which had been in insurrection until they ratified that article by a formal vote of their legislative bodies.

"Before we proceed to examine more critically the provisions of this amendment, on which the plaintiffs in error rely, let us complete and dismiss the history of the recent amendments, as that history relates to the general purpose which pervades them all.

"A few years' experience satisfied the thoughtful men who had been the authors of the other two amendments, that, notwithstanding the restraints of these articles on the state, and the laws passed under the additional powers granted to Congress, these were inadequate for the protection of life, liberty, and property, without which freedom to the negro was no boon. They were in all those states denied the right of suffrage. The laws were administered by the white man alone. It was urged that a race of men distinctly marked as was the negro, living in the midst of another and dominant race, could never be fully secured in their person and their right without the right of suffrage.

"Hence the Fifteenth Amendment, which declares that 'the right of a citizen of the United States to vote shall not be denied or abridged by any state on account of race, color, or previous condition of servitude.'

"The negro, having by the Fourteenth Amendment been declared to be a citizen of the United States, is thus made a voter in every state of the Union.

"We repeat, then, in the light of this recapitulation of events almost too recent to be called history, but which are familiar to us all on the most casual examination of the language of these amendments, no one can fail to be impressed with the one pervading purpose found in them all, lying at the foundation of each, and without which none of them would have been suggested: WE MEAN THE FREEDOM OF THE SLAVE RACE, THE SECURITY AND FIRM ESTABLISHMENT OF THAT FREEDOM, AND THE PROTECTION OF THE NEWLY MADE FREEMAN AND CITIZEN FROM THE OPPRESSION OF THOSE WHO HAD FORMERLY EXERCISED UNLIMITED DOMINION OVER HIM.

"It is true that only the Fifteenth Amendment in terms mentions the negro by speaking of his color and his slavery. But it is just as true that each of the other articles was addressed to the grievances of that race, and designed to remedy them, as was the Fifteenth."

This clean-cut, invincible decision of the highest tribunal of the republic destroys every contention of the enemies of liberty and makes impregnable the position of its friends.

CHAPTER VI
THE NEGRO IN POLITICS

THREE pen pictures have been made of President Roosevelt which, taken together, show us the man. One is drawn by the Honorable John D. Long, a political partisan and personal friend, formerly Governor of Massachusetts, and Secretary of the Navy during the Spanish-American War. Another is painted by the New York *World*, a political opponent, but honestly critical. The third is drawn by a non-partisan, or independent, President Eliot of Harvard University, the foremost educator in the land, the Dean of American scholars. There are no more discriminating nor more trustworthy sources by which a true estimate of a man may be formed.

These are the pictures presented. John D. Long, depicts him as follows: "Theodore Roosevelt. What an American career! What a fitting for his present great place! Child of the great metropolis, graduate of our own Harvard, a citizen of the Western plains, touching indeed every phase of our national life, a student of our history, a soldier of our army, Governor of the Empire State, honest, earnest, brave, high-minded, direct, forceful, and always, let us say here, a true Republican, whoever else falls off! The people like him. He preaches them sermons of manliness and right living, fidelity to duty, and they believe that he is himself even a better sermon than his sermons. There is no great question that he does not face, whether it be the trusts, or the tariff, or our duty to Cuba and the Philippines, or the purity of the civil service, or the development of our trade, or the welfare of the East, or West, or North, or South! He voices even more than the spirit of a party — he voices the spirit of the people."

The New York *World*, his most powerful political opponent, paints him thus: "President Roosevelt does not
carry his ideas of democratic equality quite so far as Thomas
Jefferson did. He respects all the conventions of official
society in public, but in his private and personal relations he
is a pretty thorough-going democrat. He often goes to
shake the grimy hand of an engine-driver who has carried
him safely on a railway journey. He is 'hail-fellow well
met' with his old friends among the cowboys and the Rough-
Riders. And just now he has in Washington, as his guest,
his old Maine woods guide, with his wife and some friends,
who have all taken lunch with the President and Mrs.
Roosevelt in the White House.

"It is safe to say that none of our mushroom aristocracy,
and very few even of the older growth, would be thus familar
with their 'plain' friends — though a good type of the
independent native guide of the Adirondacks or the Maine
woods is at heart as thorough a gentleman, in the real meaning of the word, and is certainly much better company than
one half of the vapid men-folk who help to make up what is
called 'society.'

"Yet, Mr. Roosevelt could boast, if he were weak enough,
of fine old 'Knickerbocker blood,' and, though not rich in
the modern meaning of the word, he has always lived in an
atmosphere of wealth, refinement, and culture.

"That he still believes, in respect to sterling worth un-
adorned with either wealth or book-learning or social graces,
that 'a man's a man for a' that,' and that, though occupying
the highest station in the land, he has the courage of his
likings and the fortitude of his friendships, is a trait of his
character which explains something of that popularity which
the politicians do not understand and which even his mistakes
do not seriously impair. A very few Americans may 'dearly
love a lord.' The great mass of them love and admire a
democrat like Lincoln, Grant, McKinley, and Roosevelt."

And President Eliot draws this portrait of him : "Theodore Roosevelt, President of the United States, from his youth a member of this society of scholars, now in his prime a true type of the sturdy gentleman, and the high-minded public servant in a democracy. Harvard delights to honor him."

These three pictures, taken together, faithfully and clearly represent the man.

The Right Honorable James Bryce of England, perhaps the greatest living student of history — learned, dispassionate, and philosophical — says of President Roosevelt: "He is among the greatest presidents America has had, and is to be mentioned only with Washington and Lincoln."

It would naturally be supposed that in a republic of free men where — in President Roosevelt's own words — "no man is above the law and no man below it," the whole citizenry would have a just pride in such a chief-magistrate. But the fact is that no President of the United States, with the exception of Lincoln, has been so roundly abused, and so heatedly denounced, as Theodore Roosevelt.

It has happened repeatedly in the South that the mere mention of his name, or the presentation of his pictures in theatres and public halls has brought forth storms of hisses. He has even been burned in effigy. Southerners who take part in such performances or approve or condone them, or fail to protest against them, injure themselves, by forfeiting the respect of law-abiding people. Lincoln! Roosevelt! — these are the two men seemingly appointed of God to face the hate and rancor of Southern leadership. Lincoln's victory was complete, absolute. Roosevelt's triumph has come in the overwhelming majority by which he has been elected to succeed himself in the presidency. God and the right were with Lincoln ; God and the right are with Roosevelt.

There are also noteworthy coincidences in the lives of these men.

Lincoln was born in the South. Roosevelt is of Southern extraction on his maternal side. But in this the South finds no appeasement.

Again, Lincoln stood between the colored race and their continued enslavement. Roosevelt stands between the colored race and a debasing and hopeless serfdom which does not even afford the protection of slavery. Both stand firmly on the Gospel of Christ and the Declaration of Independence. In the lives of both, the laws of God and the laws of the republic find their high exemplification.

What, then, is the head of the offending of President Roosevelt, that he should be the object of such abuse and resentment?

These are facts : There are ten millions of colored people in the United States, one-eighth of the entire population. The vast body of them reside in the South. Though equal citizens under the law, they are yet in an abnormal condition — subject to great wrongs, hardships, and inhumanities, not of their own making. Mr. Roosevelt wished to consult with some well-known, responsible persons with reference to the condition of these people ; for he is the President of the South as well as of the North, the President of the colored people just as he is of the white people. No man who is worthy to be the President of the United States would fail to have a deep concern for the welfare of ten millions of loyal, patriotic American citizens, especially were they seen to be under grievous burdens, serious disadvantage, and debasing inequalities. He therefore invited Principal Booker T. Washington's presence at the White House for consultation.

Mr. Washington is the most widely known educator in the colored race ; a man of sterling character ; conservative almost to a fault, many think to the injury of his race ; of remarkable mental gifts ; an executive of great ability ; a genius in diplomacy. No white man in the South surpasses him ; few, if any, equal him. In fact, a leading Southern white educator has declared that he is the greatest man the South has produced since the masterful Robert E. Lee.

Mr. Washington, in compliance with the President's invitation, travelled hundreds of miles to meet him in Washington City. What was more natural or becoming than that the President should invite him to dinner?

This was President Roosevelt's first offending. It was a simple act of courtesy as a gentleman; it was an act which any ruler or high official in any country might have performed with perfect grace and propriety. Yet it set the South ablaze with rage. And oh! how the big "Jim Crowites," and the little "Jim Crowites," and the "me too" "Jim Crowites," and the wee wee "Jim Crowites" did smite the air with clenched fists and denounce the President!

The following quotations show the exact nature of their utterances : —

Senator Carmack of Tennessee fires this hot shot : "It is an out-and-out damnable outrage!"

Senator Tillman of South Carolina, true to his nature, demands blood and declares : "Now that Roosevelt has eaten with that nigger Washington, we shall have to kill a thousand niggers to get them back to their places."

The *Scimitar*, a paper published at Memphis, Tennessee, makes this declaration: "The most damnable outrage which has ever been perpetrated by any citizen of the United States was committed yesterday by the President, when he invited a nigger to dine with him at the White House."

The *Commercial Appeal*, Memphis, Tennessee, says : "The example of president or potentate cannot change our views. If some coarse-fibred men cannot understand them it is not the concern of the Southern people."

The *News*, Richmond, Virginia, declares : "At one stroke and by one act he has destroyed regard for him. He has put himself further from us than any man who has ever been in the White House."

THE AFTERMATH OF SLAVERY

Governor Candler of Georgia, with vulgar assumption, thus explodes: " No self-respecting man can ally himself with the President, after what has occurred. . . . And no Southerner can respect any white man who would eat with a negro."

The *Times-Democrat*, New Orleans, Louisiana, makes this plaintive appeal: " The President of the United States has entertained a negro at dinner in the White House. White men of the South, how do you like it? White women of the South, how do you like it?"

Governor McSweeney of South Carolina declares: " No white man who has eaten with a negro can be respected; it is simply a question of whether those who are invited to dine are fit to marry the sisters and daughters of their hosts."

But Japanese, Chinese, and Indians have eaten at the White House without raising the thought of a marriage. Is it in vogue among any order of society, that an invitation to dine carries with it the expectation or the obligation of marrying off sisters and daughters?

The Enterprise, Birmingham, Alabama, says: " The incident of counselling with a negro and dining him establishes a precedent humiliating to the South."

His reverence, Bishop Kelly of Savannah, Georgia, uses the following intemperate language: " The recreant son of a Southern mother, who can hobnob with the Kaiser's brother and sit cheek by jowl with an Alabama negro."

And Senator Money of Mississippi, with a hypocrisy that is at once amazing and amusing, declares: " Any white man who should sit down to a meal with a negro would be everlastingly disgraced in the eyes of the South."

Bishop Kelly well knows, Senator Money well knows, and the whole country well knows that white men of the South have come into closer relations with negroes and committed far grosser sins than that of sitting down to meat with a reputable and representative colored person; and in the eyes of their fellows they suffered no disgrace. So that in this particular they are certainly guilty of the charge of "straining at a gnat and swallowing a camel."

During the sessions of the Congress, especially, and also at other times, the President is accustomed to give receptions at which the Supreme Court justices, the foreign ambassadors, senators, and members of the House of Representatives, officials of the army and navy, and high government functionaries and distinguished individuals may be bidden to come. There are series of such receptions. To one of these receptions the President invited Mr. Lyons, the Register of the Treasury of the United States, who happens to be a colored man. The reception was given to officers of his class. Would it have comported with the dignity and honor of the President of the United States to invite every other government official of this particular class and deliberately ignore the Register of the United States simply on the ground of color?

If he was unworthy to be invited to the reception, he was not worthy to be the Register of the Treasury. President Roosevelt only fulfilled the considerations of official etiquette and propriety and his duty as the President of *all* the people when he invited Mr. Lyons.

This simple, gentlemanly act is the second offending of the South on the part of the President. But the haters of the negro railed at the President, in a manner shown by the following brief quotations.

Judge William E. Eve, Augusta, Georgia, said: "The invitation is a blow aimed not only at the South, but at the whole white race, and should be resented, and the President should be regarded and treated on the same plane with negroes." He seems to be oblivious of the fact that the whole white race outside of the South most heartily commends and applauds the President.

Governor Terrell of Georgia declared that he looked upon the President and such a scandal with silent contempt.

Ex-Attorney-General Boykin Wright said: "It has done great harm and is the greatest mistake ever made by a president."

Representative Martin Calvin declared: "It is a blow at every white man and woman."

Senator J. Rice Smith said: "The invitation was the most ᵈⁱˢᵍᵘⁱⁿᵍ act ever heard of on the part of any public man."

The News, Richmond, Virginia, prints the following: "There is just one thing for the Southern people to do. They can and should hold themselves absolutely aloof from any social recognition of Mr. Roosevelt. He should be treated by Southern people precisely as if he were a negro.

"Our representatives in Congress should confine their dealings with the President to the strictest formality. If he should come South, he should be left to associate with the negroes, whom he has chosen to regard as equals. He should be treated in all respects by Southern people precisely as if he were a negro, and with absolute indication that he is not of our race or in any respect socially an equal with us or a fit associate for us or any of us."

The country is familiar with various forms of the boycott, but with nothing like this. What audacity! what arrogance! A social boycott is declared against the President of the United States by the lordly aristocracy of the South, and the President is to be "treated in all respects by Southern people precisely as if he were a negro," and with direct intimation that "he is not of our race, or in any respect socially an equal with us or a fit associate for us or any of us"— because he invited the Register of the Treasury, who happens to be a colored man, to an official function!

The third offence of the President is political in its nature. The colored people compose about one-third of the total population of the South. In some of the states they are pre-eminently the tax-makers; in all, their varied labors and toils are valuable contributions to the public weal; yet they have been ruthlessly brushed aside by intimidations and by the shot-gun policy, and have been denied representation in the government. That the 557,807 whites of South Carolina should by brute force seize the government of that state and deny all representation to the 782,321 colored people who make the taxes which support the government; or that the 641,200 whites of Mississippi should by murderous methods seize that state and refuse all representation to the 907,630 colored people without whose fruitful toil the state would be in hopeless decay and bankruptcy, is a wrong that cries to Heaven.

The colored people are thus denied all representation in the state and local governments. If, now, in addition to this, they should be denied representation in the Federal Government the door of hope would be closed hard and fast against them. The influences which hold them to the political and civil life of the nation would be broken; ceasing to be citizens, they would cease to be treated as men. They would become nondescripts, without a definite status. They would be derelicts on the political sea,.and the nation would have a far greater problem than ever before.

All other things being equal, the colored man has identically the same right to office as the white man. The strong arm of the Federal Government cannot be used to destroy his status as a citizen of the United States, completing the work of his enemies who have already sought to eliminate him as a citizen of the state. The appointment of colored men to Federal offices is not only just, but is absolutely necessary to maintain the status of the race as citizens of the United States.

President Roosevelt recognized this principle by appointing to Federal offices properly equipped colored men as a just and righteous act, where their numbers and importance as toilers warrant it. The appointment of Dr. William D. Crum as Collector of the port of Charleston, South Carolina, was entirely just and proper, but it stirred up a tempest of wrath among the Southern leaders.

If the Federal Government should for one moment concede that a citizen shall be denied the right to hold a public office on the ground of his color or race, it would by such concession negative the amendments to the Constitution, and thus become a violator of the laws it has sworn to uphold and enforce, and play directly into the hands of the lawless elements. The right of citizenship and the ballot carries with it the right to hold a public office. Nothing could be more absurd, foolish, and even suicidal than the proposition which is sometimes made to the effect that the colored man should waive his right to public office and the ballot for about fifty years with the hope of appeasing the implacable elements of the South. Such a waiver would be tantamount to alienation, and would put the race outside the pale of citizenship. What guaranty is to be given, and who is to give it, and how is it to be made secure, that political suicide to-day will be incarnated into the blessings of liberty fifty or a hundred years hence? This, indeed, is the paradise of a fool. Liberty is gained by eternal vigilance, and not by political suicide. The upward struggles of mankind show that the liberty and political and civil rights of a people are to be regarded as more precious than meat or drink, or houses and lands, and are more to be valued than even life itself. Liberty and their manhood rights being established, these and all things shall be gradually added. Profiting by his past experience the colored man will not waive a single right of an American citizen for fifty years, nor even for fifty *seconds*. What free man would waive his liberty and his rights at the behest of a class that is bent on forging the chains of servitude around his neck? Connivance with the South in violating the Constitution would prove embarrassing to the government and perilous to the social organism. The upheavals which are shaking the foundations of Russia, and the cry of the proletariat for liberty cast their shadows and point their lessons. America! the greatest and freest country in the world will eschew the civilization that degrades manhood and will hold true to her ideals of liberty and the equality of her citizenship.

The fourth cause of offence by the President was also of a political character. The post-office at Indianola, Mississippi, a small town, three-fourths of its inhabitants being colored people, had been filled for seven or eight years by Mrs. Cox, an estimable and efficient postmistress. She is a refined woman of unblemished character, and thoroughly competent to discharge the duties of her office. She had given entire satisfaction in the performance of all the obligations of this little office for over seven years, and there was no complaint against her. But she is colored, and the men who had carried through the wholesale disfranchisement of the colored race and had decided on its subjugation, held a public meeting and demanded her resignation, — not because she was incompetent, but on the ground of color alone. By brutal and lawless intimidation she was expelled from her office and exiled from the town.

The President declined to approve this flagrant violation of law and unreasonable assault on an officer of the United States Government, or to accept under such conditions the resignation of the exiled postmistress, and requested that the law-abiding element give her protection of the law. Less than this he could not have done. Nevertheless, this simple stand for law and order caused the most bitter hostility throughout the South.

Senator Money of Mississippi declared: "No colored man, no matter what his qualifications may be, should hold a Federal office;" and he added that the white people of the

South would have all colored men excluded from the army and navy.

Mr. W. C. Chevis, editor of the *Daily States*, New Orleans, said: "The Indianola incident and the Crum appointment, determined upon after mature consideration on the part of the President and his cabinet, cannot be interpreted as meaning anything else than a determination to cram an insult down the throats of the white men of the South, and it is accepted in this spirit here."

Mr. Charles W. Miller, editor of the Nashville *Democrat*, said: "There is no doubt the action of President Roosevelt in these two cases has severed the last connecting link in the chain of sympathy which bound him to the South."

Mr. J. S. McNeily, editor of the Vicksburg *Herald*, said: "If there were a poll now, it would be found that the President has completely alienated Southern sympathy by the Crum appointment and closing the Indianola post-office."

Mr. J. C. Hempill, editor of the Charleston *News-Courier*, declared that "The opening of the 'door of hope' to Crum, President Roosevelt's selection for Collector of the Port of Charleston, will be the closing of the 'door of hope' to many of Crum's race. In a thousand ways and in no way that will be in violation of law, Crum's race will be the sufferer." This is a distinct threat that the whites will take reprisal on the colored people. That is, if they are not permitted to snuff out the liberty of that race, destroy their citizenship, and force them into serfdom, they will in a thousand ways harass and torment them and make their life unbearable.

The press despatches reported that "Messages are hourly coming in from all parts of the surrounding country offering assistance, arms, money, and men if they are needed."

Mayor J. L. Davis of Indianola said: "Conditions are such that I would not advise Mrs. Cox to open the post-office."

THE NEGRO IN POLITICS

Major M. C. House, commanding the First Squadron of Cavalry of Arkansas, sent this telegram to the governor of the state : " Subject to your order, I tender my services with one hundred and fifty cavalry to the good people of Indianola for their protection against negro domination." Such is the Southern chivalry in the twentieth century. This gallant, brave, and heroic major offers to march his squadron of cavalry, one hundred and fifty strong, across the state of Arkansas into the state of Mississippi, to prevent one little, lone, helpless woman, who with her heart in her mouth had taken flight, and whose life was at the mercy of a Mississippi lynching mob, from forcing negro domination on Indianola, and maybe from compelling all the whites of the state to pass under the yoke. This valiant major is verily a subject for caricature.

The Atlanta *News* said: " The *News* has repeatedly stated its reasons for objecting to the appointment of negroes to Federal office ; it gives the negro a hope that he shall continue as a political factor."

Senator Tillman said: " There might be no alternative for the Southern people but to kill negroes to prevent them from holding office. There are still ropes and guns in the South."

The Atlanta *Journal* declared : " No matter how worthy certain members of the African race may be in character and capacity, yet they are unacceptable as office-holders to the white people of the Southern States." The press despatches reported " great excitement," " high feelings," " threats " against " all negro postal clerks, letter carriers, and other officials, in different parts of the South." A New Orleans newspaper boldly demanded the assassination of colored men appointed to Federal offices.

Governor James K. Vardaman of Mississippi declared that " Anything that causes the negro to aspire above the plow handle, the cook pot, in a word the functions of a servant, will be the worst thing on earth for the negro." But the Boston *Herald* warns the Governor that "hitching a negro to a mule will not settle the race question."

This same Governor Vardaman published in his own newspaper the following insult to President Roosevelt: "It is said that men follow the bent of their geniuses, and that prenatal influences are often potent in shaping thoughts and ideas in after life. Probably old lady Roosevelt, during the period of gestation, was frightened by a dog, and that fact may account for the qualities of the male pup that are so prominent in Teddy. I would not do either an injustice, but am disposed to apologize to the dog for mentioning it."

In reference to Principal Booker T. Washington, Governor Vardaman has this to say: "I am opposed to negro voting; it matters not what his advertised moral and mental qualifications may be. I am just as much opposed to Booker Washington as a voter, with all his Anglo-Saxon reinforcements, as I am to the cocoanut-headed, chocolate-colored, typical little coon, Andy Dotson, who blacks my shoes every morning. Neither is fit to perform the supreme functions of citizenship." Governor Vardaman denounces the education of negroes and publicly advocates murdering and lynching; concerning which the Boston *Herald* says: "It is a safe judgment that the white men of Mississippi who want liberty to murder negroes with impunity, or to beat them, or condemn them to the slavery called peonage, or to cheat them of the wages of their labor, or to debauch their daughters are, as a rule, supporters of Vardaman."

These criticisms and denunciations of the President, although not the hundredth part of those which have appeared, are sufficiently indicative of the dominant Southern sentiment. Well might these people offer the prayer —

> "O! wad some power the giftie gie us,
> To see oursel's as ithers see us."

At the recent Constitutional Convention of South Carolina, called for the purpose of annulling certain provisions of the

Constitution of the United States by cancelling the citizenship of the colored race, an influential politician of the state delivered the valedictory address after the convention had completed its work, saying: " We can all hope a great deal from the Constitution we have adopted. It is not such an instrument as we would have made if we had been a free people. We are not a free people. We have not been since the war. I fear it will be some time before we can call ourselves free. I have had that fact very painfully impressed upon me for several years. If we were free, instead of having negro suffrage, we would have negro slavery; instead of having the United States Government, we would have the Confederate States Government; instead of paying $3,000,000 pension tribute, we would be receiving it; instead of having many things that we have, we would have other and better things. But to the extent that we are permitted to govern ourselves and pay pension tribute to our conquerors, we have framed as good an organic law, take it as a whole, as the wisdom and patriotism of the state could have desired."

These utterances were received with hearty and prolonged applause and cheering.

The presiding officer of the Louisiana Constitutional Convention, which was called for the same purpose, used these words in his closing speech: " What care I whether it [the Constitution] be more or less ridiculous or not? Does n't it meet the case? Does n't it let the white man vote, and does n't it stop the negro from voting? — and is n't that what we came here for? "

And another leading Southerner has declared with great warmth and in language strenuously emphatic, if not elegant: " We have got our heel on the neck of the niggers and we can hold them down; and we have got a clutch on the craw of the Yankees, and we can choke down their throats our sentiments on the negro question."

In the midst of all these things President Roosevelt stands calm, firm, serene. He could borrow the language of the Apostle Paul and say: " None of these things move me." He has beaten no retreat, evaded no responsibility, made no apologies, but has met the issues in the only way thát a man worthy to be the President of the United States could meet them and has defined his position as follows: "If I could be absolutely assured of my election as president by turning my back on the principles of human liberty as enunciated by Abraham Lincoln, I would be incapable of doing it and unfit for president if I could be capable of doing it. I do not expect to be elected president by those who would close the door of hope against the Afro-American as a citizen. If I am elected to this high office it must be on my record as the executor of the law without favors or discriminations.

"The great majority of my appointments in every state have been of white men. North and South alike, it has been my sedulous endeavor to appoint only men of high character and good capacity, whether white or black. But it has been my consistent policy in every state where the numbers warranted it to recognize colored men of good repute and standing in making appointments to office. I cannot consent to take the position that the door of hope — the door of opportunity — is to be shut upon any man, no matter how worthy, purely upon the grounds of race or color. . . . Such an attitude would be, according to my convictions, fundamentally wrong. . . . It seems to me that it is a good thing from every standpoint to let the colored man know that if he shows in marked degree the qualities of good citizenship — the qualities which in a white man we feel are entitled to reward — then he will not be cut off from all hope of similar reward."

President Roosevelt further says: " In this country of all others, it behooves us to show an example to the world, not by words only, but by deeds, that we have faith in the doctrine that each man should be treated on his own worth as a man, without regard to his creed or his race."

The line of cleavage between the President and the dominant Southern sentiment is unmistakable. Which of these sentiments represents American civilization? Which represents American Christianity? Which represents the spirit of humanity and the ideals of republican government? Is there the slightest doubt that if the American people were to be judged by the dominant Southern sentiment, they would be regarded in the eyes of the civilized world as a backward, retrograde people? But happily there is a wide gulf between "Jim Crowism" and Americanism. In no sense does "Jim Crowism" represent American public opinion. It does not represent even the sober second thought of the South. It is the outgrowth of a diseased mind, — a mind infected by the virus of slavery; and by a combination of circumstances it has wrought much havoc. Although the Southern leaders have organized secret, oath-bound societies sworn to destroy the negro as a man, as a citizen, and as a member of the social organization, yet, it is as certain as fate that an aroused Southern conscience, and an enlightened moral sense, and the irresistible public opinion of this republic will ultimately triumph.

In this conflict, forced on the President by the reactionary and retrograde elements in the South, the people of the nation at large have not been indifferent spectators. They have given him emphatic endorsement, and he has not been without whole-souled supporters among the more thoughtful and conservative Southerners. The spirit of the North, as in the case of that at the South, is best represented by quoting the actual words of some of the opinions that have been vouchsafed.

President Eliot of Harvard has thus expressed himself: "Harvard dined Booker Washington at the table last commencement, and Harvard conferred an honorary degree upon

199

him. This ought to show what Harvard thinks about the matter."

President Hadley of Yale, President Tucker of Dartmouth, President Angell of the University of Michigan, and other leading educators give Mr. Roosevelt unqualified endorsement. They have entertained Mr. Washington and sat at meat with colored guests.

Bishop Potter of New York said: "He is fit to sit at any table in the land. Yes, I see the Bourbons are in a fit again! As I entertained Mr. Washington at my table last winter, and know that no more courteous and exact man exists, I naturally feel that there is no reason in the outcry."

The Methodist ministers of Philadelphia and vicinity, at their regular meeting, commend the "courageous and broad-minded act of our President, and we hail it with joy as an auspicious omen that the weight of the great office of the President of the United States is to be cast in the interest of the equal rights of all our citizens before God under the laws of the land." Other religious bodies in Chicago and in every part of the North strongly uphold the President; many churches, separately, also endorsed his actions.

Governor Richard Yates of Illinois, son of the great war governor, has said: "When we were in the crisis of a great war we were not so particular about social equality, whatever that is. We needed the negro and he helped us, and now we will stand by him. All things being equal, he has exactly the same rights to the courtesies of the White House that a white man has."

Some additional personal opinions are equally to the point: —

"It is time for Northern justice to demand that the negro citizen be accorded the same honor and privileges which are accorded to the white citizen. . . . I marvel at the patience of the negro. . . . He is demanding his rightful citizenship and must have it." [Reverend G. S. Rollins of Minneapolis.]

"Our President, following in the wake of the immortal Lincoln and the crowned McKinley, has contended and still contends for the rights of the colored citizens. This has called forth a storm of abuse in certain quarters. Two million men gave themselves to help the negro to freedom, and millions are ready to maintain him there." [Reverend E. J. Smith of Cleveland, Ohio.]

"Every good citizen of the country admires President Roosevelt, and every good citizen admires his guest." [Reverend George A. Gordon, D.D.]

"I have invited Booker Washington to my house. He has been my guest at my table. When he comes to Boston I shall be glad to do it again." [Major Henry L. Higginson.]

"I uphold the President in the bold stand he has taken." [Professor Charles Eliot Norton.]

"The President is just right." [Moorfield Storey.]

"I think that President Roosevelt did perfectly right in inviting Booker T. Washington to dine with him. The President did a gracious act in inviting him to partake of his hospitality." [Mrs. Mary A. Livermore.]

"If I were in Roosevelt's place, I would do the same thing myself." [Professor Nathaniel S. Shaler, Dean of the Scientific School of Harvard University.]

"I heartily approve of President Roosevelt's course." [Colonel Thomas Wentworth Higginson.]

"The President did just right." [Reverend Paul Revere Frothingham.]

"I think the action of President Roosevelt in entertaining Mr. Booker T. Washington at the Executive Mansion was eminently wise, timely, and proper." [Henry B. Blackwell.]

"The President should have the privilege of inviting any citizen of the United States to his dinner table, regardless of race, color, or creed." [Major Charles G. Davis.]

"It was a fine object lesson and most encouraging. It was the act of a gentleman, an act of unconscious, natural simplicity. A democracy should be color blind." [William Lloyd Garrison.]

"It is not necessary for me to defend the conduct of the President of the United States. He is well able to do that himself. I cannot understand why men should criticise the Christian act of a Christian magistrate in breaking bread with one of the foremost figures of this age, simply because of his color." [Reverend George C. Lorimer.]

"Our President at Washington recently invited to his table a good man, a Christian man, a scholar, a gentleman; and any man who is privileged to have Booker Washington to eat with him at his table should feel himself honored." [Reverend Charles M. Sheldon, Topeka, Kansas.]

And the following expressions may be regarded as representing the press of the North. The Boston *Herald* says: "There has been no incident in politics for a score of years that has so united the men who originally comprised the Republican party in opinion with regard to a subject as the attack upon President Roosevelt for calling Booker Washington to his dining-table. Incidents which induced a lower tone as regards public affairs have notoriously parted many men of character and ability from that party association during that time; but the raising of the color issue in this way has been to them like a rallying note to the old standard. . . . Here is genuine Republicanism of better days. They stand by the President in being true to it. No men endorsed his action in this matter more promptly and unreservedly than those who have felt compelled to separate from the Republican organization because its course has been objectionable in other respects. . . .

"Booker Washington is a superior man without regard to his color. No man can see him and escape the feeling that here is a superior example of human nature in its best development, aside from accidental conditions as to race or birth. The man rises above these, and appeals to something they cannot seriously affect. He illustrates their unimportance, as weighed in the scale of intellect and manhood, with an effectiveness which makes race prejudice appear at its worst when brought into operation against him."

The New York *World* says : " The President has right and reason on his side in insisting upon a vote by the Senate upon the nomination of Dr. Crum, the colored man whose nomination as Collector of Customs at Charleston has been reported adversely by the Committee on Commerce. His position is that he made the nomination deliberately, after ascertaining the fitness of Dr. Crum for the office, and that as no objection except his color is urged against the nominee he desires to have a direct expression of the judgment of the Senate upon the question at issue — whether men, the representatives of 8,000,000 citizens equal in political rights, are to be debarred from office at the South, on account of ' race, color, or previous condition of servitude.' We certainly hope that the President will adhere to this attitude. The Republican senators should not be permitted to escape a record upon this question. If they are prepared to abandon these principles and professions of their party in the past, they ought to have the courage of their apostasy. If they are ready to stand with the President in refusing to consent that ' the door of hope, the door of opportunity,' is to be shut upon any man, no matter how worthy, purely upon the grounds of race or color, they ought to be willing and even anxious to let the country know it.

" The *World* does not hesitate to say that it thinks the Southern whites are making a serious mistake in reviving the race issue in its extremest form against a President who has made fewer appointments of colored men to office than any of his predecessors."

The *Evening Sun* says : " The Indianola post-office row seems to be a tempest in a teapot. Mississippi will hardly secede or the South fly to arms, because the negro postmistress has retired to Alabama and the office is temporarily closed. That excitable New Orleans sheet which accuses the President of deliberately ' offending and insulting the white people of the South ' does not understand Mr. Roosevelt's position, and it seems to forget that the postmistress at Indianola was an old incumbent who had shown herself capable and trustworthy. The appointment and protection of postmasters is a Federal matter and the Government must not show weakness or vacillation in asserting its authority."

The *Press* says: " Those who applaud the President's militant chivalry, however, must gain no little compensation from the savage attitude struck by such organs as the New Orleans *States,* which says: ' If President Roosevelt has made up his mind to outrage and insult people of the South by appointing and keeping in office obnoxious negroes [not incompetent or corrupt negroes, mark you, but merely obnoxious negroes, for all negroes are obnoxious to those people of the South for whom this New Orleans paper speaks], *his negro appointees will be killed,* just as the negro appointees of other Republican Presidents *have been put out of the way.*' Yet if the enemies of his race policy will range themselves alongside those for whom the New Orleans assassin is spokesman the difficult road he must travel will be made much easier."

The *Tribune* says: " The President has chosen exactly the right moment to send to the Senate his long contemplated nomination of Dr. Crum, to be Collector of the port of Charleston. The persecution of the capable and respectable postmistress of Indianola, Miss., solely on account of color, has made an issue to be faced. The office of Collector is considered too sacred to be profaned by an occupant with a black skin, just as the postoffice at Indianola is considered too sacred to be profaned by a woman with black skin, though she profaned it for several years to the satisfaction of the white community, until some of the loafers thought it was time to assert their aristocratic Caucasianism and teach th 'niggers' their place. Under such circumstances the dignity of government and respect for the principles of its Constitution call for an emphatic stand, not for negro office-holding in general, but for the Government's right to appoint negroes to office when it sees fit. The agitation against Dr. Crum has practically amounted to a denial of that right, and the President correctly judges that the way to defend the right is to exercise it."

"Eternal vigilance is the price of liberty." The republic has not been vigilant in the safeguarding of the liberty of its citizens. In this matter it has fallen into apathy, and this apathy was the opportunity of the reactionists.

In 1890 Mississippi violated the Constitution of the United States, defied the national Government, and disregarded the decision of the Supreme Court of the United States, by the wholesale disfranchisement of the colored race. If this movement had been promptly met by the reduction of her representatives in the Congress and the electoral college to the basis of her white population plus the actual number of registered colored voters, no Southern state would have followed her example. Nor would the white people of Mississippi have consented to the reduction of their representatives in the Congress and the electoral college simply for the glory of disfranchising the negroes.

If in the early stages the republic had displayed the same horror over the various acts of violence in the South that they did show over the Kishineff shame in far-off Russia, mob rule and lynch law would not have become so firmly intrenched on American soil. But the nation has remained quiescent, notwithstanding the repeated nullification of its organic laws, and the long train of frightful horrors that followed. This quiescence has been interpreted by the reactionists as acquiescence, and they feel emboldened to proceed to crush and keep in subjugation the colored race.

In dillydallying with the reactionists, the nation has been playing with fire, and it is being burnt. These reactionists are so well organized into secret clans that by the mere "touch of the button" they can bring forth complaints and threats at any time from every Southern centre in the form of interviews on the necessity of "teaching the negroes their place." It is, however, all for effect.

The attempt to "Jim-Crow" the President of the United States and coerce the Government of the United States to disregard its own citizens on the ground of color alone and deny them all share in the government is preposterous. But neither Mr. Roosevelt nor the many thousands of people in the North, churchmen, professional men, capitalists, bankers, men of affairs, educators, sons of toil, and in fact representatives of all classes who have broken bread at a feast where there was a colored guest, will feel alarmed at the threats of violence, or be degraded by the social "boycott" declared against them by the Southern aristocrats.

The race problem has reached an acute stage in its development. The serpent of slavery was coddled and nursed in the nation's bosom and warmed into life; it gained in strength and power until it all but stung the republic to death. If the more subtle and treacherous monster, serfdom, shall be allowed to wind itself around the vitals of the republic, it will strangle liberty and constitutional government. Its sting may be even more destructive than that of the serpent of slavery.

It ought not to be admitted even for a moment that any class of citizens is above the law or any class is below the law. Nor, on the ground of color alone, shall a citizen — otherwise entirely worthy and capable — be denied the right to participate in the government or hold an office under it.

It is true that any interference with plans of the reactionists to subjugate the colored race may produce more or less trouble. Expressions of defiance are to be expected. Reprisals threatened on the colored people may be carried out to some extent. But all that they can do is inconsequential in comparison with the great national object to be attained. To use the language of the decision of the Supreme Court of the United States, " *We mean the freedom of the slave race, the security and firm establishment of that freedom, and the protection of the newly made freeman and citizen from the oppression of those who had formerly exercised unlimited dominion over him.*" The path of duty is plain.

We have now to consider the political conditions in the South which may be included under the significant term " Lily-whitism." For . some years there has been much speculation about the organization of a new republican party in the South. The old organization had rendered signal and invaluable services to the republic in the hour of its greatest need. To it belongs the credit of the establishment of the first free governments in the South. It also gave the South its first system of free public schools. Through it the nation reconstructed the Southern states at the close of the War of the Rebellion, and without it reconstruction with free government would have been impossible, and the fruits of the war could not have been preserved.

But its constituency was largely colored men ; its leaders were conservative Southerners and Northern men who had settled in the South. Naturally these became a mark for the great body of the Southern white people, because they stood athwart the purposes of the latter and foiled their plans. Nevertheless, these Republicans elected presidential electors, and United States senators and representatives in Congress ; notwithstanding the fact that in recent years they have been opposed by the shot-gun policy.

Gross and serious charges of corruption were laid against the old organization, but not always justly. For when one considers the surrounding circumstances, the inflamed passions, and chaotic conditions at the close of a great war, the cross purposes of the contending parties, and how the organization was hedged about and hampered by the great mass of the whites — it will be seen that great blunders and venality were invited. But the organization was republican in principles ; it was patriotic, it was liberty-loving, and it was just to colored and white men alike.

The "Lily-white" Republican party which assumes in some of the states to take the place of the old Republican party is composed mainly of disappointed Democrats, men whose ambitions for power and thirst for office were not satisfied in their own party. After bitterly opposing the Republican party for years, and not receiving the recognition they sought in the Democratic organization, they deserted to the Republican party and proceeded at once by the same oppressive methods formerly employed to harass and defeat republicanism, to seize control of the Republican organization and oust those who had been loyal and true to its standards for forty years.

There is absolutely nothing to choose between the democracy of Tillman and Vardaman and this "Lily-whitism." They are equally brutal, unrepublican, unmoral. The chief aim of both is to oppress and degrade the members of the colored race, destroy their manhood and citizenship, and appropriate the offices.

In the course of American history there have arisen a number of political parties, but each party has hitherto stood for some definite principle, even though it may have been some wild fad or quack nostrum, to be enforced as the policy of the government. The Federalists, the Democrats, the Whigs, the Free-Soilers, the Republicans, the Green-backers, the Populists, the Prohibitionists — these all stand for certain governmental policies.

But what do the " Lily-white" Republicans stand for ? Their platform might be expressed in a single sentence. Condensed into common Southern speech, it would be :

THE NEGRO IN POLITICS

"*Down wid de niggers; gin us de offices; dat's what we stan' fer.*"

The "Lily-whites" have demanded the control of the Federal patronage as a necessary condition for voting the Republican ticket. They plaintively appealed to McKinley and took the public into their confidence, — promising that, if they only had control of the Federal offices in the South, they " would build up a respectable white Republican party."

The idea that these politicians, who publicly repudiate the cardinal doctrine of republicanism — the equality of rights before the law for all American citizens — and who have assumed the name Republican for purposes of revenue only, will " build up a respectable white Republican party " through the use of the Federal patronage, is absurdly chimerical. This " Lily-white " party is unique in American politics. Its emblem should be the buzzard. It deserves to be known as the " buzzard " party. It scents the carrion of office from afar, and where the carrion is, there it will be found. Lily-whitism is the antithesis of republicanism. If the Republican leaders coquette with this party they will cause the disappearance of republican principles in the South. The few ineffective votes gained in the South — bought and influenced through the bribes of Federal patronage — will be more than offset, by the manifold loss of effective votes in the North.

The republican conscience of the North will not uphold " Lily-whitism." The logical and immediate effect of recognizing or temporizing with this political movement will be to encourage and strengthen " Jim Crowism," and thus further complicate an already embarrassing and hazardous situation.

It will always be true that honorable Southerners, or those without sinister motives, who may wish to vote the Republican ticket will do so independently of the bribes of Federal patronage. Such patronage has never built up a respectable party. The Republican party itself came into power without the possession of a single Federal office. And it has been twice "put out of action" in spite of its possession of the Federal offices.

Wherever the "Lily-whites," by their high-handed and unrepublican methods, have conquered Republican organizations in the South, they have seriously injured the Republican party. Their touch is death to republicanism. They have rejected colored delegates regularly elected by the precincts and have prohibited them from participating in district and state conventions, solely on the ground of color, and have expelled them from the floor of the convention. They have in some cases obtained offices and used the power thereof to oppress and degrade the colored voter, and it has been necessary for the President repeatedly to intervene for the protection of the colored citizen by dismissing them from the public service.

In the removal of a "Lily-white" from office in Alabama, Postmaster-general Payne, speaking for the President, said : "Neither the administration nor the Republican party of the North will stand for the exclusion of any section of our people by reason of their race or color, . . . and the action of the [Lily-white] Republican state convention referred to, in arbitrarily excluding them, is not approved."

These men have no respect for the principles of the Republican party. They despise its history and cherish open contempt for its great leaders and its legions of adherents. This was shown by the conduct and words of Mr. W. S. Robinson, the "Lily-white" member of the national committee from North Carolina, at the dinner given by Senator Hanna to the national Republican committee. This committee was convened at Washington for the purpose of arranging for the national Republican convention to nominate a president of the United States. Senator Hanna, the national chairman, gave a dinner complimentary to the committee, at the Arlington Hotel. One of the members of the committee, Mr. Judson Lyons, is a colored man. And it may be stated that Mr. Lyons holds the high and important position of Register of the Treasury of the United States.

Senator Hanna, with his guests — some fifty-odd members of the national Republican committee — had seated themselves around the banquet board. At this moment Mr. W. S. Robinson, the "Lily-white" member from North Carolina, arrived. And on entering the room and seeing Mr. Lyons, the colored member from Georgia, at one of the tables, he "strode out in high dudgeon," and with great show of indignation exclaimed, "I came here a gentleman, and I shall certainly go back one." He also said that no white man who was a gentleman could eat in the same dining-room where there was a negro seated at one of the tables.

This, surely, is a singular way for a gentleman to show his high breeding. Mr. Robinson could have absented himself from Senator Hanna's banquet or declined the invitation, and that probably would have been the end of the matter. But the manner in which he left the banquet-room, and the excuse he gave to the press reporter implied that Senator Hanna and his assembled guests were not gentlemen since they could sit at meat with Register Lyons. His language was, therefore, an insult to his host, an insult to every guest at that banquet board, an insult to the national Republican party in whose name they had assembled. Who will say that such a man is a fit representative of the Republican party in a state where there are 624,469 colored citizens?

The more serious aspect of the case is that Mr. Robinson has been indorsed by the "Lily-whites" of the South. These men by treachery and force have seized some of the local Republican organizations and shorn them of the Republican principles and are making an audacious attempt to stampede the national organization, or drag it from its moorings. This incident is not a matter to be lightly regarded. It shows the temper, spirit, and purpose of "Lily-whitism" — to rule or ruin. The national organization had to combat this same spirit in the South in the great crises of the Reconstruction period.

Men of this character are not Republicans, but interlopers, "wolves in sheep's clothing," who would rend and destroy the organization and trample its principles under their feet. They are a reproach to the party, an ulcer on the organization.

Under such circumstances it is clearly the duty of the national Republican organization, or the national committee, to carry out such plans as may seem wise in reörganizing the party along republican lines in the states where the organization has been conquered by unrepublican methods, and where the men who have loyally stood by the organization for forty years, and suffered untold hardships and risked their lives for its principles, have been unjustly thrown out by the interlopers, in order that the latter might place a lien on the Federal offices.

Mr. Crumpacker in a recent speech in Congress utters a warning to which it would be well for the nation to give ear: "I have said enough, Mr. Speaker, to warn the House and the country that the situation is rapidly crystallizing into a policy of complete subjugation of the colored race in all the fields of activity, . . . and slavery is its inevitable result. . . . I have been admonished that if the race question were let alone and the Constitution were ignored the 'solid South' would go to pieces politically and a white Republican party would be built upon the ruins. A white Republican party in the South is only possible by universal assent to the practical enslavement of the negro. If that imaginary party should at any time show any friendship for the colored man or any sympathy with his struggles to better his condition, it would at once fall under the ban of the hereditary prejudices, and social and business proscription would be its fate.

"If the country will consent that the 8,000,000 colored citizens shall be deprived of their rights, that lynching may go on without let or hindrance as a necessary part of the process of subjugation, there may be a white Republican party in the South, but not otherwise.

" But can we afford the price? A white Republican party? Shades of Lincoln and Seward, of Sumner and Chase! A white Republican party only a little over a generation after the death of the emancipator! It is an impossibility. The Republican party is the party of human liberty and equal rights. It is based upon manhood, and not upon race or color. The old Whig party forfeited its conscience and lost its character temporizing with wrong, injustice, and human oppression over half a century ago. The Republican party will never make that mistake. Let the South continue to be ' solid ' if it will, let the Republican party go down in defeat if it must, but it will never surrender the great principles of human liberty of which it was the born champion."

The national organization, in dealing with its loyal supporters in the South, cannot respect the wholesale disfranchisement which contravenes the Constitution of the United States. It must regard the fundamental condition of the Reconstruction. It must stand for equal laws for all. Therefore it must take the only just ground, that any citizen who has voted the Republican ticket at any previous congressional or presidential election, and wishes to continue as a member of the Republican party of his state, shall have equal rights to participate in the councils and elections of the party without regard to unlawful disfranchisements. If the " Lily-whites " shall wish in this event to return to their democratic or populistic allegiance, then let them do that.

The Charleston *News and Courier*, a leading Southern journal, very pointedly says : " There is no question about it that the men who have gone into the Republican party in the South in nine cases out of ten have gone in for the money they could make out of it, for the prominence it would give them, for the influence they would be able to exert toward the accomplishment of their mean, selfish purposes. There ought to be no room in the Democratic party for the returning ' Lily-whites.' "

And these discredited creatures boast about organizing a respectable white Republican party ! Republicanism is based on the eternal certitudes of liberty, justice, equal rights, and honest and orderly government. And in the onward sweep of civilization these principles are sure to triumph. It will assuredly prove true that no party, Democratic, Republican or other, can gain and hold the favor of the great masses of the American people which does not raise aloft and defend these principles.

In the South the Republican party can afford to bide its time. It can afford to be overborne by fraud and violence. It can stand and suffer persecution for its cause's sake. But it cannot afford to be un-American, un-republican, oppressive. As " Lily-whitism " and " Jim Crowism," twin evils of barbarism, shall wane in power, as they must, decreasing race passions and strife, and as the South shall take the second sober thought, many white people in the South will be attracted to the Republican party, not for the sake of the offices, but because they accept the righteousness of its cardinal principles and favor the great national policies of government which it would enforce.

CHAPTER VII
THE NEGRO AND THE LAW

THE colored race, like the white race, like every race, has its criminals. It has many of them. Some people think and say that it has more than its share in proportion to the other part of the population. This may be true, or it may not be true. To discuss a matter of this kind intelligently and fairly, attention must be given to the conditions and environments of the class from which the criminals come.

It is not to be disputed that while the web of the law catches here and there a member from the higher or more prosperous element of the social body, it most frequently drags in criminals from the less fortunate, poorer, laboring classes. The record of the police and other courts day by day would show scores of the latter to one of the former.

Among the Southern whites, the preponderating element consists of the higher or more prosperous class. A man who can command good wages and steady employment, even though he is obliged to work for a living, should be properly classed among the higher or more prosperous element of the community. The large majority of the whites belong to this class.

On the other hand, the man who must take the most menial places and receives small pay, at times hardly more than enough to keep soul and body together, or must depend on odd jobs and finds them unremunerative and scarce as a rule, belongs to the less fortunate, poorer or common laboring class. The great majority of the colored people belong to this class.

It is true, however, that many thousands of colored people are engaged in business pursuits, and to such an extent that there is not a field of business in which they are not engaged ;

and many have achieved remarkable success, some having even gained a competency. Scores of thousands are the owners of their own homes and farms and may be justly rated as prosperous.

Many occupy commanding places in the professions, law, medicine, theology, dentistry, and pharmacy. Some thirty thousands of them are teachers in the public schools and institutions of higher learning. Thousands are also in the employment of the National Government, from the Register of the Treasury of the United States and other important Federal offices down through the various grades of clerkships to the scrub-women. Some thousands are in the army and navy.

Indeed there is not a walk or calling in American life in which the negro has not forged ahead and won success. But nevertheless, it would be unreasonable to suppose that in the brief forty years of struggle in the rise from abject, demoralizing slavery,— in the face of tremendous odds and difficulties,— the proportion of negroes commanding first-rate positions and receiving remunerative wages would be as great as among the whites with their long line of free ancestry.

The general progress of the American negro has not only been commensurate with his opportunities, but to many it has been one of the wonders of the age. Nevertheless it must be admitted that the great body of the colored people belong to the less fortunate, the poorer or ordinary laboring class. Their very condition — the entailment of slavery — bears heavily upon them ; their lack of means and the denial of remunerative employment and a fair chance for advancement handicaps them enormously in the race of life; and their environments are a serious detriment to them, living as they do under degradingly oppressive laws and among a people hostile to the recognition of their manhood and citizenship.

THE NEGRO AND THE LAW

Inasmuch as the great majority of the whites are included in the more fortunate element of the community, and the larger body of the colored people — through no fault of their own, but because of the greed, avarice, and oppressions of the whites — constitute the less fortunate class, it is obviously unfair and unreasonable to judge the Southern negroes without regard to their opportunities, relations, and surroundings. The many and disheartening disadvantages under which they labor materially affect the question of crime among them.

If, then, the total number of colored criminals — waiving for the time being the blighting and deadly effects of the operation of race prejudice — should be compared with the total number of criminals who come, not from the whole white race, but from that portion of it nearest to the colored people in opportunities and circumstances, and which constitutes the ordinary laboring class of the whites, it may or it may not be shown that the colored people have more than their proportional share of criminals. But, be this as it may, there are forces, manifold forces, irresistible and deadly forces, such as no white man ever feels, no matter how ignorant, depraved, or even dirty he may be, that are brought to bear day by day upon every member of the colored race, and which are productive of criminality. Satan could hardly devise a scheme better arranged for manufacturing criminals in the largest numbers and with the greatest expedition and thoroughness, than the policy and methods adopted towards the negro by the reactionists who at present are supported by the dominant elements of the white people of the South.

The colored people are equal citizens ; they are copartners in the government ; they are a material factor in its support and defence ; they are peaceful and law-abiding. When, therefore, a wide-spread reign of terror, violence, and blood-shedding is inaugurated to accomplish their abasement and degradation ; when they are stripped of the protection of the law, their manhood is trampled in the dust, and they are made the victims of open, unremitting, and flagrant persecutions by a religious people, — conditions exist which inevitably tend to the multiplication of criminals and the increase of crime. The whites thus place themselves above the law, and force the colored people below it.

Two immediate results follow. First, the whites, regarding themselves as above the law, will hold it in contempt and will be a law unto themselves — recognizing and being controlled by no law, save their own unrestrained passions, in dealing with the colored man. They will feel free to treat him according to their whims, whether good or evil. In the second place, it depresses the colored man; it blunts his moral perceptions; it confuses his moral conceptions; it deadens his sense of security under the law; it chills in his heart respect for the law and his faith in the honesty of the whites; his faith in the justice of the courts is undermined; he is enveloped in an atmosphere of doubt, distrust, despair, or desperation.

Many of the weaker-minded among the negroes are driven into crime; some of the stronger-minded are perverted. Is it not plain that when the idle, thriftless, or weaker-minded negro, or the one criminally bent, sees the white people treat with scorn, contempt, and even violence the legitimate aspirations and ambitions of the negro of probity, substance, and intelligence, and refuse him the considerations due an honest man and good citizen, simply because of the color of his skin, he should naturally conclude that these things are of little or no value, that being a " good negro " is of no moment, and that the bad one is just as well off as a good one?

The white people of the South are the only people in the history of the world — aside from the Boer republics of South Africa, which a just and avenging God has removed from the face of the earth after exacting a terrible and bloody atonement — who with deliberation and premeditation have sought to prevent a people as free as themselves under the law of the land from making the most of their opportunities to advance in a Christian civilization.

The Holy Scriptures say that out of the mouth of two or three witnesses shall the truth be established. But any number of Southerners, men in the highest stations of life, may be put in the witness chair to testify against the South in the wilful, deliberate, and violent persecution of the colored people.

Mr. George W. Cable, formerly of Louisiana, and probably the foremost literary man that the South has produced since the War of the Rebellion, says : "There is scarcely one public relation of life in the South where the negro is not arbitrarily and unlawfully compelled to hold toward the white man the attitude of an alien, a menial, and a probable reprobate by reason of his color " ; and that the white man "spurns his ambition, tramples upon his languishing self-respect and indignantly refuses to let him either buy with money or earn by excellence of inner life or outward behavior the most momentary immunity from these public indignities, even for his wife and daughters. Steamboat landing, railway platform, theatre, concert hall, art display, public library, public school, court-house, church, everything — flourish the hot branding iron of ignominious distinction."

Mr. J. Temple Graves of Georgia says : "The negro, whom a million died to free, is in present bond and future promise still a slave, whipped by circumstances, trodden under foot of iron and ineradicable prejudice ; shut out forever from the heritage of liberty, and holding in his black hand the hollow parchment of his franchise as a free man looks through a slave's eyes at the impossible barriers which imprison him forever. Straighten the hair and whiten the skin of the negro, and the issue is closed."

Senator McEnery of Louisiana says : "The negro is inferior in every essential of manhood ; he ought not to aspire

219

to office ; he will be compelled to occupy an inferior and subject place."

Mr. A. F. Thomas, of Lynchburg, Virginia, in discussing the race question in a booklet written especially to influence the recent Constitutional Convention of Virginia, says : " The negro has progressed wonderfully ; his relative position is much nearer the white man's standard of civilization now than thirty years ago ; yet the fact is apparent that the races are farther apart than they were the day the negro was emancipated. The nearer the negro approaches to the white man's standard of civilization, the less love there is between them. Looking backward to the time when our black mammies were, in our esteem, second only to our mothers, and when we played in perfect harmony with the negro children, and contrasting it with the clearly defined relations that exist between the races to-day, we readily see the difference. . . .

" A black man who has never committed a crime, who has always lived up to his highest ideals, who has cultivated his mind, whose moral character is roundly developed, who has been frugal and industrious, and has accumulated wealth, goes to a soda fountain to slake his thirst ; he offers in exchange his money, but is refused for no other reason than that he is black and belongs to a different race. A man, in the land of his nativity, with the money to pay for the goods, cannot, on account of race, buy the articles that are publicly offered for sale. This condition exists to-day, thirty years after the United States Constitution had proclaimed the civil and political equality of all of its citizens. . . .

" If we take the view that the negro will remain here indefinitely, then the only solution consistent with existence is entire subordination. If this be true, it is the greatest folly to educate him further than education may make him more efficient in the sphere which he must occupy. Viewed from this standpoint, he should be educated, not with a purpose of lifting him to a higher plane, but to increase his power to do those things which would make him most useful to his masters. It should be an education of the hand rather than the head. This condition, however much freedom the race might nominally have, would be practically a mild form of slavery."

Thus Mr. Thomas admits that the Southern leaders are aiming at the establishment of "a mild form of slavery." But the old system of slavery began as a comparatively mild condition and gradually descended into the grossest form, and almost wrecked the republic. A new "mild form of slavery" would degenerate into even greater cruelties and inhumanities, and its inauguration would mark the beginning of the end of republican government. It would be the death-knell of free institutions.

At a recent meeting of the State Medical Association of Georgia, one of its members, Dr. E. C. Ferguson, read a paper intended to demonstrate that the negro is not a human being. He attacked the negro's skin, mouth, lips, chin, hair, nose, nostril, ears, and navel; and compared him with the horse, cow, and dog, and other animals. He declared that the "negro is monkeylike; has no sympathy for his fellow-man; has no regard for the truth, and when the truth would answer his purpose the best, he will lie. He is without gratitude or appreciation of anything done for him ; is a natural born thief,— will steal anything, no matter how worthless.

"He has no morals. Turpitude is his ideal of all that pertains to life. His progeny are not provided for at home and are allowed to roam at large without restraint, and seek subsistence as best they can, growing up like any animal."

Some of the things that Dr. Ferguson said in his address are really not fit to print. And yet a body of scientific men — Southern gentlemen — listened with approval and heartily applauded this foul assault on a people who nursed with the tenderest affection and all of a mother's love, their fathers and grandfathers, mothers and grandmothers, and themselves ; and whose devotion, fidelity, and kindheartedness were never challenged in two hundred and fifty years of service. If Dr. Ferguson had a sense of humor, he would realize that his sweeping and unqualified statement makes him not only a dangerous competitor with the ablest negro in the art of fabrication, but marks him as a man who may eclipse the cleverest negro who " will lie even when the truth would answer his purpose the best."

The Reverend Thomas Dixon, Jr., of North Carolina, speaking at a church in Baltimore, said : " My deliberate opinion of the negro is that he is not worth hell-room. If I were the devil I would not let him in hell."

This same divine, in a book that he published, says : " The more you educate, the more impossible you make his position in a democracy. Education ! Can you change the color of his skin, the kink of his hair, the bulge of his lips, the spread of his nose, or the beat of his heart, with a spelling-book ? The negro is a human donkey. You can train him, but you can't make him a horse. Mate him with horse, you lose the horse and get a larger donkey called a mule, incapable of preserving his species." The moral obliquity, the want of charity, the absence of dignity indicated by these words, mark off their author as seriously beneath the standards of thousands of educated colored men, whose life, words, and conduct shame these critics into insignificance.

The Reverend Henry Frank advocates the re-establishment of slavery, and further says of the negro : " His native sluggishness, and the evidence of his general extinction since his emancipation, his imperceptible improvement since liberation, his startling lapse into barbarism, all must incline thinking people to conclude that the freeing of the negro was a disastrous failure."

Senator Tillman of South Carolina, the Mad Mullah of American politics, has used on the floor of the United States

Senate and on the lecture platform these expressions: "Yes, we have stuffed ballot-boxes, and will stuff them again; we have cheated niggers in elections, and will cheat them again; we have disfranchised niggers, and will disfranchise all we want to; we have killed and lynched niggers and will kill and lynch others; we have burned niggers at the stake and will burn others; a nigger has no right to live anyhow, unless a white man wants him to live. If you don't like it you can lump it."

Cruel and scurrilous attacks and defamations of this character against the colored people could be quoted in sufficient quantities to fill a volume. But those just mentioned, taken in connection with others recorded in these pages, may serve to indicate the fierce and consuming flames of persecution in the midst of which the colored man lives and moves and has his being.

A people so vilely abused and outrageously persecuted are made an easy mark for malevolence and race hatred. Unrestrained abuse of the colored man leads surely to unrestrained oppression and violence. And these are not conditions which inspire a high morality or favor the upbuilding of character; they rather tend to strangle the self-respect and debase the souls of the hapless victims and shape many of them into criminals. The whites cannot sow to the wind without reaping the whirlwind.

As might be expected, illustrations in the concrete of the operation of this bitter persecution abound on every hand. Laws are enacted and enforced in the spirit of persecution, and the colored people are the victims of such laws; often they are condemned without even the form or semblance of law.

Regarding the latter, planters have combined or conspired — in defiance of the law — to arrest under false charges the number of colored men needed for service, hold mock trials, one of the conspirators acting as judge, condemn and sentence the helpless creatures to penal servitude; and then divide the laborers among themselves, put them in chains, and work them for long periods of time on their plantations. And this crime is committed against liberty and humanity rather than pay the small wages which agricultural laborers command in the South!

And as to the former, it would be difficult to find more striking examples of " man's inhumanity to man " than some of the crimes committed in the name and under the forms of law on the colored people. In Alabama, Mississippi, Georgia, South Carolina, Louisiana, and some of the other states, labor and contract laws are deliberately framed with the view of facilitating the seizure of colored men and selling them into practical slavery.

In a speech recently made in Congress touching this matter, Mr. Edgar D. Crumpacker of Indiana said: " Under existing conditions the standard of living among the colored people of the South is low, and the rate of wages is on the same basis. The colored laborer is completely at the mercy of the employer. In the state of South Carolina to-day there is a qualified condition of industrial serfdom. Farm laborers are compelled by the penal laws of the state to carry out their contracts of employment, however unjust and unfair they may be. They must perform all 'the labor reasonably required' of them by the contract or go to jail. If any one knowingly shall employ a laborer in any kind of service who is under contract to labor for another, he, too, is liable to fine and imprisonment, even though the workman or his family may be on the verge of starvation."

Under these laws the great mass of the colored laborers are placed in the merciless grasp of the planters, who can readily force them to accept any form of contract whatsoever. Some of the planters, under a carefully devised system of paying the laborers off in plantation " scrip " or " checks," which are heavily discounted mediums, or by compelling the laborers

224

to buy their supplies at the " plantation store," where exor-
bitant rates are charged, or by " padding " the accounts of the
laborers, manage to bring them out in debt at the close of
each year.

And this system is carried on year after year, and the
colored man never gets ahead and so cannot leave his plantation prison-pen. The planter holds the laborer in debt as
long as it suits his convenience to do so. The laborer has
no relief in the law of the state. Such hardships drive many
colored people from the plantations to the cities.

In the name of the law, colored men may also be arrested
for debt and sold at public auction, into servitude. And
those laborers are compelled to work without pay while their
families are exposed to want and made to suffer ; the wages
which they ought to receive being divided between the
planters and the magistrates.

The following press despatch throws some light on this
matter : " The Federal grand jury at Montgomery is expected to return indictments against ten prominent ' slaveholders ' to-morrow. They will be charged with the almost
forgotten crime of peonage. Robert M. Franklin is already
under indictment on the charge of keeping a negro in servitude for a year.

" The system was called to the attention of the Department
of Justice a month ago, and Chief Wilkie sent Captain
Dickey to Montgomery to investigate. His reports indicate
collusion between magistrates and plantation owners who
wanted cheap help.

" The plan is for a negro to be brought before the magistrate on charges on which he is heavily fined. Some white
man offers to pay his fine and save him from jail if he will
agree to work for him until his wages reach the amount of
the fine. The negroes, it is alleged, are herded together and
treated like convicts. When they protest, so it is charged,
they are whipped and beaten until they are cowed, and when

they run away they are chased with dogs, and in case of recapture, compelled to work in chains. They are constantly under the eyes of armed guards, and are driven to the limit of human endurance. They are fed only enough to keep them alive."

As a further illustration of the operations of the system the following press despatch will prove of interest: "The evidence in the case of Samuel W. Tyson in the Federal court which ended yesterday makes it plain that slavery still exists in the United States. Tyson was ordered to pay a thousand dollars fine, but he handed over only one hundred and fifty dollars and the remainder was suspended by the sympathetic judge.

"Tyson runs a lumber mill in Coffee County. There were three cases against him. He was charged with holding Will Brown, Will Thornton, and Nick Anderson, all negroes, in peonage. Anderson was fined five dollars for assault and battery. E. L. Warren, a white man, confessed judgment for Anderson. He sold Anderson to a white man named Crumpler for sixty dollars, who in turn swapped him to Tyson for a negro, Jerry Stoval, and a money consideration.

"The case of Brown was that Brown borrowed a dollar from H. B. Crumpler and failed to pay it back. He was arrested, put in jail, handcuffed, and sold to Tyson for ninety-six dollars and fifty cents. Tyson later sold Brown to George Stephens for thirty-six dollars and fifty cents. Thornton owed C. D. Clemens some money that he could not pay. Clemens got him and sold him to Tyson, who worked him under guard for three months."

And again other press despatches, which are fully sustained by the best authority, reveal with circumstantial detail the criminal practices of planters, who, with the connivance of the magistrates, imprison both colored men and women on their plantations and rob them of the fruits of their labor. "The Department of Justice is preparing to take up again the subject of peonage in the South. Additional reports have been received indicating that negroes are held in servitude. Assistant Attorney General Purdy has issued instructions to the United States attorney for the western district of Louisiana to investigate a number of alleged cases of peonage on plantations near Monroe, Ouachita parish, and other points in that vicinity. Information regarding these cases came to the department from Judge McDaniel, assistant attorney for the southern district of Texas, to whom complaint had been made by relatives of a number of negroes alleged to have been illegally held. Some of the stories told are sensational in the extreme.

"In addition to the charges made by negroes, the Texas officials have forwarded the statement of a white man living in Houston, who has made several trips through northern Louisiana recently, and who says that many colored people of both sexes are being illegally restrained of their liberty in that region.

"A feature of the affair which makes it of unusual interest is the intimation that some of the peace officers are in collusion with those who are alleged to be holding the negroes. One man, who claimed that he had escaped from a plantation south of Shreveport, asked Judge McDaniel's assistance in securing the release of his brother, who was still detained there. This person asserted that whenever negroes who tried to escape were caught, they were soundly beaten and taken back.

"If they succeeded in getting as far as Shreveport, he said, they were taken in charge by the officers and immediately returned. The owner of the plantation lived at Shreveport, he claimed, and the officers worked in collusion with him.

"Not long ago A. D. Crenshaw, a negro, who lives at Ledbetter, Texas, showed Judge McDaniel and Marshal Hanson a letter from his brother, who, it was alleged, was held in bondage near Monroe. This communication told of awful conditions among the negroes there.

"Crenshaw gave Marshal Hanson a sum of money, which Hanson forwarded to the marshal of the western district of Louisiana, with instructions that it be given to Crenshaw's brother. Later the money order was returned by a man who said he was the deputy marshal and was acting in the place of the marshal, who had died, but that he could do nothing in the premises, since the order was not payable to him. The necessary change was made and the order sent on again. Considerable time has elapsed and nothing has been heard of it.   •

"A negro named Johnson, whose character has been vouched for by white people who knew him in Texas, has also written to Houston, claiming that he and his wife are being held in bondage and are refraining from attempting to escape because they fear they will be recaptured and beaten or killed.

"All such letters have been sent out surreptitiously, the writers being afraid to forward them through the regular channels.

"Judge McDaniel expresses the opinion that hundreds of negroes are being held in the region indicated."

The *Independent* of New York City, a leading family journal, commissioned one of its representatives to examine into this new form of slavery in the South, and it spreads before its readers in a recent issue a typical case of a colored man held in slavery for thirteen years. The narrative is harrowing indeed, and the saddest reflection is that it is only one of many thousands that may be chronicled in the same state in which this occurred.

An additional feature is that a state senator, a maker of the laws, was the owner of the slave camp, and thus the oppressor of those who were equal citizens, subjecting them, men and women, to the most humiliating treatment, and filching from them all the fruits of their hard and exacting toil. The experiences and observation of this colored man, who was held in bondage and treated as a slave for that length of time, as told by himself, are in part as follows : —

"The senator had bought an additional thousand acres of land, and to his already large cotton plantation he added two great big saw-mills and went into the lumber business. Within two years the senator had in all nearly two hundred negroes working on his plantation. . . .

"Two or three years before, or about a year and a half after the senator had started his camp, he had established a large store, which was called the commissary. All of us free laborers were compelled to buy our supplies — food, clothing, etc. — from that store. We never used any money in our dealings with the commissary, only tickets or orders, and we had a general settlement once each year, in October. In this store we were charged all sorts of high prices for goods, because every year we would come out in debt to our employer. If not that, we seldom had more than five or ten dollars coming to us — and that for a whole year's work. Well, at the close of the tenth year, when we kicked and meant to leave the senator, he said to some of us with a smile (and I never will forget that smile — I can see it now): 'Boys, I'm sorry you 're going to leave me. I hope you will do well in your new places — so well that you will be able to pay me the little balances which most of you owe me.'

" Word was sent out for all of us to meet him at the commissary at two o'clock. There he told us that, after we had signed what he called a written acknowledgment of our debts we might go and look for new places. The store-keeper took us one by one and read to us statements of our accounts. According to the books there was no man of us who owed the senator less than $100 ; some of us were put down for as much as $200. I owed $165, according to the bookkeeper. No one of us would have dared to dispute a white man's word — oh, no — we were after getting away ; and we had been told that we might go, if we signed the acknowledgments. We would have signed anything, just to get away. So we stepped up, we did, and made our marks. That same night we were rounded up by a constable and ten or twelve white men, who aided him, and were locked up, every one of us, in one of the senator's stockades. The next morning it was explained to us by the two guards appointed to watch us that, in the papers we had signed the day before, we had not only made acknowledgment of our indebtedness, but that we had also agreed to work for the senator until the debts were paid by hard labor. And from that day forward we were treated just like convicts. Really we had made ourselves lifetime slaves, or peons, as the laws called us. But, call it slavery, peonage, or what not, the truth is we lived in a hell on earth what time we spent in the senator's peon camp.

" My wife fared better than I did, as did the wives of some of the other negroes, because the white men about the camp used these unfortunate creatures as their mistresses. When I was first put in the stockade my wife was still kept for a while in the ' Big House,' but my little boy, who was only nine years old, was given away to a negro family across the river in South Carolina, and I never saw or heard of him after that. When I left the camp my wife had had two children for some one of the white bosses, and she was living in fairly good shape in a little house off to herself. But the poor negro women who were not in the class with my wife fared almost as bad as the helpless negro men. Most of the time the women who were peons or convicts were compelled to wear men's clothes. Sometimes, when I have seen them dressed like men, and plowing or hoeing or hauling logs, or working at the blacksmith's trade, just the same as men, my heart would bleed and my blood would boil, but I was powerless to raise a hand. It would have meant death on the spot to have said a word. Of the first six women brought to the camp, two of them gave birth to children after they had been there not more than twelve months — and the babies had white men for their fathers!

"The stockades in which we slept were, I believe, the filthiest places in the world. They were cesspools of nastiness. During the thirteen years that I was there I am willing to swear that a mattress was never moved after it had been brought there, except to turn it over once or twice a month. No sheets were used, only dark-colored blankets. Most of the men slept every night in the clothing that they had worked in all day. Some of the worst characters were made to sleep in chains. The doors were locked and barred each night, and tallow candles were the only lights allowed. Really the stockades were but little more than cow-lots, horse-stables or hog-pens. Strange to say, not a great number of these people died while I was there, though a great many came away maimed and bruised, and, in some cases, disabled for life.

"It was a hard school, that peon camp was, but I learned more there in a few short months by contact with those poor fellows from the outside world than ever I had known before. Most of what I learned was evil, and I now know that I should have been better off without the knowledge, but much of what I learned was helpful to me. Barring two or three severe and brutal whippings which I received, I got along very well, all things considered; but the system is damnable. A favorite way of whipping a man was to strap him down to a log, flat on his back, and spank him forty or sixty times on his bare feet and limbs with a shingle or a huge piece of plank. When the man would get up with sore and blistered feet and an aching body, if he could not then keep up with the other men at work he would be strapped to the log again, this time face downward, and would be lashed with a buggy trace on his bare back. . . .

"One of the usual ways to secure laborers for a large peonage camp is for the proprietor to send out an agent to the little courts in the towns and villages : and where a man charged with some petty offence has no friends or money, the agent will urge him to plead guilty, with the understanding that the agent will pay his fine, and in that way save him from the disgrace of being sent to jail or the chain-gang! For this high favor the man must sign beforehand a paper signifying his willingness to go to the farm and work out the amount of the fine imposed. When he reaches the farm he has to be fed and clothed, to be sure, and these things are charged up to his account. By the time he has worked out his first debt another is hanging over his head, and so on and so on, by a sort of endless chain, for an indefinite period ; as in every case the indebtedness is arbitrarily arranged by the employer. In many cases it is very evident that the court officials are in collusion with the proprietors or agents, and that they divide the 'graft' among themselves. As an example of this dickering among the whites, every year many convicts were brought to the senator's camp from a certain county in South Georgia, way down in the turpentine district. The majority of these men were charged with adultery. . . .

" I have been here in the district since they released me, and I reckon I 'll die either in a coal mine or an iron furnace : it don't make much difference which. Either is better than a Georgia peon camp. And a Georgia peon camp is hell itself ! "

This unfortunate man also relates the cruel and revolting manner in which colored women were thrown across a barrel and brutally flogged.

The New York *World* prints a picture of a "Stockade Pen" in South Carolina, showing the hapless negroes at work in convict garbs, surrounded by bloodhounds and guards. And after stating that the negroes whom Abraham Lincoln emancipated and whose emancipation a million men died to seal are still held and treated as slaves, proceeds to give these details : " Convict slaves are traded freely among the land owners. They are forced to labor, for which they receive no pay; they are flogged, made to work when ill, made the victims of 'man-hunts,' and otherwise ill-used. Women are treated with similar cruelty.

"When the stock of convicts gives out, innocent negroes, it is now proved, are railroaded into the penitentiary, and thence obtained by the men who become their masters. The system has continued for years in open defiance of law and humanity. These are facts now officially verified.

"The offenders are so well protected by money and influence that it is doubtful if they can be punished, or even that the practice can be stopped. If these proceedings are not at first clear, here are the details: William A. Neal, of Anderson, who was superintendent of the state penitentiary, and who was tried in court for being short in his accounts, was the first man to introduce the convict lease system in Anderson County. A stockade was built and convicts from the penitentiary, which was overcrowded with criminals, were sent under guard to the place; it being arranged that the state was to receive a revenue.

"The plan worked splendidly for the planters. The expense was small, and the lash, freely administered, made the negroes give the best of their efforts for the managers.

"At this time plans were quietly put on foot to seize ignorant negroes, have mock trials, and commit them to the stockades where their labor could be had for the scant food offered and the expense of the convict garb and shackles.

"From the state stockade relatives of the managers built private prisons on the big farms and a ransom was paid for every negro seized and sent in. It was the same system of 'shanghaiing' transferred from the sea to the farm.

"Recent developments have given an inside view into the operation of the prisons, and the discovery of the private stockades has shown a more terrible condition than was at first imagined. . . .

" Not one of the freed slaves has dared to testify against the man who outrageously ill-used him. There are too many sharp eyes about, too many pistols, too many bloodhounds, and the unfortunate creatures were long since cowed out of every likeness to their manhood. More potent than any law on earth is the unreasoning fear which the brutal slave owners have succeeded in infusing into the very life-blood of the creatures they have deprived of liberty. . . .

" The death of Will Hull, a poor negro, who had been seized on a trumped-up charge and illegally committed to the stockade, led to the investigation. Hull protested against his incarceration, asked for a fair trial, and got a blow from a club. Then the negro planned to escape, and at night, with the chains still binding his legs, he stole forth.

" But the guards had orders to watch him. As Hull was going away, a bullet from a 54-calibre rifle bored its way into his brain and he fell dead. . . .

" The most appalling of the abuses is that women were seized and made to work. They were whipped with cat-o-nine-tails because they failed to scrub and work when common humanity showed that they should have been in hospitals; and there was no protest. . . .

" When sport got dull on the stockade plantations, the bloodhounds were called forth, and the speediest negroes were unshackled.

" Sunday was the big day for sporting blood to boil, and this thirst could only be satisfied with a vicious ' man-hunt.' The negroes were unshackled and sent running through the swamps and over the hills. There was no danger of making an effectual escape. Two hours after the negroes left the pen, the dogs were unleashed. Men on horseback were ready for the start, and with yelping and crying the trail was followed and the ' man-hunt ' was on. Once a negro failed to reach safety in a tree, and he was mangled fearfully.

"The so-called contracts by which these negroes were jailed gave the owners the right to sell or trade them as they saw fit. They were used and handled as convicts, when in fact they were free citizens. But laws are not a figure in these dens of iniquity.

"The men had to wear stripes; and they had to bear shackles; When night came and work had to stop they were sent to the pens, locked in, and guarded. Long before daylight they were called out, and with the first dawn they were toiling in the fields. When sickness made them unfit for work, they were whipped and lashed for trifling. Even the hot iron is said to have been used, and the grand jury is searching for the slaves who were branded like wild cattle."

The *World* also says that the grand jury by its "verdict accuses scores of wealthy South Carolinians of practices of atrocious villany."

The Chicago *Tribune* of recent date prints this press despatch: "A special to the *Tribune* from Savannah says that state senator Foye of Egypt, Georgia, has been brought here under arrest by Federal officers on a charge of holding negroes in bondage. Foye is one of the wealthiest men in south Georgia and is a Democratic leader. He conducts several large turpentine farms near Egypt, and Federal officers assert that he is holding many negroes as slaves. The negroes are confined at night in stockades and are worked in chains during the day."

The gravity of the situation is emphasized in a recent event. The Honorable William H. Moody, Attorney-General of the United States, in filing a brief with the Supreme Court of the United States, in a peonage case recently brought before that high tribunal from Georgia, uses these startling words: "Immediately upon the certification of this case to the supreme court, several of the district judges in the fifth circuit, in which numerous prosecutions for violations of this statute were pending, refused to try any of the cases, and postponed the same to await the decision of the court in this case. It is therefore quite evident that the executive arm of the law, so far at least as the enforcement of this statute is concerned, is practically paralyzed, even in the most typical and flagrant cases. We think we may truthfully say that upon the decision of this case hangs the liberty of thousands of persons, mostly colored, it is true, who are now being held in a condition of involuntary servitude, in many cases worse than slavery itself, by the unlawful acts of individuals, not only in violation of the Thirteenth Amendment to the Constitution, but in violation of the law which we have here under consideration."

Thus it is shown that forty years after the destruction of slavery, a new system of servitude is in operation, concerning which the Attorney-General of the United States informs the Supreme Court of the United States that the executive arm of the Government is paralyzed in dealing with it. If the Southern leaders are given a free hand for fifty or a hundred years more, the fate of the colored man will be worse than in the blackest day of slavery.

The legislature of Georgia, a few years ago, appointed a committee to investigate the operations of the penal system of the state. The committee reported a shocking state of affairs, both in chain-gangs and in many convict stockades scattered over the state. It showed that colored men and women were poorly fed; worked to the limit of human endurance and beyond it; that the sick forced to work, in some cases, had died while at the task; that men were held for years after their sentences had expired, because they were profitable workmen; that convicts were brutally flogged — in some cases whipped to death; that they were shot to death at times without justification; and that they were subject to many other inhumanities. But it appears that the condition of these unfortunate people has not been bettered.

An official investigation of the penal system of Florida disclosed even greater abuses. In this state it was shown that convicts were murdered because they dared to protest against being held after their sentences had expired ; and any complaint meant floggings and probable death.

The chain-gangs in Atlanta, Georgia, reek with horrible inhumanities. In that city colored girls of tender age, who were guilty of no other offence than that of " sassing back " at the "Missus," have been sent to the chain-gang stockade. The lesson of abject submission must be enforced. In this stockade colored men and women are brutally beaten on the slightest pretext.

Another horrible feature of the terrible system is that colored women and girls are used for the purpose of training the bloodhounds. These unfortunates, in some cases so poorly and lightly clad as to sicken the moral sense of the ordinary citizen, are summoned to " quarters," and at the crack of the driver's whip they flee to the woods, and must climb trees before the yelping bloodhounds can overtake them, or else their bodies will be fearfully mangled. This is oft repeated.

A writer in the Springfield (Massachusetts) *Republican* says : " As one who has been in close contact with the social systems of the Southern states and knows very well the workings of this penal system, particularly of Georgia, let me say to you that the system of criminal justice, or rather injustice, applied to the negro is but a system of the worst slavery in itself. It is justified in the minds of men by the seldom spoken, yet because silent, nevertheless potent, belief and conviction that the ' nigger ought to be a slave anyway.'

" Slavery fostered and has bequeathed to the population of the South a cruelty and a crudity of criminal punishment foreign to the humane spirit of our age ; and so outrageous is the system that it would long ago have been abolished if it were not for the fact that it is the negro who suffers most by it. The penitentiaries, or convict settlements, for there are no penitentiaries, are simply unspeakable. And the treatment of the convicts in the camps by lessees who pay the state eleven dollars a year for an able-bodied man, is such that an average of three years and five months of life in one of these camps is the record, while no man has ever been known to survive more than seventeen years.

" A few of the many cases that came under my personal observation might be of general interest. I saw a boy twelve years old sent to one of these camps for larceny, for a term of three years. There are no places for juvenile offenders, and it is not strange if their own chickens come home to roost in the shape of rape and theft and general cussedness by young criminals who have been schooled in these prisons.

" I saw a man who had served a term under a convict lease in a brick company's camp and the condition of that man's hands from handling hot bricks, and the condition of his back from stripes received were suggestive of the very limit, not only of human cruelty but the limit of human endurance as well.

" I saw a man returned after a term of four years, and the sides of the fellow, his elbows, his shoulders, hips, and the side of his legs were hard and calloused from lying on his sides in the mine, where the opening was not allowed to be made sufficiently large for comfortable work, and where, he told me, he had often worked far into the night, to send up his ' stint ' before the bucket came down with the order to get in and come up ; only to return at sun-up in the morning.

" A mother, half white, with her daughter lighter still, about fifteen years old, came to me one day to inquire if any redress could be had against the convict authorities for the inhuman treatment of the girl, while serving a year's sentence in the stockade for some trivial offence. She had been whipped unmercifully, as scars on her shoulders and upper back plainly showed, and I was afterward told by the physician to whom I sent her for treatment that she had a running sore on her hip, caused by a cut made by a strap in the hands of the ' whipping boss.' The ' whipping boss,' be it known, is a legal functionary and an invariable and much overworked adjunct to every convict settlement. This child, for she was not more, and frail at that, was at the time I saw her, shortly after her release, four months pregnant by one of the guards; which one she did not know. The mother's grief was pitiful. There was nothing to be done. It is easy to surmise what the remedy would have been had the color of the skins of the respective parties been reversed.

" Two stalwart fellows came with a friend one night to consult me about their situation. It was a sorry plight, indeed. They had escaped from the chain-gang, after being unmercifully beaten. Both were so cut and bruised across the back that their shirts stuck in places to the open sores. They were desperate and frantic with fear lest they should be apprehended, and declared they would rather die than return to the camp. This friend, at a loss to know what to do for them, fearing to be seen in their company, brought them to me. I could do nothing for them, but advised them to get out of the country. They took the hint and started.

" The one least injured was overtaken by the bloodhounds next day, and brought into court to be resentenced as an ' escape,' which means, under the law, doubling his sentence. He was shot a few weeks later, as it was said, in an attempt to escape. The other I never heard from. This is no tale of sixteenth-century barbarity, but of living, existing facts of our own day and in our own land. I can make no more telling comment on the negro-convict-lease system than to quote the language of one of Georgia's men, who sees in it a blot upon our civilization and a disgrace to humanity. Dr. Felton, a few years ago, while a member of the Georgia legislature, said : ' If the fiends of hell had undertaken to devise a penal system, devilish, barbarous, and malignant, they could not have succeeded more fully than Georgia has succeeded in her system.' And what is true of Georgia is also true of the whole South on this subject. Such a system is only possible where two centuries of slavery have blunted human hearts to all the finer instincts concerning the rights of the subject race. One is prone to believe with Samuel Clemens that, 'while there are many humorous things, one of the most ludicrous is the fact that the white man thinks he is less savage than the other savages.'"

So the penal system in the South, which ought to be operated for the punishment or correction of criminals, is proved by the records of the United States courts and competent witnesses to be itself an organized system of crime; and is administered in many instances by criminal officials who are more deserving of punishment than the criminals in stripes. These records also show that the makers of the law, the magistrates of the law, and the sheriffs or guardians of the law are in many instances *participes criminis* in the breaking of the law and the violation of the liberty of citizens.

After a colored man or woman has passed through the hands of such "schoolmasters" and such a "school of crime," what hope is there for such a being? The state courts take no cognizance of these things. The white people have all the power necessary to blot out these terrible evils in a week.

This must be conclusive, if one would but consider what would be done if the case was reversed? Suppose that colored farmers were arresting white men and women on trumped-up charges and working them by day in chains and sleeping them in stockades and subjecting them to the same abuses which colored men and women are now compelled to endure. Would the whites submit to such conditions for twenty-four hours? If necessary, to wipe out such crimes, would not negro blood flow as free as water? These evils can be remedied and that quickly, if there were a disposition to accomplish it.

They are allowed to exist because they are tributary to the plans of the reactionists, to depress the spirit of the colored people and aid in making them a subject race by closing " the door of hope " to them. The leaders are acting on the principle that every humiliation, oppression, or outrage inflicted on the colored people helps to undermine the *morale* of the race and make alienation and subjugation easier.

There are illustrations in the concrete of other and more sanguinary persecutions of which the colored people are the helpless victims. These are riots and lynchings. The reactionists through secret societies, on the order of the Ku Klux Klan, are thoroughly organized. They can produce riots and lynchings as by clockwork. At Wilmington, North Carolina, after rioting and shooting down colored men on the streets for three days, the rioters were called off as suddenly as they had assembled.

When the leaders pass the word for the rioters to act — they act. When they say stop — the rioters stop. If they decide that a lesson must be taught and negroes must be lynched — lynching takes place. If they think that there is no particular need for lynching and the courts may act in a given case — the courts act. The white people can put down lynchings and curb riotings whenever and wherever they may make up their minds to do so.

These lynchings and riots are a fearful strain on the nerves of the colored people. No one is safe when the mob starts out on its bloody work. Innocent people, who had not even heard that a crime had been committed and who were not suspecting the existence of the mob and by mere chance came within its sphere of operation, have been done to the death.

The lynchings in Statesboro', Georgia, on the 16th and 17th of August, 1904, show order and method in the performance — they were directed by a leading mind. A murder had been committed. Two negroes were condemned to death. Others were under arrest in jail awaiting trial. The judge congratulates the community on its respect for law and order. All was quiet the night before. All is quiet in the morning. But suddenly the mob appears, the two negroes convicted are seized and burned alive at the stake. There were guards on hand; they had guns, but no bullets, and so were brushed aside. The negroes were taken from the court house — the temple of justice. The judge and others protested. But what does a Georgia mob care for judges, justice, or law? Members of the secret clans can get on the jury and save their fellows from the penalty of the law.

The affair is described in part by the following press despatch to the New York *Sun:* "Men, as they passed on the street during the evening, looked at each other significantly, as men lately initiated into the same mysteries, but there was little said or heard in public. . . .

"There was no effort of any sort made on the part of the mob at disguise. Everything was done in the broad open daylight, without masks or other concealment. Men who represented the wealth and the worth of the town openly joined in the work of leading the mob. These were the ones who led the rush on the court house and up the stairs to the little room in which the prisoners were confined. The mob, with its victims closely hemmed in, then proceeded to the place of execution. Everything had been prepared. The stake was a light-wood stump about seven feet high. The negroes were bound to this by a stout chain. At their feet light-wood knots were piled, and brushwood and splinters reached to their waists.

"This done, a man mounted the top of the stump and can after can of kerosene were handed up to him. Probably twenty gallons were poured over them in liberal quantities and they were ready for fire. Without a pause these preparations had gone on. As they were finished a man stepped forward and applied the match. The flames rose over the negroes and they uttered a simultaneous groan.

" Reed seemed to bear the torture with fortitude and died quickly. Within three minutes he had ceased to utter sounds, and the only sign of life was the convulsive bending of the left arm at the elbow. This soon ceased and he was burned to a crisp.

" Cato seemed to die harder. Long after the life had left Reed's body he continued to utter cries and to writhe in the flames, which seemed to have less play at him than Reed. Finally one of the mob leaned over and with a bludgeon smashed Cato's head open and he seemed to give up the ghost. His body then turned and took a horizontal position in the fire and slowly burned to a crisp and then to ashes."

After its work, the mob dispersed. The town was again quiet until the next day, when the mob suddenly renewed its work and lynched three more negroes.

A special despatch to the New York *World* says: " ' Regulators' are riding Bullock County ; one unidentified negro has been riddled with bullets, two others perhaps fatally shot, and everywhere negroes are being unmercifully whipped by the bands.

" An absolute reign of terror exists throughout the country. A crowd passed the house of Albert Roberts, an old negro, living near Register, and fired a broadside into it. The old negro, a thoroughly peaceable man, was mortally wounded, and his seventeen-year-old son, Raymond, was struck by several bullets. The negro was seventy-odd years of age. . . .

" Wild spirits from surrounding counties have flocked to Statesboro' and are aiding in the whipping and assaulting of the inoffensive negroes. . . .

" The unidentified body of a negro was found lying by the roadside riddled with bullets eight miles from here. It was at first believed to be that of Handy Bell, but men who know him say that it was not he."

The *World* editorially says:

"The burning of negroes by a mob at Statesboro', Georgia, yesterday, was one of the most barbarous and wanton crimes ever committed in the name of lynch law.

"The victims had been convicted of murder, after a prompt and fair trial, and had been sentenced to be hanged on September 9th. So that the usual excuse of uncertain or delayed legal justice was not present. Yet the mob ' overpowered the militia ' — without a shot having been fired, apparently — and took the condemned prisoners to the woods and burned them at the stake. If ' Darkest Africa ' is any blacker than this, travellers have failed to report it. Even the savages' rude forms of justice are respected."

The Southern leaders and their apologists are accustomed to justify lynchings on the ground of the protection of womanhood. Whenever they speak in public, in Congress or elsewhere, the blood of negroes lynched is spattered on the head of womanhood. To push womanhood to the front and make it bear the brunt of barbarous crimes committed on the negroes from " stark blood-lust overwhelming the appeal to reason," which is absolutely true of the great majority of lynchings, is unwise and merits the condemnation of chivalric manhood. Negroes have been lynched in the South for every crime ; and they have been lynched when no crime whatever has been charged. The negro man, the woman, the youth fourteen years of age, the child three years of age, the babe in the mother's arms who could not lisp the word " mamma," have been the victims of the lynching mobs.

The records of lynchings kept by the Chicago *Tribune*, a reliable authority, show that only two or three out of every ten colored persons lynched are even charged with the nameless offence. It has been proved that some of those charged with the crime were innocent. In a particular instance a white man who killed his wife while in a passion charged one of the negroes who worked on his place with having assaulted and murdered his wife. And this white man headed the mob which lynched the negro. He made a full confession on his death-bed of the negro's innocence.

Riotings and lynchings have become dominant features in Southern life and their reflex influence has caused the enactment of bloody deeds in a few Northern communities. It does not help matters to say that in Illinois, Kansas, or Delaware a mob can burn a negro at the stake with all the cruelties of a Georgia, Mississippi, or Texas mob. It is due to Southern example; and it has been proved that men from the South have been the leaders of Northern mobs. It is also true that many Southern men residing in the North, and also visiting Southerners, seize every opportunity to discredit the colored man and inflame passions against him.

Senator Tillman, while on a visit North, referring to the violence committed by a Northern mob, said : " I see you are learning how to kill and burn ' niggers.' That's right; let the good work go on. Keep it up; you are getting some sense." Other Southerners, through the press and in addresses, have made statements calculated to inflame certain elements, and doubtless have caused much mischief. The good people of the North can and should call a halt to those Southerners who are seeking to create strife between the races in the North. The "strikes" among a few school children against colored teachers or pupils are due to the barbarous teachings of these Southern leaders.

The truth remains, however, that lynch-law does not dominate any Northern state. It does dominate Southern states. It has become a part of Southern civilization and is publicly defended by many leading Southern men. The Northern man in public life who should advocate lynching would be disgraced. The Southern men who defend or endorse it, like Tillman, Carmack, Vardaman, Richardson, Graves, and Money, are honored in public life and kept in high places.

To indicate how general lynchings have become in the South, and to emphasize, if possible, the infamy of it, the following cases may be cited: At Carrollton, Louisiana, a negro man and two women were lynched: they were suspected of being implicated in a murder. In Smith County, Mississippi, four negro men and one woman were lynched, and eight or ten badly beaten, and most of the negroes ordered to leave: they were suspected of wounding two white men. In Mississippi, a negro woman was lynched; "the mob visited the woman's house and after tying her hands behind her, took her to the bridge over Lick Creek. Here she was shot through the head and her lifeless body was thrown into the stream": her offence was that her brother was charged with stealing a pocket-book and she could not tell the mob of his whereabouts, and so was lynched.

In Louisiana, a young negro was lynched because he could not tell the whereabouts of his brother, who was charged with theft. At Lewisburg, Tennessee, a negro was lynched in the court-house yard: he was suspected of murder. In St. James Parish, Louisiana, a negro charged with murder was burned at the stake. At Florence, Alabama, a negro was lynched by being "hamstrung, hung up by the heels like a hog, and allowed slowly to bleed to death": his offence was that he had protested loudly against the killing of innocent negroes. At or near Tuscombia, Alabama, three negroes were lynched, because one had resisted arrest.

In South Carolina, a negro man and wife were intercepted while on the way to Abbeville jail, taken from the sheriff, and hanged on a bridge, and their bodies riddled with bullets: they were suspected of murder. At Langley, South Carolina, two negroes who had been wounded in a fight in the "Jim Crow" car set apart for colored people, and which had been invaded by whites, and whom the doctor said could not possibly live, were taken from the jail and lynched. At Newbern, Tennessee, two negroes were lynched: they were suspected of murder. At Memphis, Tennessee, four negroes were lynched for starting a grocery store, in competition with a white man, in a colored settlement.

At Joplin, Missouri, several negroes were lynched, a number of their homes were burned, and over a thousand were driven out in one day. The home of postmaster Baker, of South Carolina, was surrounded at night; oil was poured on the house and it was set on fire. When the family attempted to escape, the mob opened fire on them. Mr. Baker was killed; his young babe in his arms was killed; his wife and two daughters and a son were also shot. His only offence was that he was a negro who held a Federal office. In Louisiana, a leading negro minister was lynched because he advised the colored people to become the owners of their own homes and farms. In the same state, near Girard, a negro was lynched; the only offence that he was charged with was the stealing of a bottle of " pop."

At Hodenville, Kentucky, a negro was lynched on the court-house steps: he was charged with causing a white boy to steal. At Brookside, Alabama, three white men shot down an inoffensive negro just for fun — one saying, " Watch the ' coon ' jump." The negro was shot dead.

In one case a young white girl was made the executioner. She put the rope around the victim's neck; he was then placed on the back of a horse; the end of the rope was thrown over the limb of a tree, and the little girl took hold of the bridle of the horse and led it away, leaving the victim hanging. The body was then riddled with bullets. Where else in civilization could such a spectacle be witnessed?

At Beach Still, Georgia, the negroes were having a dance, when the hall was fired upon by white men; two negroes were killed, and nine wounded, including three women. In Gunterville, Alabama, a negro was lynched; the charge was barn-burning. In South Carolina five negroes were lynched:

they were suspected of having burned a barn. It was afterwards proven that they were innocent.

The Boston *Journal* cites this case: "Viewed from any standpoint the lynching of negro Robert White in Alabama was a cowardly murder. A white man had killed all of White's chickens. This resulted in a row and shots were exchanged. No white participant in the affair was troubled, but the negro was arrested, and while in the hands of an officer, going to jail, he was seized by a mob of white men and put to death. Every man in that mob was nothing less than a murderer and should be so treated; but the victim was only a 'nigger' who had no rights which white folks of that sort respect, and the murderer will go scot free."

In Salisbury, North Carolina, two negro boys were taken from the jail and lynched : they were suspected of murder.

Pierce City, Missouri, shows this record: "For nearly fifteen hours to-day this town of 3,000 people has been in the hands of a mob of armed men, determined to drive out every negro. In addition to the lynching last night of William Godley, accused falsely, it is believed, of murder, and the shooting of his grandfather, French Godley, the mob to-day burned Peter Hampton, an aged negro, alive in his home, set the torch to the houses of five blacks and with the aid of state militia rifles, stolen from the local company's arsenal, drove dozens of negroes from town. After noon the excitement died down, the mob gradually dispersing, more from lack of negroes upon whom to wreak their hatred than from any other cause. Many of the negroes who fled the city are hiding in the surrounding woods, while others have gone greater distances in seeking safety."

A colored camp-meeting in Mississippi was raided by whites; thirty colored people engaged in the worship of God were killed, including the pastor, his wife, a daughter twelve years of age, his younger child three years of age, and a minister who was assisting in the meetings. The whites interfered with the meeting. The killing was wanton; there were no charges against any of the colored people.

In South Carolina a number of colored men appeared at the polls to vote, and a riot was started. Seven of the colored men were captured and made to stand up on a log, and were there shot to death: their offence was that they had attempted to vote. The white man who was running for Congress and for whom they wanted to vote was also shot. In Arkansas, fifteen negroes were lynched as a result of a dispute in which a colored man doubted a white man's word over a grocery bill.

The New York *World*, reviewing the crimes of 1901, says: " Lynchings show one hundred and seven cases in the South, all colored . . . Race hatred is the cause of many crimes . . . Thus ten persons were killed for no other cause than race prejudice in the South last year." Many of those lynched for " cause " were innocent of crime.

The New York *Journal* describes a case in these words: " Call to your mind the picture of the negro, with a rope hanging around his neck, escaping from the mob the other day and running to the sheriff with his face battered in. The mob had wanted to lynch him because he would not confess that some one else was guilty of arson." The *Journal*, referring to another case, said: " Negroes are lynched for being born into the world."

The Nashville (Tennessee) *American* gives an account of a lynching in Mississippi as follows: " But there was a lynching in that state that for fiendish brutality has not yet been surpassed, even when the victims have been roasted at the stake. It occurred at Doddsville, recently, and these are the circumstances as related by local newspapers: Luther Holbert, a negro, had a quarrel with a white man and, following the usual Mississippi method, they exchanged shots, the negro escaping and the white man being killed. The negro, knowing the penalty for killing a white man in that section, fled, of course, accompanied by his wife, who had had no part in the quarrel. They were captured by the mob and this is what was done to them, according to the statement of an eye-witness in the Vicksburg *Herald.*

" ' When the two negroes were captured they were tied to trees, and while the funeral pyres were being prepared they were forced to suffer the most fiendish tortures. The blacks were forced to hold out their hands while one finger at a time was chopped off. The fingers were distributed as souvenirs. The ears of the murderers were cut off. Holbert was severely beaten, his skull was fractured, and one of his eyes, knocked out with a stick, hung by a shred from the socket. Neither the man nor the woman begged for mercy, nor made a groan or plea. When the executioners came forward to lop off fingers, Holbert extended his hand without being asked. The most excruciating form of punishment consisted in the use of a large corkscrew in the hands of one of the mob. This instrument was bored into the flesh of the man and the woman, in the arms, legs, and body, and pulled out, the spiral tearing out big pieces of raw, quivering flesh every time it was withdrawn.

" ' After these tortures the mutilated bodies were burned. Had this negro outraged a white woman ? Oh, no ; he had merely killed a white man who was shooting at him. His wife had committed no crime, but simply fled with her husband. Yet she was made to share his fate, and with him to suffer the most cruel and brutal tortures the devilish ingenuity of the degraded savages could devise.' "

During the last ten years lynchings have averaged one hundred and fifty a year. Many of the victims were known to be innocent at the time, but when the mob starts out it must have blood, whether the victims are guilty or innocent. Numerous riots and expulsions have also taken place.

A feature in connection herewith, worthy of note, is that the coroner's jury, impanelled to uphold the law, as a rule renders the stereotyped verdict that "The party or parties came to their death at the hands of persons unknown." And this in the face of the fact that the press publishes the names of the leaders of the mob, and of the man who fires the first shot or lights the fire to burn the victim. Sometimes the jury treats the matter as a joke; in one case they rendered the verdict that " the deceased came to his death by swinging in the air." Again, that "the deceased came to his death by taking too great a bite of hemp rope." At other times their verdict is a direct incentive to crime; as for instance this: " We do not know who killed the deceased, but we congratulate the parties on their work." Members of the mobs have also served on the coroner's jury. A grand jury returned this verdict in Louisiana: " The men who participated in the burning were among the best citizens of the county, and nothing but a desire to protect those who are nearest and dearest to them would move them to undertake such measures." As to the savagery of the tortures inflicted upon the victims, these additional facts may be given: Red-hot iron has been used to burn the tongue from the mouth ; to burn the flesh from the breast and back ; to burn out the eyes ; to burn the flesh from the arms and legs ; to burn off the ears and nose. The heart and the liver have been removed from the body and cut into small pieces and sold as souvenirs of the lynching. Repeatedly, events have occurred which showed that the negroes who were lynched were entirely innocent.

Press despatches gave the following case : " Charleston, South Carolina, March 2, 1904. After taking a prominent part in lynching three negroes, section-foreman Jones, of the Atlantic Coast line, to-day confessed to the murder of his wife, for which the innocent men were mobbed.

" One morning during the early part of May, 1902, the body of Mrs. Jones was found in the dog house, in the rear of her yard, at Ravenel. Her throat was cut from ear to ear and her head crushed in.

"The news of the terrible crime soon spread over Coîleton county and armed parties were organized and the woods were scoured for negroes, it having been stated that three negro men were seen in the vicinity of the Jones house the morning of the tragedy. The description of the negroes corresponded with that of Jim Black, James Ford, and Thomas Pryer, who had been in the neighborhood, but who had suddenly disappeared.

"After searching for the negroes for a week they were arrested, taken to the scene of the crime, and swung to the limbs of trees. Jones was present and was given the opportunity of firing the first shots into their bodies.

"Several weeks ago section-foreman Jones was taken sick, and Dr. Willis was called in to treat him; but he had passed all medical aid, for the disease with which he was afflicted had wrecked his constitution, and he began to sink. Realizing that he was about to die, Jones confessed to killing his wife.

"'I know I am going to die, but I can't die until I tell all about killing my wife,' he said to his physician. He then recited the details of the crime, declaring that he killed his wife in a moment of passion that morning in May before he left for his work. He then carried the body from the house and dumped it into the dog house, where it was found by his little daughter a few hours afterward. Immediately after making the confession he expired."

The first thought that may impress the average mind from these recitals is that the negroes are not the only, or the chief, or the worst criminals in the South. Colored criminals may outnumber white criminals in the penal institutions, but they may not be numerically stronger outside the penitentiary. Practically all colored criminals, and many not criminals go to the penitentiary, but many white criminals go to Canada, or into political offices, or become "guards" or "bosses." Crime has increased among the colored people since emancipatiou, but it should be remembered that there are nearly

252 .

three times as many colored people now as were emancipated. Crime has also increased among the whites. Forty years ago there were practically no whites in penitentiaries in the South, but now there are thousands ; besides, there are hundreds of white females in prison, — a condition unheard of before the War of the Rebellion. One of the greatest scandals of recent times in the South was the brutal flogging of a white woman in a prison in Georgia.

Another thought that will suggest itself is: Why are these inhumanities permitted to exist in Christian, civilized communities? The answer is : It is because of the virus of slavery in the brain of the whites, called into activity by the leaders to compass the subjugation of the colored race. It is a part of a carefully evolved plan by the leaders. It is designed to put the race under the contempt of the whites and to destroy its *morale*.

Thomas Wentworth Higginson, in the *Atlantic Monthly*, shows that the reign of terror and lynchings are in defence neither of law nor of chastity, but " It is in defence of caste." And he further says : " What the whole nation needs is to deal with the negro race no longer as outcasts, but simply as men and women." The Boston *Herald* says : " In all the years since the war it is probable that fifty negroes have been murdered by white men for every white man murdered by negroes, and a hundred negro women have been debauched by white men for every white woman outraged by a negro."

Miss Caroline Pemberton, of one of the first families of Philadelphia, in a communication to the *Public Ledger* of that city, says : " In the first place, the crime of assault is not peculiar to the negro race. It is practically unknown in the West Indies, in South Africa, and South America, and was never charged against the Southern negro until political and social conditions ripened in the minds of Southern whites a frantic desire to stigmatize the whole negro race as unworthy to possess the rights of men. The crime of assault so frequently charged against the negro as a race is part of the political conspiracy to deprive him of his legal rights. It has been proved over and over again that only a very small proportion of negroes who are lynched in the South are even charged with this crime; and of those who are charged with it, it is safe to conclude that a fair proportion is innocent. I reach this last conclusion from knowledge of the fact that the charge is often made against men of all races under conditions that make their comparative innocence almost a foregone conclusion.

"In regard to negro criminality, let me assure you that I speak from personal experience when I assert that the average working negro is as free from pronounced criminal tendencies as the white man of the same class. I have for years employed colored people in my own household, and found them both trustworthy and efficient. . . .

"I have travelled over the muddy roads of Eastern Virginia for many miles, and through the Black Belt of Alabama for several days, with no other protector in each case than a negro driver, and with no thought of harm coming to me. I have visited colored schools in the South, taught by white Northern women whose sole protectors were their black students and a few colored instructors. The only people these gentlewomen feared were the white men of the neighborhood, whose threats against the school had at one time caused them grave anxiety. The loyal devotion of the blacks to these white women was something beautiful to see, and was proof enough that the faithful character of the negro has not changed since slavery."

Mr. James S. Stemons, in the Philadelphia *Record*, says: "Shame! But who can point to any negro crime so loathsome as the assault and murder by four white men of Jennie Bosschieter, in Paterson, New Jersey, four years ago; or as that of the two men in Wheeling, West Virginia, who, two years ago, took a seventeen-year-old girl from her escort at the point of a pistol, assaulted and murdered her, and threw her body into the Ohio River; of the nine men who a few days ago assaulted a young girl in this city; of the two brothers who assaulted a five-year-old child; or that of the more than a dozen men who have within the past four years assaulted, in some cases at the point of a pistol, their own daughters, nieces, and cousins?"

All these cases were committed by white men. And it may be noted here that the Confederate Congress, in resolutions formally adopted in October, 1862, made this same charge against the soldiers of the Union army. It was unjustly pressed then; it is unjustly pressed now, against the colored people. No large body of people should be held responsible for the acts of a few brutal individuals. All races have developed brutal men. But neither in the North nor in the South has the colored race developed the most elusive, dangerous, and brutal criminals.

The colored race has produced no criminals or desperadoes of heartless cruelty like the James brothers; or the man Holmes, who killed so many people, including several wives and his own children, that he did not keep trace of them; or the Chicago boy bandits; or the trained nurse who wiped out several families by poisoning; or some of the guards and officials of the stockades or penitentiaries and the leaders of the lynching mobs.

The Chicago *Chronicle*, referring to an editorial in the Atlanta *News*, edited by Mr. John Temple Graves, in which he advocates the systematic establishment of a reign of terror and lynching, says:

"In his leading editorial last Friday he advocates not only lynching, but a revival of the Ku Klux Klan. In that editorial he declares that 'neither law nor statutes, nor public opinion, nor armed forces, nor Federal courts, nor any other courts will prevent the stern expression of the popular horror' of crime when it is committed by a negro — expression by burning at the stake the negro suspected of the crime without trial or proof of any kind.

" This man threatens to revive the masked night-riding murderers if an attempt is made to invoke national law and courts for the protection not only of negroes but for the preservation of Southern society from lapsing into that savagery and anarchy into which by admission of the Governor of Georgia it has almost fallen in that state already."

In order to accomplish the subjugation of the colored race and the destruction of its citizenship, these leaders would plunge the South into a state of anarchy.

For forty years the negro has been harassed and harried on the right and on the left, in front and behind. He has been on the run, and has not had a moment to pause and catch his breath or take his bearings. He has been, and is, fearfully handicapped. Some of the whites of the South have been kind, friendly, and helpful to him ; many have sympathized with him in his tribulations and woes, but lacked the courage to manifest it ; and a few have spoken out boldly against the outrages and outlawry of which he has been the victim. But the leaders and the organized South have allowed him no quarter, shown him no mercy.

The proscriptions and oppressions which are laid on the colored man either North or South on the ground of color alone have made him extremely sensitive to any infraction of his rights and liberty. And in desperation he has at times struck back at the oppressor, although the lyncher's noose was dangling in his face.

Much of the violence of which he is guilty, especially in the North, is due to resentment that certain elements in the North should seek to outrage him simply because of his color. A community which denies a man a fair chance to earn an honest living because of his color, thus driving him into idleness, is in a manner responsible for the increase of its criminals.

256

Every municipal or state law bearing on him enacted in the South since his emancipation has been to degrade, ostracize, and alienate him, and deprive him of his liberty, or restrict him in the realization of his dreams of freedom. On the other hand, it is a cheering truth that every law passed in the North touching the negro has been to confirm and make secure his freedom, protect his civil rights, guarantee his ballot, and put him on the same footing with all other citizens before the law.

In the passage of such laws in the North, Democrats and members of other political parties have nobly aided the Republicans in achieving the security and firm establishment of the liberty and rights of the colored citizen.

In the South, in the state of Texas, a colored man who had been carrying the mail to and fro from the State House to the post-office for fifteen years was discharged under the new order of things, which prohibits the negro from being recognized in any public or semi-public relation in the South. Such repression is general. The Richmond, Virginia, city council passed a resolution prohibiting the negro from being employed in any position around the City Hall. The brotherhood of locomotive and steamboat firemen of the South at their meeting at Norfolk, Virginia, passed resolutions protesting against the employment of negroes as firemen on locomotives or steamboats. Other labor organizations have placed the boycott on him. He is being driven to the wall. The increase of crime is coincident with the increase of oppression and outlawry. The organized South is responsible for the growth in crime.

How far — how long — are these things to go on?

Ella Wheeler Wilcox has published in the New York *Journal*, a poem which, in part, runs as follows: —

> " Out of the wilderness, out of the night,
> Has the black man crawled to the dawn of light;
> Beaten by lashes and bound by chains,

A beast of burden with soul and brains.
He has come through sorrow and need and woe,
And the cry of his heart is to *know*, to *know!*

" Red with anguish his way has been,
This suffering brother of dusky skin,
For centuries fettered and bound to earth.
Slow his unfolding to freedom's birth —
Slow his rising from burden and ban
To fill the stature of mortal man.
You must give him wings ere you tell him to fly —
You must set the example and bid him try ;
Let the white man pay for the white man's crime —
Let him work in patience and bide God's time.

" Out of the wilderness, out of the night,
Has the black man crawled to the dawn of light ;
He has come through the valley of great despair —
He has borne what no white man ever can bear —
He has come through sorrow and pain and woe,
And the cry of his heart is to *know*, to *know!* "

CHAPTER VIII

THE RISE AND ACHIEVEMENTS OF THE COLORED RACE

PRESIDENT ALDERMAN of Tulane University, New Orleans, Louisiana, a well-bred, high-minded, and highly cultured Southerner, who holds his equipoise even in that city which is the storm-centre of "Jim Crowism," in a public address said: "Progress is measured by the distance one has travelled as well as to the point one has reached." He was speaking on the race question. The colored race, judged by this standard, measured by this mete-wand, may confidently invite comparison in their forty years of struggles and ascent in civilization with any people in the world's history.

Another Southerner, the Right Reverend Bishop Haygood, one of the greatest men, greatest in heart, greatest in brain, that the South has produced, speaking of the progress of the colored race, said: "It's a marvel. It overturns all of our preconceived ideas about the negro. We thought we knew him, but we did n't. We must in honesty confess that he has surprised us and taught us much we did not know and would not have believed."

The Reverend A. B. Curry, D. D., of Memphis, Tennessee, who at present represents a small but important class in Southern life, but a class like "the mustard seed" of the parable, that will certainly multiply and predominate as the South shall take the sober second thought, preached a sermon in his home city on the 27th of November, 1904, in which he pays a deserved tribute to the colored man and paints a word portrait of him which should command consideration because of its truthfulness. The sermon was published in the Memphis *Commercial Appeal*, and carries its own commendation of the mind and heart of the minister.

Dr. Curry said in part: "I am not ashamed to say that I have a tender feeling in my heart for the negro. I believe I would be an ingrate if I did not have such feeling. My helpless infancy and early childhood were watched over with a tender care and affection second only to those of the mother who bore me, and it was those of my faithful negro nurse on the old plantation home in southern Georgia. . . .

"We criticise him and complain of him, but we don't want to give him up. Let a labor agent go through the South, seeking to induce the negroes to leave the country and he becomes at once, to say the least, *persona non grata*. I have known such agents in some localities to be fined and imprisoned. That means that our country needs him. He is the best laborer, for the kind of labor that needs to be done in the South, that we have ever found. . . .

"A year ago, when there was a disagreement between our steamboat companies' and their negro roustabouts, an effort was made to replace the latter with white men; but it was not successful. The white men could not do the work satisfactorily; and when I went up to St. Louis the past summer on the river, I understood it. I do not believe there is the white race living or any other race, not even the patient Chinamen, who either could or would do the work the negro roustabouts do, in the way they are required to do it. The negro's great muscular-strength, his powers of endurance, his healthfulness in a Southern climate, and his docility of spirit make him an invaluable factor in the labor problem of the South, and the present material development of the South is due in no small measure to the brawn and muscle and willing industry of the negro. . . .

"Twenty white tramps come to my door, begging, to one negro. An able-bodied negro is almost never a beggar. What he asks, and what the white man owes him, is a chance to work along every avenue for which his mind and his hand capacitate him, with a fair wage fully and promptly paid. . . .

"There is no more docile man, nor loyal friend than the negro, when convinced of your disinterested love for him.

"But we are told by some that the game is not worth the candle; that after all, the negro is incapable of a high civilization and of valuable achievement; that he is destitute of the noble traits of human nature. I cannot believe this, for I remember when, during the Civil War, my two oldest brothers, both still in their teens, went to the front, and my father was called away on a similar mission, leaving my mother and her little children to the care and protection of the negro slaves, that sacred trust was kept with the utmost fidelity; and there were men among them who, if need arose, would have laid down their lives through devotion to their trust. . . .

"I have heard of a negro man, who, after freedom, removed from his old home in Virginia to Macon, Georgia. There through industry and thrift he amassed a nice amount of property. Hearing that his old master and mistress in Virginia, unable to adjust themselves to changed conditions, had become homeless and poor, he built them a comfortable little home in Macon, brought them to it, and cared for them till they died, and then carried their bodies back to the old Virginia home for burial.

"When I was in the Palace of Fine Arts in St. Louis this summer, I saw a picture before which I stood and wept. In the distance was a battle scene; the dust of tramping men and horses, the smoke of cannon and rifles filled the air; broken carriages and dead and dying men strewed the ground. In the foreground was the figure of a stalwart negro man, bearing in his strong arms the form of a fair-haired Anglo-Saxon youth. It was the devoted body servant of a young Southerner, bearing the dead body of his young master from the field of carnage, not to pause or rest till he had delivered it to those whose love for it only surpassed his own; and underneath the picture were these words: 'Faithful Unto Death'; and there are men before me who have seen the spirit of that picture illustrated on more than one field of battle.

"I do not think a race possessed of such qualities of heart, capable of such noble, unselfish deeds, is to be despised among the families of the earth. There is a place for it, and a work for it to do, in the world. Is it asked, what will be the final destiny of the negro in America? We cannot tell, but let us do our duty to the poor man at our gate in the spirit of Christ, and leave results with God. We need not fear; they will be satisfactory."

Mr. Sarge Plunkett of Georgia, a sane Southerner on the negro question, writing to the Atlanta *Constitution*, says: "No matter how others may feel or have felt, the negro in the South has been such a surprise to me that I am slow to say what he will or will not accomplish; I am even slow to say that he is as inferior as we have heard he was. The negro must lift himself, and while it goes mighty hard with me to acknowledge it, he is lifting himself, and he will keep on lifting up and up at every opportunity. On lines of accumulation, the negro has done better than an old timer would have ever thought he could do. I know negroes, and we all know negroes, who could 'buy,' as the saying goes, every child of his old master. And I can tell you, as a truth, that negroes who are able to do this that I have hinted have more prestige, are more respectable if you please, than these children I have mentioned. Sit down coolly and contemplate the negroes as they were at the end of our war and as they are to-day; do this, after laying aside the prejudice that you have and I have, and I feel more than a great majority will have to acknowledge that the negro is not so inferior as we thought he was.

"How well can many now living remember what a picture they made about the time of Lee's surrender!

" I admit that I was fooled about their capacity, and I know that thousands of others were the same. If we had been told then that there would be a black man developed into what we know that Washington is, we would have honestly thought it foolish and passed it as a joke. When I pass out about the big negro colleges around Atlanta and look upon the students there, I am bound to admit that they are beyond anything that I ever dreamed they could be."

And speaking of the possibilities of a great foreign war, and the availability of the negro for service in the United States army, Mr. Plunkett further urges : " If we should have such a war as is contemplated, I take it that the negroes will join our armies just as white men join. They will march under the same flag, wear the same uniform, and are bound by right to be accorded all the honors that their actions may deserve. It is more than probable — it is certain — that there will develop heroes and heroines from out of the race of whom the poets will sing, and when this is accomplished, then many other things will belong to them by right and the natural consequences. When we get up such a war as will call for the need of these negroes, and they are formed into regiments and brigades, put on the blue, rally around the flag, charge batteries, and do all the duties in a soldierly way, then they will feel that they have rights here that they never had before, and millions of people outside of their race will feel the same about the matter."

This is precisely true. In the wars in which the negroes have worn the blue, they have rallied around the flag, charged on batteries even unto the jaws of death, and performed all their duties in such a soldierly way that millions of people outside of their race believe them to be entitled to all the honors that their actions may deserve — even the full enjoyment of American citizenship.

But it must be evident to Mr. Plunkett that the dominant leaders of the South are not the kind of men who could be moved by the influences of which he speaks, or by humane or Christian or patriotic impulses. Neither the negro soldier who charged Fort Wagner or San Juan Hill, nor the negro educator who has been pronounced to be among the greatest of living men, would be recognized by them as an American among Americans.

What then becomes of the contention that it is the white man of the South alone who knows the negro?

The rise and achievements of the race have not been along one line, or two lines, or three lines, but they have been witnessed in every vocation, avenue, and calling of American life. In the brief space of a single generation, the manumitted race has conquered places in all the multiple phases of modern activities. Verily, " the republic is opportunity."

The abolitionists, philanthropists, Christians, and humanitarians of the North, and those scattering, but greatly deserving Southerners who in wisdom " faced the rising sun," probably built better than they knew — guided and upheld by the wisdom and power of Jehovah, God — when they decided on the kind of education that should be open to the colored race at the close of the war. They refused to regard the colored race as a special race, and therefore needing a special kind of education. They acted on the principle that as the colored people were a part of the human race, then any kind and every kind of education that was good enough for a white man, was good enough for them. The putting in force of this simple, common-sense idea made possible the wonderful success of the colored people.

If they had yielded to a " craze " for industrial education and devoted their strength to it, the colored race could not have gained in a hundred years the great advance in civilization and the splendid achievements which now stand to its credit after only a single generation of endeavor. For emphasis on industrial education would have circumscribed the mental vision, limited the aspirations, narrowed the ambitions, stunted all higher and broader growth, and held the race close down to the lines of hewers of wood and drawers of water, which was the endless routine under the slave régime. The colored race can work, it knows how to work, it will work, and in an experience of two hundred and fifty years it proved its value as the hardiest of toilers in every Southern community.

The South acknowledged the value and profitableness of the negro as a toiler and producer when it went to war and fought four years with vast loss in blood and treasure to hold him as a part of its system. It was divinely wise that the colored race in beginning its new life of liberty was taught to look also on the higher and greater things of life ; that the mind was taken beyond its accustomed sphere ; that the things denied it in slavery were open to it in freedom ; that the mind might expand with the height and breadth of the universe.

Schools were planted : the lower grades ; the preparatory schools ; the normal schools ; the colleges ; the professional schools. They began work almost simultaneously, — in some cases while the shock of war was still on ; in other cases the instant that peace was declared. The work was carried on with such rapidity and thoroughness, and there was such hearty and overwhelming response from the colored people — who crowded and overflowed school-houses with their children, and, for lack of room in-doors, sessions were held out-of-doors under the oak and elm trees — that the white people of the South stood sullenly surprised, and the people of the North gladly amazed. It meant a revolution in the Southland irresistible, sweeping, all-embracing. It meant a New South !

For a time this work of education was supported by the National Government, supplemented by Northern benevolence and by a nominal fee which was charged the colored parent for each child. The people of the North contributed money for this cause without stint; chiefly through the several religious denominations. In this work the Congregationalists, Methodists, Baptists, Presbyterians, Episcopalians, Unitarians, Friends, and other denominations, and hosts of individuals heartily co-operated. But greater and better than the money contributions, they gave thousands of their consecrated, devoted, self-denying sons and daughters to this humane, patriotic, Christ-like work. The brave men, and it may be said, braver women, who left comforts, luxuries, refinements of their Northern homes and went to the South at the close of the war to teach and lift up a despised and prostrate people, performed a service for humanity, for the republic, for the kingdom of God in the world that will go on with ever-increasing power and beneficent fruitage through all the countless ages to come.

True, they were frequently hampered in their work by irreconcilable Southerners; their school-houses were sometimes burned to the ground; their homes stoned in the night; they were insulted on the streets; they were, and still are, socially boycotted; they were sometimes murdered. But their work went on. They conquered. The best South to-day, notwithstanding the clamor and outlawry inspired by "Jim Crowism," is being converted to the education of the colored people. Some have materially assisted in the work; others have given it the support of tongue and pen; and still others have become efficient teachers.

Among the Northern men who rendered distinguished and lasting service in the uplifting of the race was the Reverend William W. Patton, D.D., late President of Howard University, Washington, D. C. He was a man with a history; and the impress of his great life was stamped on thousands of colored youths. He left school an ardent and uncompromising abolitionist. His father was a distinguished Presbyterian minister. But he entered the Congregational denomination, as it offered and encouraged the greatest freedom for the expression of his antislavery views. For ten years he was the pastor of the Fourth Congregational Church at Hartford, Connecticut, and made it a great antislavery centre.

In 1856, because of his antislavery reputation, he was called to the First Congregational Church at Chicago, Illinois. His sermons, lectures, and addresses soon made him a great favorite in the West among all antislavery elements. He aided in the organization of the American Missionary Association, which was an organized protest against slavery, and which, through its numerous schools, colleges, universities, and churches has bestowed countless blessings on the South and the nation. He also aided in organizing the Chicago Theological Seminary. He was editor of the *Advance*.

Dr. Patton is the author of the words of the famous " John Brown " song, which " express the moral issues of the war in relation to slavery." It was as follows: —

I

"Old John Brown's body lies a-mouldering in the grave,
While weep the sons of bondage, whom he ventured all to save ;
But though he lost his life in struggling for the slave,
His soul is marching on ! O Glory Hallelujah !

II

" John Brown he was a hero, undaunted, true and brave,
And Kansas knew his valor, where he fought, her rights to save,
And now, though the grass grows green above his grave,
His soul is marching on ! O Glory Hallelujah !

III

"He captured Harper's Ferry with his nineteen men so few,
And he frightened " Old Virginny," till she trembled through and
    through ;
They hung him for a traitor, themselves a traitor crew,
But his soul is marching on ! O Glory Hallelujah !

IV

"John Brown was John the Baptist of the Christ we are to see —
Christ who of the bondman shall the Liberator be ;
And soon throughout the sunny South the slaves shall all be free,
For his soul is marching on ! O Glory Hallelujah ! "

The entire song was afterward printed in the Chicago *Tribune,* and became wonderfully popular in the Western army. The " Jubilee Singers," some years after, adopted two of the stanzas for their use, thus giving them yet wider currency. Wendell Phillips was accustomed at times to quote the third stanza with great effect.

When the war came Dr. Patton announced from his pulpit that the lecture-room of his church should be used for the purpose of drilling the soldiers. He was made Vice-President of the Sanitary Commission of the Northwest and became its chief executive officer, visiting the seat of war and looking after the sick and wounded soldiers and the sanitary condition of hospitals. He was the inspirer of, and chief figure in, the great mass meeting at Chicago which sent a memorial to President Lincoln, urging him to issue a proclamation freeing the slaves. He was chairman and spokesman of the committee which bore the memorial; and he was ably assisted by Dr. John Dempster and the Honorable Charles Walker.

President Lincoln talked with them freely. After the conference Secretary Stanton said to Mr. Medill of the Chicago *Tribune :* " Tell those Chicago clergymen who waited on the President about the Proclamation of Emancipation, that their interview finished the business." It was even so. The Emancipation Proclamation was issued shortly afterward. Scholar, preacher, editor, lecturer, organizer, teacher, president of a university, invincible foe of slavery. Behold him!

This recital will give some insight into the mental and moral stamina and high character of the men and women who planned and laid the foundation for the education and the uplifting of the colored race. Among the pioneers in this work, there should be mentioned: the Reverends M. E. Strieby, James Powell, Simeon Gilbert, E. M. Cravath, E. A. Ware, John G. Fee, G. W. Andrews, John Braden, John W. Alvord, S. C. Logan, Luke Dorland [and his wife], R. S.

Rust, J. M. Walden, A. Webster [and his wife and son], L. M. Dunton [and his wife], J. C. Hartzell, J. W. Hamilton, E. F. Williams, Amos Billings [and his wife], Samuel Loomis [and his wife], Richard H. Allen, Alfred Owen, Theodore E. Balch, D. W. Phillips, M. R. Miller, E. C. Mitchell, E. P. Cowan, Isaac Rendall, A. Wescott, Dr. Tupper [and his wife]; Professors C. W. Francis, A. K. Spence, Henry S. Bennett, C. H. Richards, John A. Cole, A. J. Steele, Helen C. Morgan; Miss Cahill, Miss Welles, Miss Kate Moorehead, Miss Helen Bayden, Mrs. S. J. Neil [widow of a Union officer]; Generals Clinton B. Fisk, George Whipple, E. Whittlesey, Charles H. Howard, S. C. Armstrong, Alvord, William Birney; and Doctors G. W. Hubbard, D. S. Lamb, and N. F. Graham, who have had such great success in promoting the education of colored youths in medicine, dentistry, and pharmacy. Bishops Haven and Mallalieu were also potent forces. General O. O. Howard who was at the head of the Freedmen's Bureau was the mentor and rendered invaluable services. It was a work in which thousands were engaged, so that the above mention of a few individuals to show the character of the whole will not appear invidious. Every man and woman who enlisted in this second army of invasion of the South, with spelling-books instead of muskets, is worthy of mention and deserving of praise. All of them faced ostracism, some fell martyrs.

In certain instances the law of compensation operated most directly. Libby prison, which had become infamous because of great cruelty inflicted upon Union soldiers imprisoned within it, was occupied and used as the first school for the education of the colored race in Richmond, the Capital of the Confederacy. The school which was started in this former prison pen by the Reverends Nathaniel Colver and Charles H. Correy has grown into Union University, the leading institution conducted for the education of colored youths by the Baptists of the North.

Hampton Institute, which has the name of General Armstrong so inseparably connected with it, had its beginning under a colored teacher, Mrs. Mary S. Peake, who was employed by the American Missionary Association to open and conduct this school. General Armstrong afterwards took charge of it and gave it wide and deserved fame, but it was organized by a colored person.

It was also in harmony with the law of compensation that a number of colored people who had escaped from slavery and settled in the North or in Canada and had taken advantage of the schools, as also some who had been born free or set free by the slaveholders, and some others who despite the watchfulness of the master class had stolen a knowledge of the three "R's" in the dead of the night by the light of the light-wood torch — that these, with more or less intellectual preparation, should have entered with enthusiasm upon the work of educating their race. Among such may be mentioned: Bishops Daniel A. Payne, H. M. Turner, and J. W. Hood; Reverends H. R. Revell, J. B. Reeves, T. W. Henderson, and Henry Highland Garnett; Professors R. T. Greener, F. L. Cardoza, John M. Langston, J. M. Gregory, W. H. Crogman, and William S. Scarborough, the latter being well known as a Greek scholar; and William H. Jones, James A. Bowley, John Shackelford, and P. B. S. Pinchback.

Naturally, this class was not large in numbers, but it was important and forceful, and a great inspiration to the colored people in their entrance upon the new life of liberty. Some of these, and many other colored men whose chief qualification was "mother wit," became leaders in religious and political affairs among the colored people. Robert Brown Elliot and Joseph H. Rainey, as members of Congress from South Carolina, and Major Martin R. Delaney of the Black Regiment, are among the most conspicuous colored men of this period.

The graded schools and universities established were numerous and strategetically distributed. It is to these workers and to these schools, and to the workers and to the schools that followed, that may be attributed the regeneration of the colored race which has been wrought. As a result of this impetus the colored man can make this showing in a single generation :

Educationally, his illiteracy has been cut down forty-seven per cent, although there are nearly three times as many colored people to-day as were emancipated. He fills the common schools with 1,200,000 of his children ; 30,000 are in schools for higher learning, and trade schools ; over 200 are pursuing studies in Northern universities, or taking special courses in European institutions.

There are about 2,000 negro graduates from colleges ; more than 400 of these have graduated from white colleges in the North or from institutions in Europe. Among the Northern colleges and universities that have sent out colored graduates are : Harvard, Yale, Michigan, Oberlin, Dartmouth, Columbia, Brown, Kansas, Stanford, Iowa College, Ohio, Illinois, Bates, Williams, Indiana, Boston, Middlebury College, Minnesota, Wellesley, Smith, Bowdoin, Denver, Amherst, Beloit, New York University, Northwestern, Nebraska, Olivet, Vassar, Radcliffe, Adelbert, Colby, Rutgers, Chicago, and the Catholic University ; there are besides a score of others.

A number of negro students have won honors in Northern colleges, as for instance R. T. Greener, W. M. Trotter, R. C. Bruce, at Harvard, Marshall at Michigan, Pickens at Yale ; and there are others that might be mentioned.

It may be noted that 278 colored women are among the graduates of colleges ; many of them from colleges at the North. American negroes have graduated from French, German, and English institutions and some have prosecuted successfully studies in Rome.

The following leading theological seminaries of the North have sent out colored graduates : Andover, Princeton, Oberlin, General Theological Seminary, Yale, Newton, Drew, Episcopal

Theological School of Cambridge, Union, Hartford, Boston, and others. In all about two hundred colored men have graduated from Northern theological seminaries.

The *Central Christian Advocate*, one of the organs of the Methodist Episcopal Church, pertinently remarks : " What kind of negroes does America want? The negro is here. Nothing can uproot him from our soil. He is multiplying rapidly. He is millions strong. He is walking about amid our institutions, our rights, our constitutional guarantees. What kind of a negro does America want? That is a question that a generation hence will make the republic pause.

" No country is safe where vast masses of its citizens are forced down under the proper exercise of their capacities. That is but damming the flood that presses heavier on what is, with each new repression and scorn.

" The long and the short of it is : The negro is capable of being a man, and therefore he has a right to a man's chance. Professor Shaler of Harvard says : 'The negro has mastered the English in a very remarkable manner. There are tens of thousands of untrained blacks in this country who, by their command of English phrase, are entitled to rank as educated men. I believe, in general, that our negroes have a better sense of English than the peasant class of Great Britain.'"

Secretary Thirkield, in his address at the annual meeting at Lincoln, Nebraska, said further : " The capacity of the negro for genuine scholarship has never been more strongly stated than by the Reverend J. E. Edwards, D.D., of the Methodist Episcopal Church, South, in the *Methodist Review* for April, 1882 : ' In many instances it must be admitted — and examples are in this city (Petersburg, Virginia)— that not only do they make as rapid advances as the whites, but really acquire thorough scholarship in the different departments of learning and carry off medals for proficiency in mathematics and in the languages that would be creditable to any one of any race or color. It is idle, and only shows the inveteracy of our prejudice, to shut our eyes to the fact that the negroes of the coming generation are just as capable of scholarship and culture as the whites.'

"There is but one way to measure a man — and that is by his capacity. We did not do that when we kept the negro in slavery. Let us beware failing to do it now, lest the God whose thunderbolts are hot bring the republic once more to a judgment day."

The colored man and woman quickly learned to put their education into service ; it was not allowed to become a drug on the market : about thirty thousand of them are now teachers in the public and other schools, and hundreds are filling professorships in institutions devoted more especially to the higher education of their race. They have organized and have complete control over a number of colleges, academies, and industrial schools conducted by the several denominations, as well as some independent schools. They are the patrons of fifty high schools, five law schools, five medical schools, and twenty-five theological schools devoted to the education of the race.

About two thousand negroes are now engaged in the practice of law ; perhaps fifteen hundred are in the medical profession, in which some have become specialists along various lines; some have built and are conducting hospitals, as Doctors Williams in Chicago, Boyd in Nashville, McClennan in Charleston, Mossel in Philadelphia, Purvis in Washington, and others in other cities. There are several hundred dentists and pharmacists. They have written and published four hundred books ; they own and publish three hundred newspapers, and twelve magazines, some illustrated, and others devoted to higher literature and criticism.

In the public service, individual distinctions have been numerous. Two negroes have been members of the United States Senate, Revells and Bruce ; and in the House of Representatives these have seen service: Elliot, De Large, Cain, Haralson, Lynch, Nash, Rainey, Ransier, Wells, Rapier, Smalls, Turner, Ling, Lee, Cheatham, Murray, and White — and not one of these violated the decorum of his environments by fisticuffs, or brought other scandal on himself or his race. There have been in the diplomatic service of the United States, in foreign countries: Bassett, Langston, Douglass, Greener, Van Horne, Garnet, Smyth, Astwood, Turner, Powell, Grimke, and Lyons. Negroes have filled the offices of Register of the Treasury of the United States and Recorder of Deeds of the District of Columbia; Terrell and Hewlett are now exercising judicial functions in the city of Washington. A number have served as postmasters; a few as collectors of ports — as Dancy, Smalls, and Crum.

Negroes have been employed in the United States secret service and in other important positions. W. H. Lewis is now assistant district attorney of the United States Court at Boston, Massachusetts. One of the complaints of the reactionists is that the people of the North are forcing negro office-holders on the white people of the South, but do not sanction the election or appointment of negroes to office in the North. In discussing this matter the Atlanta *Constitution* has repeatedly referred to the Northerners who hold that all things being equal the negro has the same right to hold office as the white man, as "Yankee long-range philanthropists." This complaint is entirely without foundation. The liberty, the civil and political rights of the colored man, so far as impartial laws can make them secure, are absolutely assured in the North. Under them the colored man is working out his destiny. Besides, the people of the North have encouraged every effort he has made to free himself from the blighting evils of slavery and rise to the stature of a man.

Colored men have been repeatedly elected or appointed to offices in the North by the white people. D. A. Straker was elected and re-elected to a judicial office in Detroit, Michigan; Ruffin was appointed a judge at Boston, Massachusetts; Mathews was elected a judge at Albany, New York; Carr is an assistant in the district attorney's office of New York City; a colored lawyer fills a similar position in the city of Chicago; the city of Cleveland, Ohio, has elected Green and Smith, colored men, to the state Senate and the House of Representatives respectively; Chicago has elected Morris to the legislature of Illinois; Detroit elected Pelham and others; Boston has repeatedly elected colored men to the legislature: Reed, Teamoh, and others; and colored men are enrolled in her city council; a colored man was chosen a member of the governor's council in Massachusetts; Philadelphia has elected colored men to her city council, and hundreds have been appointed on her police force and to various lines of service in the city government. Rhode Island has repeatedly elected colored men to her legislature, and Pennsylvania in the last national election chose a colored man, J. W. Holmes, as a presidential elector.

The Boston *Herald*, referring to the colored men who have held positions in Cambridge, Massachusetts, says: "The list includes an alderman, two representatives in the legislature, seven members of the common council, a chief of the fire department, where he was the only man of African blood, a policeman in the service for nineteen years, a municipal bacteriologist, a commander of a white post of the Grand Army of the Republic, a trustee of the public library, and a woman almost purely African in blood as principal of a public school in a first-class residential district, with six white teachers as her subordinates and with several hundred white pupils. Besides, Harvard University has paid distinguished honors to not a few men of color who have studied there. Cambridge is a city which in its rank as a civilized community can certainly compare with any south of Mason and Dixon's line. And yet none of its citizens would ever dream that in thus honoring certain of their fellows with negro blood in their veins they would render themselves liable to have a negro ask the hand of their daughter in marriage — a contingency that proverbially is submitted for consideration as a poser when questions as to negro equality are asked in the South. The thing is that in Cambridge, as in many other intelligent and correspondingly unprejudiced communities, a man, whatever his race, is regarded according to his capacity as a human being, and not by the color of his skin, any more than by the color of his eyes or hair."

These are but a few of the instances of the election and appointment of colored men to office in the North; and they are alike complimentary to the colored man, as evidence of his rise in civilization, and to the broad, patriotic, and benevolent policy of the people of the North in dealing with him.

Practically in every Northern state from the Atlantic to the Pacific, and from the Mason-Dixon line to the Great Lakes, colored men have been and are enjoying political preferment with the sanction of the great body of the people.

The number of colored men and women who are in the employment of the Government of the United States in the departments at Washington, and other places, will probably be a surprise to many people. These colored men and women reached the positions held, not through political pull or favoritism, but by merit — generally through the civil service examinations.

The table on page 277, compiled from official data, shows the number of colored employees in the service of the Government, exclusive of the United States Capitol and the judiciary.

In the activities of church life the colored man has probably scored his greatest success. As a minister he was unhampered by race prejudice; his work was among his own people. To this work he gave himself with an earnestness and a spirit of self-sacrifice difficult to surpass. He freely offered to God and his people the service of the best talents he

ACHIEVEMENTS OF THE COLORED RACE

COLORED OFFICERS, CLERKS, AND OTHER EMPLOYEES IN THE SERVICE
OF THE UNITED STATES GOVERNMENT, 1904.

	No.	Salaries
Diplomatic and consular service	13	$32,000
Department service :		
State	10	7,600
Treasury	596	391,834
War	122	94,910
Navy	42	29,736
Post-Office	103	66,840
Interior	219	167,260
Justice	17	13,520
Agriculture	100	53,272
Commerce and labor	125	78,856
Government Printing Office	320	210,874
Interstate Commerce Commission	4	2,280
District government, Washington, D. C.	1,891	847,055
Recorder of deeds	22	14,050
Service at large :		
Customs and internal revenue	258	205,047
Post-Office at large	750	611,140
Land Office, New Orleans	3	7,800
Miscellaneous	5	2,400
Army Officers	10	17,260
Total	4,610	$2,853,734
Recapitulation by localities :		
At foreign stations	13	$32,000
At Washington, D. C.	3,663	2,056,727
At New York City	188	153,982
At New Orleans, Louisiana	108	96,740
At Atlanta, Georgia	94	65,780
At Savannah, Georgia	42	32,766
At Augusta, Georgia	12	8,120
At Baltimore, Maryland	40	31,444
At Richmond, Virginia	50	37,820
At miscellaneous points	390	321,095
Army Officers	10	17,260
Total	4,610	$2,853,734

possessed. He was, and in many cases is at the present time,
deficient in book learning, but there are essential qualities of

mind and heart which he did possess and knew how to use to the glory of God and well-being of his fellow-men. Above all else, the colored minister has demonstrated the ability of the negro to organize great masses of the people into solid, compact bodies, hold them under discipline, enforce laws in the spirit of love, and make millions subservient to the teachings of the Christ.

In the religious denominations, the colored man has demonstrated his capacity for self-government. Take, for instance, the African Methodist Episcopal Church. It has 6,429 ministers, 5,715 churches, 728,354 communicants, and property valued at nearly $12,000,000; it conducts 25 schools, the property value of which is $855,000; it publishes two weekly papers and a monthly magazine; it has a publishing house for its Sunday School literature at Nashville, Tennessee, and a publishing house at Philadelphia for books and periodicals; it has over 2,000 missions and about 15,000 members in Africa, and, in addition, it has missions in Canada, Hayti, and Bermuda, and also conducts schools in Sierra Leone, Monrovia, and Cape Town, Africa, and in Bermuda and Hayti. To operate this vast machinery over $500,000 is now collected and expended annually. It has twelve bishops and thirteen general officers; one of the bishops is assigned to Africa to watch over the work on that continent.

Another denomination, the African Methodist Episcopal Zion, close in name and closer in sympathy and work to the African Methodist Episcopal Church, operates along similar lines. It has 3,810 ministers, 2,985 churches, and 542,422 members; it has all the machinery of its sister body, and its Christian Endeavor work is especially prosperous — having over 600 societies with more than 30,000 members. It has seven bishops, a full complement of general offices, publishing plants, and twelve colleges and schools, with Livingstone College, Salisbury, North Carolina, founded by the eloquent J. C. Price, at the head of its educational system. There are several other colored Methodist bodies working along these same general lines.

The colored Baptists are numerically the strongest denomination among the colored people, having 10,726 ministers, 15,583 churches, and 1,615,321 communicants. It carries on important missionary work in Africa, and has a large printing and publishing plant at Nashville. And a unique fact is that about forty-five newspapers in various cities are published in the name of this denomination. It conducts a number of schools. Not only in those just mentioned but practically in all the denominations, the colored man has found a home congenial to himself for the worship of God.

Dr. H. K. Carroll reports the following membership of negro church bodies in the United States, not including foreign mission membership, for the year 1903:

Denominations	Ministers	Churches	Communicants
Baptists	10,729	15,614	1,625,330
Union American Methodists . . .	180	205	16,500
African Methodists	6,500	5,800	785,000
African Union Methodist Protestants	68	68	2,930
African Zion Methodists	3,386	3,042	551,591
Congregational Methodists	5	5	319
Colored Methodists	2,159	1,497	207,723
Cumberland Presbyterians	450	400	39,000
Total	23,477	26,631	3,228,393

A number of colored people are connected with separate churches which are not independent denominations, but are in fellowship with white denominations, and these may be recorded as shown in the table, page 280.

These figures vary so slightly from those of another authority as to be practically the same. It is a matter of great significance that colored men should be operating great organizations, co-extensive with the jurisdiction of the republic

Denominations	Ministers	Churches	Membership
Methodists (Methodist Episcopal) .	. . .	. . .	245,954
Congregationalists	139	230	12,155
Episcopalians	85	200	15,000
Presbyterians	209	353	21,341

and reaching beyond into foreign countries, touching in the most direct way the hearts, interests, and welfare of millions of people. This work goes on year after year so smoothly that even many who are influenced by it scarcely realize its proportions. These colored denominations own $41,000,000 in church property. A large percentage of the college-bred colored men are in the colored ministry. Many thousands of the colored ministers have had high, normal, or preparatory school training, and several thousands have had thorough theological training. There are colored physicians with incomes of $5,000 a year and upwards, and colored lawyers who earn equally large sums.

The colored race has successfully applied its education in all the vocations of life; in business enterprises in various lines: life insurance; building associations; organized charities; slum, prison, and temperance work; kindergartens, and mother's meetings; hospitals, nurseries, orphanages, and homes; benevolent club work; farming and truck-gardens; savings-banks; contributing to newspapers; contributing to magazines; lectures; papers before various bodies; college and student aid; fraternal societies and orders; theatricals; athletics; stenography and typewriting; telegraph operating; instrumental and vocal music; inventions; the several trades; and on through the long list of human endeavor.

In some of these it has won world-wide fame. In the colored race there is probably more pathos and humor than in any other race, probably than in all other races combined.

The Irish is the only other race that approaches it. These two races furnish the humor that kills dull and heavy cares and makes the people laugh.

The colored Jubilee singers have made their impress on the civilized world. People of every degree have been swayed and moved by them. In minstrelsy, Billy Kersands, Sam Lucas, Tom McIntosh, and others, will not be soon forgotten. Several regular theatrical companies have delighted audiences in this country and in Europe. "The South before the War," "In old Kentucky," "The Smart Set," and the superb company, "Williams and Walker," and other combinations have ministered to the public with satisfaction and profit. In these lines the negro has been frequently imitated, but not always with success.

In athletics, Harte, of Boston, won the championship as a pedestrian ; Taylor, "the whirlwind" bicycle rider, broke and made records and won fame in America, Europe, and Australia ; and in the "manly sport," Peter Jackson and George Dixon held the championship for years against all comers.

About five hundred patents have been taken out by colored men. A negro patented the first machine for pegging shoes. Elijah McCoy has taken out twenty-seven patents, mostly for lubricating ; Granville T. Woods, twenty-two, mostly electrical ; W. R. Purvis, sixteen ; Frank J. Farrell, ten. The patents taken out by negroes cover appliances in domestic and personal service, agriculture, transportation, manufacturing, and mining, and other lines of inventions.

In the fraternal and beneficial organizations the negro has gained great triumphs. The order of True Reformers is probably the leading fraternal organization. It was organized in 1881 by William H. Browne, and chartered in 1883 under the laws of Virginia, with headquarters at Richmond. It started with 100 members, and without capital. It now numbers 72,000 members ; conducts a savings-bank with a capital stock, paid up, of $100,000 ; has $300,000 on deposit; 10,000 depositors; conducts five stores in as many cities, and which do a business of $100,000 a year; it operates two hotels; it owns $400,000 worth of real estate; it employs over 800 negroes, and the total business transacted aggregates $8,000,000. In its beneficiary department, it has paid out in death claims $902,092.75; in sick benefits, it has paid out a million dollars. It publishes its own newspaper and its membership is represented in twenty-six states. Hundreds of thousands of colored people are also in other orders, including the Masons, Odd Fellows, Knights of Pythias, Foresters, Elks, Good Templars, and other societies intended to care for the sick and bury the dead.

But it is as artisans and as tillers of the soil that the negroes meet with their greatest success. The colored man has put his brain and his brawn into the trades and into farming and domestic occupations.

The largely increased crops produced by negro laborers — the cotton crop alone has been doubled since emancipation — attest their increased efficiency and industry. The millions of Afro-Americans engaged in agriculture, mining, manufacturing industries, mechanical vocations and trades, fishing, commerce, and transportation, and in domestic service and in other lines make themselves felt in the life of the nation. Mr. Henry W. Grady of Atlanta, just before his death about ten years ago, in a speech in Boston, declared that the negro through his labor contributed a billion dollars a year to the wealth of the nation. He is contributing more than that amount at the present time.

Mr. Morrell of Pennsylvania, in a speech in Congress, says: "In forty years the number of farms operated by white farmers increased 371,414, and of that number 148,601, or 40 per cent, were those of owners or managers, and 222,813, or 60 per cent, those of tenants. In the period which witnessed this addition of white farmers in the South Atlantic states 287,933 negroes had acquired control of farm land in those states, of whom 202,578, or 70.4 per cent, were tenants, and 85,355, or 29.6 per cent, were owners or managers.

"In considering these comparative figures, account should be taken of the following facts : The negroes at the close of the Civil War were just starting out upon their career as wage-earners. They had no land and no experience as farm owners or tenants, and none of them became farm owners by inheritance nor inherited money with which to buy land. Of the 371,414 white farmers added since 1860, very many were the children of landowners and came into the possession of farm land, or the wherewithal to purchase the same, by inheritance. When this difference in the industrial condition of the two races in 1860 is taken into account, the fact that the relative number of owners among the negro farmers in the South Atlantic states in 1900 was practically three-fourths as great as the relative number of owners among the white farmers of those states added in the same period marks a most noteworthy achievement.

"The statistics for the South Central states show about the same proportions.

" As already stated, the total number of farms in the United States operated by negroes in 1900 was 746,717. The value of these farms, including buildings, tools, machinery, and live stock, was $499,943,734. The value of the products of these farms, inclusive of products fed to live stock on the premises, was $255,751,145, and exclusive of products fed to live stock, $229,907,702. The value of the negro farms was about 2½ per cent of the total valuation of the farm property of the United States, while the value of the products of the negro farms was about 6 per cent of the total value of the farm products of the United States.

" Turning to the Southern states again, we find that the corresponding proportions are greatly increased. In round numbers the values of all the farm property in those states, and of the negro farm property, were in 1900 as follows : —

States	Total farm values	Negro farm values
Virginia	$323,000,000	$25,000,000
North Carolina	234,000,000	28,000,000
South Carolina	153,000,000	44,000,000
Georgia	228,000,000	49,000,000
Florida	54,000,000	6,000,000
Alabama	179,000,000	47,000,000
Mississippi	204,000,000	86,000,000
Louisiana	198,000,000	38,000,000
Texas	962,000,000	56,000,000
Arkansas	181,000,000	34,000,000
Total	$2,716,000,000	$413,000,000

" In other words, the value of the negro farm property in these ten states is about 15 per cent of the total farm property in those states, and if Texas be eliminated, a state which is in much of its area not closely affiliated with the South, and in which the negroes have comparatively small interests, the proportion would be over 20 per cent.

" The figures in regard to the relative values of farm products at the South are still more striking: —

States	Total farm products	Negro farm products
Virginia	$73,000,000	$8,000,000
North Carolina	79,000,000	13,000,000
South Carolina	62,000,000	25,000,000
Georgia	92,000,000	27,000,000
Florida	16,000,000	3,000,000
Alabama	81,000,000	27,000,000
Mississippi	91,000,000	47,000,000
Louisiana	66,000,000	19,000,000
Texas	209,000,000	21,000,000
Arkansas	66,000,000	16,000,000
Total	$835,000,000	$206,000,000

" Here the proportion of the products of negro farms, as compared with the total farm products of the ten states, is seen to be nearly 25 per cent, or, taking out Texas, nearly 30 per cent.

" In all parts of the country except the far West the percentage of improved lands on farms operated by negroes is greater than those of white farmers. In the South Central states the farms of negroes had 68.3 per cent, while the whites had but 28 per cent. The total acreage of negro farms is about 40,000,000 acres."

The New York *World*, speaking of the achievements of the colored man since his emancipation, says : " He owns 137,000 farms and homes worth $725,000,000 ; he has personal property to the value of $165,000,000 ; and he has raised $10,000,000 for his own education ; his *per capita* possessions amount to $72.50. To propose that the nation shall step backward in the face of such a stepping forward, is a curious way to argue the superiority of the dominant white man."

This is a practical age, and in such an age, it is the results that count. The achievements briefly outlined above are the direct results of the system of education which was planned and executed by the pioneers who laid the foundation for the rise of a race. They were men and women of mature thought, ripe experience, broad-gauged intellect, great faith in God and in the colored man as responsive to the same influences as other men ; and their mental vision swept the whole field of life rather than one phase of it. They acted on the advice of Colonel Higginson forty years before he phrased it, to wit : " What the whole nation needs is to deal with the negro race no longer as outcasts, but simply as men and women." The Afro-American must not permit himself to be " specialized." Frederick Douglass was accustomed to say : " It is vastly better for the race to be a part of the whole American people, in the same sense as other races, than to be a little whole unto itself." The splendid record which has been made would have been absolutely impossible if emphasis had been put on industrial education and the race had been treated as a special order of humanity.

The leaders of the South ofttimes make the claim that the white people are taxing themselves to educate the negroes, and that they have spent on negro education over a hundred million dollars since the emancipation. This is not a fair statement; it is not the truth; it is a myth. While the bulk of the taxes in the South is paid by the white people, it is also true that the productivity of the labor of the colored race on farm and field, in the rice swamps and wooded lands, in mines, factories, and workshops, and in all the diversified forms of toil, constitutes an important element in those taxes. The New York *World* is authority for the statement that 19,000 persons own the property of that city. Suppose these 19,000 people should claim that they were taxing themselves to educate the children of that city. The reply would be quickly made that labor pays the taxes.

There are towns and cities in New England where one family or a few families own the industries which give prosperity to the communities. If the members of such family or families should proclaim that they are taxing themselves to educate the children of the thousands of working people — the answer would be given that labor pays the taxes.

In the South the masses of colored people are laborers; and the colored man's labor in the South pays the taxes for the education of his children, exactly in the same sense that a white man's labor in the North pays the taxes for the education of his children. It may also be borne in mind that the colored man contributes more than a billion dollars a year, by his labor, to the wealth of the nation. So that he contributes in a single year, ten times as much to the common weal as the South has expended on his education in forty years. Besides, much of the accumulated wealth of the South represents the two hundred and fifty years of the unrequited toil of the negro. In all fairness it can be said that the colored man by direct and indirect taxes and by the productivity of his toil is carrying his share of the burden in educating his children. For generations his labor educated the masters.

In the evolution of the home life the colored man has accomplished notable triumphs.

The chief curse of slavery was the obliteration of the home. As the home is the foundation of the social organism, the colored people had to unlearn many things which the master class had taught by precept and example for two and a half centuries, before it was possible to begin aright the development of the home life.

Under the old régime the country life was darker intellectually, morally, and spiritually than the city life, and the closer contact of city life had its leavening influence.

Barriers apparently unsurmountable have been overcome. The newly awakened desire for homes became a strenuous passion, which has led to the secure establishment of the family life on the legal and scriptural foundations.

While the colored man has been the master of his own home for only forty years, yet in this brief period he has bridged the chasm which divided him from his wife and separated him from his children — has unlearned the lessons taught day by day in the years of his bondage — has met with heartiness all the responsibilities involved in the family life, and now reaps and realizes to the full its joys, fruitage, and blessedness.

No others among the cosmopolitan population of the republic make greater sacrifices for the care and education of their children, or are more solicitous about their future, or take greater pride in their successes than these humble people.

The colored mother, almost too poor for her poverty to be understood, yet with a mother's love and anxiety for her children will waste herself away in the kitchen or over the wash-tub that her offspring may have the advantages of the schools. Unmindful of herself, the pittance she earns goes almost wholly to assist her children through college and into the professions.

The illiterate father lengthens his hours of toil on the plantation and practises economy and self-denial in many directions in order that his promising sons and daughters may receive an education and enter upon a life of broad usefulness.

To this true appreciation of the home and the recognition of its obligations may be ascribed not only much of the prosperity, progress, and happiness which freedom has brought to the colored race, but it is also the rock on which the race must build to insure its salvation and a glorious future.

The negro race is struggling upward. It should have the kind, the sympathetic hand. It has surpassed the expectations of its friends; and it has put to confusion its enemies who have taken their last stand on the ground of color alone. The rise and achievements of the race in American life and civilization overthrow all their preconceived ideas. But color cannot be a perpetual barrier in a republic. Manhood, patriotism, thrift, and the nobler qualities of mind and heart are superior to color and will break down such a barrier.

The colored people need only to continue to develop along all lines and stand firmly for liberty; be faithful to the Church, patronize the school, support the colored press, encourage professional men, cultivate the home life, practise thrift and economy, be helpful to each other in all the lines of endeavor, honor those North and South who champion the cause of freedom, and love the flag of their country, and these shall be unto them the forces of the Lord of Hosts which shall overturn the oppressor and redeem a people.

It is noteworthy that no dangerous or un-American tendency has developed among the negroes. They are Americans of Americans, and national to the core.

ACHIEVEMENTS OF THE COLORED RACE

The late Reverend Dr. J. E. Rankin, for many years President of Howard University in the city of Washington, a man as strong and inflexible in character as the granite hills of his New England home, and whose presence was the balm of light and sweetness, and who has accomplished a grand and noble work to the uplift of humanity and the glory of God, wrote these beautiful lines:—

> "I know no difference of race,
>   Of African or Saxon,
> Of tawny skin, or rose-cheek face,
>   Of hair of crisp, or flaxen.
> The soul within, that is the man,
>   There is God's image hidden,
> And there He looks each guest to scan,
>   The bidden, and unbidden.

> "One God in love broods over all,
>   One prayer to Him is taught us,
> One name for mercy when we call,
>   One ransom Christ has brought us;
> One heart of meekness, lowly mind,
>   Life's counter-currents breasting,
> One Father's house, we hope to find,
>   In God's own bosom resting."

M. Taine, in his "History of English Literature," Chapter I, gives a description of a certain people who may not now be readily recognized. It is as follows: "Huge, white bodies, with fierce, blue eyes, ravenous stomachs, of a cold temperament, slow to love, home stayers, prone to brutal drunkenness; pirates at first, sea-faring, war, and pillage their only idea of a freeman's work. Of all barbarians the most cruelly ferocious. Torture and carnage, greed of danger, fury of destruction, obstinate and frenzied, bravery of an over-strung temperament, with a great and coarse appetite. To shout, to drink, to gesticulate, to feel their veins heated and swollen with wine, to hear and see around them the riotous orgies, this was the first need of the Barbarians.

"They left the land and flocks to the women. They sold as slaves their nearest relatives, and even their own children. The Latin race never at first glance see in them aught but large gross beasts, clumsy and ridiculous when not dangerous and enraged."

To what people does M. Taine refer? This language describes in one stage of their evolution the proud and powerful Anglo-Saxon race, who are to-day the leaders and light-bearers in the world's thought and civilization. In the blaze of this bit of history, there is no ground for despair of the American negro.

Christian education wrought the change in the Anglo-Saxon. It will in any people. Let the adherents of the Christian faith and the advocates of the commonalty of man push the work of Christian education, and every step of its advancement will strengthen the foundations of the republic, promote the peace of society and the purity of the Church, and multiply and realize the grand possibilities of Afro-American citizens. And they and the whole nation may sing, with a new meaning and power, Julia Ward Howe's Battle Hymn of the Republic: —

" Mine eyes have seen the glory of the coming of the Lord ;
He is trampling out the vintage where the grapes of wrath are stored ;
He has loosed the fateful lightning of his terrible, swift sword ;
His day is marching on.
Glory, Glory, Hallelujah.

" He has sounded forth a trumpet that shall never call retreat ;
He is sifting out the hearts of men before his judgment seat ;
Oh ! be swift my soul to answer him, be jubilant my feet ;
His truth is marching on.
Glory, Glory, Hallelujah.

" In the beauty of the lilies, Christ was born across the sea,
With a glory in his bosom that transfigures you and me ;
As he died to make men holy let us die to make men free ;
His word is marching on.
Glory, Glory, Hallelujah."

CHAPTER IX

THE NATIONAL DUTY TO THE NEGRO

THIS work would be regarded as incomplete if it did not at least venture to point out a way to some practical and substantial relief, and thus help to pave the path for the amelioration and ultimate obliteration of intolerable conditions. That something can be done, that something ought to be done, is the verdict of every patriotic citizen. The unwisdom of permitting matters to drift along until a dangerously acute state of affairs shall exist in the South, breeding serious trouble, must be patent to all.

The Springfield (Massachusetts) *Republican*, the Chicago *Tribune*, and the New York *Evening Post*, three of the most important and conservative journals in the country, have repeatedly called the people's attention to the painfully anomalous and threatening conditions in the South. Other journals and leading citizens have sounded the alarm. The nation remains amazingly apathetic, seemingly believing that somehow in the order of Providence these evils will " pass away."

It was so with regard to slavery. But deep-seated evils do not cure themselves, and seldom die of their own corruption.

Is it either common-sense or prudent patriotism to drift on until a settled condition, in essential respects worse than slavery, disastrous and volcanic in its possibilities — shall be established in the South ? Is it not far better to face these evils and eliminate them ? The manhood, the womanhood, the statesmanship, the all-pervading principles of Christianity of the mighty republic are entirely competent to bring this question to an equitable and righteous settlement. No other settlement will be enduring. Compromise may postpone, but it cannot settle fundamental questions of liberty and human rights.

> "Truth crushed to earth shall rise again :
> Th' eternal years of God are hers."

The journals above mentioned have shown that the colored people are becoming restless under long continued persecutions, ostracisms, and outrages. Here and there they are beginning to take a stand under pressure. They have been wonderfully blessed with conservative and Christian leaders, who have succeeded in restraining all attempts at retaliation. "Have faith in God : trust the American people : continue to develop along all lines : all things are sure to come right" — this is the teaching of the colored leadership.

No people have ever displayed greater forbearance and long-suffering than the free men of color. Colonel Higginson, in an interesting magazine article, has taken great pains to show that the colored man is "intensely human" in all things and at every point. And here lies the danger, for there is a limit to human endurance.

The dominant elements in the South make a fatal error in assuming that they alone must have the final word on the question — utterly ignoring the colored man whose interests are coequal with their own, and contemptuously disregarding the nation whose interests, of necessity, are paramount.

If the final word were in harmony with the Constitution and laws of the United States there would indeed be no problem. But when the final word contravenes or supersedes the Constitution and laws of the United States, neither the colored people nor the nation can or will accept its finality. The lesson of history should impress itself here : slavery was forced on the nation by a radical and minor element determined on building up a peculiar institution, and which finally dragged the whole South into its support.

The War of the Rebellion was made on the life of the republic by a radical and minor element determined on perpetuating this peculiar institution, and which dragooned the whole South into it.

The peace of the nation is now blasted by a radical and minor element determined on the destruction of the liberty of the colored citizen and the building up of a new peculiar institution ; and which has by incendiary speeches and writings and by the machinations of secret conclaves, working more stealthily than the Ku Klux Klans, united the white people of the South against liberty and human progress, without regard for the majesty of the law.

The Honorable Josiah Quincy, referring to the early days of slavery, said : " Disgust at it was so general as to be little less than universal. Among slaveholders, the language and hope of putting an end to the evil as soon as possible was on all tongues ; but alas! it was far from being in all their hearts. Some of the leaders saw the advantages derived from it by the unity and identity of action and motive to which it tended, and its effect in making Slave states move in phalanx over the Free states. They clung to the institution for the sake of power over the other states of the Union, and while they were open in decrying it, they were assiduous in promoting its interests and extending its influence. By constantly declaring a detestation of slavery, they threw dust into the eyes of the people of the Free states, while they never ceased to seize every opportunity to embarrass the measures which would advance the interests of the Free states, and at the same time to strengthen and extend the interests of the Slave states. We can trace their policy in history. We now realize the result. With all their pretensions, the leading slaveholders never lost sight for one moment of perpetuating its existence and power."

There may be discerned a sameness in the methods of the *ante-bellum* and the *post-bellum* leadership of the South.

"Dust," much dust, is being thrown into the eyes of the people now by stock-phrases, dire threats, and bald subterfuges. In the " Solid South " now there is the same "unity and identity of action and motive," and its power in the government is unduly magnified. Equal laws for all is the antidote. In the light of history it is clear that a majority of the American people did not at any time, from the beginning up to the present time, approve or justify the institution of human slavery. Yet it grew and flourished and all but brought death and destruction to the republic.

The vast majority of the American people are now uncompromising in their opposition to a new and peculiar institution. The fierce fires of war consumed the dross in the Constitution, and that grand instrument as it stands, and the laws made in connection therewith, leave no room for doubt that the people demand a truly free republic with equal rights for all Americans.

This simplifies the question and indicates the remedy.

First : The people should zealously and jealously guard the offices of president and vice-president, and preserve them from defilement and desecration by any persons tinctured with caste or sectional prejudices, and who would exalt these above the Constitution and laws of the land.

It is axiomatic that no citizen is worthy to be the president of the whole people who does not stand for equal laws for the whole people. The Constitution and laws of the United States are the paramount plank of any platform on which a president may be elected : these make all citizens equal before the law, and positively and absolutely forbid all discrimination on account of race, color, or previous condition of servitude. Race or color should be neither a credential to public favor or participation in the government, nor a bar against the full enjoyment of any immunity or privilege under the government.

The people should see to it that only such men as measure

up to the constitutional standard shall be elevated to the presidential office, or to the vice-presidency.

In guarding these offices, they will also be guarding the various cabinet chairs, and thus the administration of the government will be uninfluenced by the brutalism of the traditions of slavery, or the "Jim Crowism" which at present rules the South.

It is a travesty on free institutions, a jeer and sneer at a righteous national sentiment which demands equality of rights for all under the law, that the very men who are foremost in working for the wholesale disfranchisement of the colored people contrary to justice, reason, and the Constitution, and subjecting these people, who are equal citizens with themselves, to gross humiliations and degradations, and inflicting on them many inhumanities — that these men are now contending that one of their own number shall be placed in the presidential or vice-presidential chair. Is this not a mockery on civilization, — a burlesque on republican government?

At the Virginia State Convention to elect delegates to the National Democratic Convention, Governor Montague in an address advocated the nomination of a Southern man on the ticket, and at the very same time President Roosevelt was roundly denounced because "he eateth with negroes and drinketh with them."

Mississippi, at her state convention, nominated the Honorable John Sharp Williams for vice-president, and yet this Southerner, in a recent speech in the Congress, vociferously declaimed against the recognition of the political and manhood status of the colored man. Yoking the negro to a mule is his loftiest idea of Americanism and humanitarianism. Such a man the leader in a republic!

It may interest the country to know that Mr. Williams was elected by a *total* vote of 1,433, scarcely enough votes to elect a constable in a Northern township. This shows the farcical character of a Mississippi election. Think of it: 1,433 votes elect a member of the Congress from Mississippi when the population basis is nearly 200,000.

Other Southern states are also urging favorite sons for these highest offices, without a sign of compunction of conscience at the general nullification of the organic law and the shameful injustices and persecutions forced on ten millions of American citizens.

These men have already wrought the general ostracism of the colored race throughout the South, and by imposing on them systematic humiliations and degradations they seek to take heart and hope out of the race and bring about its utter demoralization, and then plead these very conditions which they designedly created as the justification for harsher and more oppressive laws. The possession of the office of president or of vice-president would greatly stimulate them in putting the final touches on the heinous work, for it would be construed as an endorsement by the *people*.

The Atlanta *Constitution*, a leading Southern journal, with a snarl demands that the South be represented in one of these offices. General Montague of Virginia cynically inquires: " Is this not a reunited nation? "

The following statement from the Boston *Herald* would seem to cover the issue: " The people of the Northern states do not carry their willingness to forgive and forget to the extent of ignoring the attitude of a representative Southern man toward questions of personal rights and public duty that are living questions.

" For example, the people of the North, as a rule, believe in the supremacy of the laws of the land and of the orderly processes of the courts of justice in dealing with violators of the law. They are not upholders of mob government and lynch law, and they will be likely to distrust the influence in the highest office of administration of one who has a record of approval, or of tolerance, of lynch law in his own state.

They would object to a man of that kind from any section of the country.

"But, in consideration of the notorious facts that this manner of lawlessness is more rife in the Southern states than anywhere else, that it is sustained, apparently, by a more powerful public sentiment, that vindictive murder by a mob is rarely followed by any punishment of the murderers, any Southern candidate for the chief magistracy of the nation would need to have an especially clear and conspicuous record of active fidelity to principles of orderly justice and Christian humanity in order to obtain the confidence of communities which have, and desire to continue having, assurance of the reign of law, according to the standards of civilization.'

"Again, the people of the North, as a rule, have a strong feeling that there should be equality of rights at the ballot-box. They do not object to a high standard of qualification, and especially not to an educational qualification, nor strenuously, if it be deemed necessary anywhere, to a property qualification. But they do not think it to be consistent with democratic principles that men who are otherwise qualified should be permanently debarred from exercise of this high function of citizenship, on account of race, or of accidents of birth or fortune, not necessarily involving moral turpitude nor inability to understand, exercise, and conform to the obligations and the duties of a good citizen. They believe in the equality of all men before the law, and they are afraid, not without reason, that politicians who will resort to such tricks and subterfuges as have been resorted to in several Southern states, to keep intelligent and moral colored citizens from the ballot-box, while allowing unintelligent and immoral white citizens to have the suffrage, are not to be trusted with implicit confidence to protect the rights of any citizens whose opinions may not be agreeable to them.

"Furthermore, there is a prejudice in the North, not so general and exacting as it ought to be, perhaps, that politicians should be trustworthy in the matter of keeping their formal pledges to the people. The people are disposed to hold their public men to a rather strict accountability in this respect. They do not relish being fooled by men who ask for power on a specific agreement that they will not exercise it in a certain way, and, when power is obtained, use it in precisely the way they assured the people they would not. The recent action of the Constitutional Convention of Virginia, in proclaiming a constitution without submitting it to the ratification of the people of the state, in violation of the conditions upon which a convention was authorized, is a case in point. Nothing has happened in the last ten years, hardly anything since Southern conventions chosen to oppose secession voted for it, more influential to make Northern people reluctant to trust Southern politicians. Men who will do such a thing as if it were honorable must not complain if their professions of public policy are regarded with suspicion. This is not because they are Southern men, but because of the exhibition of untrustworthiness they have given. Northern men doing a similar thing could not command Northern support as these Southern men seem to command Southern support.

"Considering the matter in another light, it is to be said that the people of the states where political opinion is free and where the public men of either party are, as a rule, mutually tolerant and regardful of the rights of all citizens, have a not unreasonable distrust of the narrowness of view and the partiality of conduct of a statesman hailing from a section where practically there is but one party, where generous toleration of differences of judgment concerning public affairs is not the characteristic of the people, a state controlled, as several Southern states are, by an oligarchy, instead of the sovereign people, a state which is not democratic in the generic sense of the term. It is not because these men belong to a geographical section, but because they are of a certain character and represent a type of statesmanship which does not stand broadly for the substantial ideals of American institutions — equal rights and equal opportunities, secured by impartial laws justly enforced."

When the South shall produce a man of broad and national instincts, a devotee at the shrine of liberty, a man whose character and public services shall give evidence that he is more an American than a Southerner, who is true to the letter and spirit of the Constitution and laws of this country, is not the slave of caste or race prejudice, upholds the principles of equal rights, regarding "no man above the law and none below it" — the American people will welcome the day as the harbinger of the era for which they have prayed and wrought, and no honor in their power would be too great or lofty for such a man.

Second : National aid for education is an imperative necessity.

Among the colored people general illiteracy was the chief heritage of slavery. Among the whites a heritage of dense ignorance existed in great areas. Statutes and penal codes prohibited the spelling-book to the colored people ; and the policy pursued to keep the negro's mind in darkness also had the effect of blackening the mental vision of the whites.

The strength of "Jim Crowism" lies largely in the illiteracy among both the white and the colored people of the South, powerfully sustained and influenced, of course, by the virus of slavery in the brain of the whites. This, in a word, is the true explanation of the distressing, disheartening, demoralizing conditions in the Southland.

Education will raise the veil of mental darkness, and chase away the clouds of ignorance, dispelling unreasonable antipathies, and ameliorating conditions generally.

It is not claimed here that education is the panacea or "cure-all" for every ill under the sun. But it is affirmed, without the least reservation or fear of contradiction, that

Christian education is the greatest force in God's universe for the regeneration and uplifting of the people and the harmonizing of a nation.

In former years the three " R's ", reading, 'riting and 'rithmetic, had the right of way in the education of the people; but in these later days these have given place to the three " H's ", the education of the *head*, the *hand* and the *heart*.

There is no risk in assuming that when this threefold, symmetrical education, the highest type of Christian civilization, shall have become as general throughout the benighted South as it is in the great, free and prosperous North — great and prosperous, because educated and free, — then truly the vile "Jim Crowism" and its attendant lawlessness will cease to disgrace the American name. This work of education in the Southland is even now advancing.

The people of the North, patrons and devotees of education, sent the spelling-book in the trail of their armies throughout their marches in the War of the Rebellion. And when a place was captured, almost before the smoke of battle had cleared away, the work of the schoolmaster was begun. Children, young people, middle-aged people, old men and old women were gathered into schools, both in the day-time and at night, and the foundation for the education of a race was laid. The barracks occupied by soldiers were, when vacated, turned over to the community to be used for schools. Out of such beginnings was developed the present school system of the South.

The Republican organizations which achieved the reconstruction of the South at the close of the war took the cue from this and gave the South its first system of free public schools. These schools have grappled with the problem and have been nobly reinforced by Northern benevolence. A vast work has been done, but a work as vast, probably more so, yet remains to be accomplished.

The financial power of the several states, ably seconded though it is by Northern benevolence, falls far short of meeting the emergency. Neither the several states nor the benevolence of the North seem to have the capacity to increase their working forces materially.

Supplemental aid from the national treasury is an absolute necessity, if the illiteracy which hangs over the South like a black pall is to be lifted, thereby eliminating the blighting and cankerous evils which are gnawing into the heart of the republic and are a constant irritation and an ever present disturber of the people's peace and prosperity.

The census of 1900 places the total number of white illiterates, above ten years of age, at 3,200,746. The total number of negro illiterates is given as 2,853,194. So that in the country at large there are more illiterate whites than negroes. It is therefore manifestly unjust to single out the negro and make him the target for denunciations and the object of oppression on the ground of illiteracy. The census also reveals the rather startling truth that while the Southern states have only twenty-four per cent of the total white population of the United States, yet they nevertheless have sixty-four per cent of the white illiterates over ten years of age. Naturally, the mass of colored illiterates are also in the South. The total negro school population — that is, from five to twenty years of age, aggregates 3,485,188. The school facilities of the South do not reach half of the negro children of school age; and a large percentage of the whites are also without school privileges. If the utter inadequacy of the length of the school term should be taken into consideration — a school term in many cases being from four to eight weeks in the year — it could be said that the large majority of the children of both races in the South are growing up practically in ignorance and will greatly reinforce the present large army of illiterates which mark the danger line in the life of the nation.

THE AFTERMATH OF SLAVERY

President Charles W. Dabney of the University of Tennessee, in an address before the Southern Educational Society, said: "Our duty to the new time in the South is the duty of educating all the people. It is the task set by Jefferson for Virginia in 1779, only changed and made more urgent by the extension of suffrage to another race. This is the real Southern problem : How shall we educate and train the people? It is the problem of the whole country, in fact. How shall we educate all the people for intelligent citizenship, for complete living, and the true service of their God and fellow-men?

"Our conception of public education has grown very greatly in these last years. It has grown in two ways : first, in content, and second, in kind. This conception now includes every human being ; we realize, now, that all must be educated — that every human being has a right to an education. God has a purpose in every soul He sends into the world. The poorest, most helpless infant is not an accident, a few molecules of matter, merely, but a plan of God, and as such deserves to be trained for its work. Every child has a right to a chance in life because God made him and made him to do something. . . .

"But we must consider our problem more nearly and in more detail. Our problem is the education of all the people of the South. First, Who are this people? In 1900 these states south of the Potomac and east of the Mississippi contained, in round numbers, 16,400,000 people, 10,400,000 of them white and 6,000,000 black. In these states there are 3,981,000 white and 2,420,000 colored children of school age (5 to 20 years), a total of 6,401,000. They are distributed among the states as follows. [See table on the next page.] Only 60 per cent of them were enrolled in schools in 1900. The average daily attendance was only 70 per cent of these enrolled. Only 42 per cent are actually at school. One half of the negroes get no education whatever. . . . In North

	White	Colored	Total
Virginia	436,000	269,000	705,000
West Virginia	342,000	15,000	357,000
North Carolina	491,000	263,000	754,000
South Carolina	218,000	342,000	560,000
Georgia	458,000	428,000	886,000
Florida	110,000	87,000	197,000
Alabama	390,000	340,000	730,000
Mississippi	253,000	380,000	633,000
Tennessee	590,000	191,000	781,000
Kentucky	693,000	105,000	798,000
Total	3,981,000	2,420,000	6,401,000

Carolina the average citizen gets only 2.6 years, in South
Carolina 2.5 years, in Alabama 2.4 years of schooling, both
private and public. . . .

" But why is it that the children get so little education?
Have we no schools in the country? Yes, but what kind of
schools? The average value of a school property in North
Carolina is $180, in South Carolina $178, in Georgia $523,
and in Alabama $212. The average salary of a teacher in
North Carolina is $23.36, in South Carolina $23.20, in
Georgia $27, and in Alabama $27.50. The schools are open
in North Carolina an average of 70.8 days, in South Carolina
88.4, in Georgia 112, and in Alabama 78.3. The average
expenditure per pupil in average attendance is, in North Carolina $4.34, in South Carolina $4.44, in Georgia $6.64, and in
Alabama $3.10 per annum. In other words, in these states,
in schoolhouses costing an average of $276 each, under teachers
receiving the average salary of $25 a month, we are giving the
children in actual attendance 5 cents worth of education a day
for 87 days only in the year. In 1900 the percentage of illiterates among males over 21 — native whites, mind you, the
sons of native parents — was, in Virginia 12.5, in North Carolina 19, in South Carolina 12.6, in Georgia 12.1, in Alabama
14.2, in Tennessee 14.5, and in Kentucky 15.5."

This exposition of the school facilities in the South, as discouraging as it is, does not expose the worst side of the question. The colored people are touched near to the heart, for the provisions for the education of the millions of colored children are woefully and alarmingly inadequate. Commissioner Harris of the Bureau of Education furnished the information that the state of Florida provides $1.89 *per capita* for a full year, for the education of colored children, North Carolina $1.02, and South Carolina only $.73. When it is considered that Massachusetts spends $38.11 *per capita* for the year on her school children, New York, $41.68, and Illinois, $25.16 — the contrast must leave a disturbing impression on the mind of every thoughtful citizen.

It is evident the South cannot handle this problem alone. More than half of its children of school age are practically without schools to attend. The nation should come to the rescue. A system of national schools under the Bureau of Education, especially in the agricultural districts, generously supported for about fifteen years, would efface illiteracy and remove the excuse for unrighteous laws. And this would add vastly more to the strength of the republic than more battleships and a larger army.

Horace Mann said: " Every follower of God and friend of mankind will find the only sure means of carrying forward the particular reform to which he is devoted, in universal education. In whatever department of philanthropy he may be engaged, he will find that department to be only a segment of the great circle of beneficence of which universal education is the centre and circumference."

Third: Equalization of representation in the Congress and the electoral college by reducing the number of Southern representatives.

In a previous chapter the in*equality* of representation has been clearly demonstrated. All that has been said there would apply here. A white man in the South is entitled to one man's share in the government, but not more than one man's share. When by circumventing the Constitution he usurps power which makes him three times as strong at the ballot-box as a man in New England, or the great West, then the equilibrium of representative government is destroyed.

The Constitution of the United States says: "Representatives shall be apportioned among the several states according to their respective numbers, counting the whole number of persons in each state, excluding Indians not taxed. But when the right to vote at any election for the choice of electors for President and Vice-President of the United States, representatives in Congress, the executive and judicial officers of a state, or the members of the legislature thereof, is denied to any of the male inhabitants of such state being 21 years of age and citizens of the United States, or in any way abridged except for participation in rebellion or other crime, the basis of representation therein shall be reduced in the proportion which the number of such male citizens shall bear to the whole number of male citizens 21 years of age in such state. The Congress shall have power to enforce by appropriate legislation the provisions of this article."

So that the Constitution imposes on Congress the duty of fixing representation and preserving the equilibrium of the states in the government.

When the white people of several of the Southern states summoned state conventions with the avowed purpose, proclaimed boldly and above-board, to disfranchise the colored voters and remove them from all share in the government, they well knew the penalty provided in the Constitution to meet such a case. They acted with their eyes wide open. They ought not to haggle or balk now that the time has come for Congress to act.

The National Republican Convention recently held in Chicago wrote this plank in its platform: " We favor such

Congressional action as shall determine whether by special discrimination the elective franchise in any state has been unconstitutionally limited, and, if such is the case, we demand that representation in Congress and in the electoral college, shall be proportionally reduced as directed by the Constitution of the United States."

This plank, which is directly in line with the Constitution, and simply seeks the equalization, the due proportioning, of the several states in the affairs of the government, has set the South ablaze.

But the country has come to know from exasperating experiences that anything and everything which would bring to the reputable, talented, prosperous colored citizen a just meed of recognition, or which would tend to prevent the South from having unfair, undue advantage in the affairs of the Government, would most certainly set the South ablaze.

The following expressions from representative Southern sources will disclose how unreasoning and unreasonable is the Southern mind on questions which may even remotely and indirectly affect the colored people.

Colonel Watterson of Kentucky says: "President Roosevelt, by injecting this dreadful racial problem into the contest, has invited inevitable defeat."

Mr. Thomas F. Ryan of Virginia says : "Its real spirit is found in that deliberate declaration about Southern representation, — a spirit which foreshadows a new force bill and makes inevitable a concerted movement to revive all the evil passions to which such an appeal is made."

Colonel Henry B. Gray of Alabama says : "It boldly declares, in effect, that the Republican party is a negro party, playing the negro above the Southern white man. It means negro domination."

The Montgomery *Advertiser* says : "But there is one result that is sure to follow this movement, and that is, that it will still further solidify the South."

Congressman Patterson of Tennessee says : "The plank in the Republican platform which threatens a reduction in the representation of the Southern states is a revival of the worst days of the bloody shirt ; is an insult to Southern manhood."

The Atlanta *Constitution* says : "The South got a slap in the face in the shape of the Crumpacker threat to reduce its representation because of local suffrage laws."

Senator Tillman of South Carolina says : "If Roosevelt wants to force negro social equality on the South, we are ready to meet that issue, and we will meet it, I think, to begin with, in our platform."

Governor Vardaman of Mississippi says : "I sincerely hope that the Democrats will accept the challenge and come out squarely for the white man's government. I do not believe that any announcement that could be made by the convention at St. Louis would go quite so straight to the heart of the white American voters as a clear-cut declaration against permitting negroes to participate in the government of the nation."

These are a few of the multitudinous comments of leading Southerners. The plank has not the remotest relation to the question of social equality. The reduction of Southern representation according to the constitutional limitations would not alter or in any way affect the standing of a single colored man in the whole South.

It would not add one single colored voter to the electorate of any of the states. It would not disqualify a single white voter. The Southern leaders could continue to carry elections unopposed or by a practically unanimous vote. For the colored man would be as much out of politics as at present.

There are two expressions bearing on this plank which are of unusual interest. The Honorable John Sharp Williams, in his keynote speech at the National Democratic Convention at St. Louis, said :

" The real object of the Republican party, in so far as the

plank is concerned, however specious the phraseology in which it is clothed, is to reduce Southern representation, without reducing that of Massachusetts, Connecticut, and other states, or wherever the negroes are disfranchised, not as such, but because of ignorance, by an educational qualification, or because of any other right reason, in any other constitutional way.

" Disfranchisement of a negro in Mississippi for ignorance is a horrible thing, disfranchisement of a white man for ignorance in Massachusetts or Connecticut is a part of New England 'higher education.'

"Let not the business interest of the country deceive itself; let those controlling it prepare, if Roosevelt is elected on this platform, for another period of uncertainty, unrest, business disturbance, and race war in the Southern states, instead of that peace and prosperity, which both races now enjoy and which has been rendered possible only by home rule and by white supremacy.

"In keeping with all this, consider the negro Santo Bambino scene in the Republican National Convention; the wild adoration of ' my little Alabama coon ', or was it a Georgia 'coon'? Why was it all thus prearranged, and by whom? Who were the two little white girls placed on the same platform with the little negro boy to march around with him carrying flags? Who pretends that it was accidental? What was the pretended lesson to be taught? What is the subtle, symbolical meaning of it all? It is the beginning over of the old scheme, revived for political advantage, to retain as a Republican asset the solid negro vote in Indiana, Illinois, New Jersey and like-conditioned states — this time without price in money paid — by disturbing all over the Southland peace and order, by demoralizing reviving industries, unsettling business and labor, disintegrating society, and, as a remote effect, if successful, hybridizing the race there and Africanizing its civilization."

Are not these the utterances of the ranting negrophobist playing to the mob to excite and inflame race passions and strife, rather than those of the calm and wise statesman handling a delicate and weighty question? Every man in this country knows, and Mr. Williams himself knows, despite his evasions, that the colored man is disfranchised in Mississippi and other Southern states on the ground of color alone. There is not a reputable citizen, white or colored, who would protest against the disfranchisement of the ignorant or degraded white or black man. The demand is that there shall be one law, applicable alike to both races. Such a law applies in every Northern state.

The people of the North have, at the solicitation of Southerners, during late years invested considerable money in the railways and street-car systems of the South, and other large sums have been invested in factories and various industries and in building up the waste places. This generous outpouring of Northern capital, coupled with Northern hustle and brains and the hard and faithful toil and drudgery of the colored people, are the two greatest factors in the development of prosperity of the former slave states — the New South.

Nevertheless, Mr. Williams has the hardihood to threaten the American people with the direst consequences if, in the exercise of their sovereign will as free men, they shall dare elect Mr. Roosevelt as the President of the United States. " Prepare," says he, " if Roosevelt is elected on this platform, for another period of uncertainty, unrest, business disturbance, and race war in the Southern states." This is a reckless challenge.

It means that if the reactionists, a radical and minor element, are not permitted to force on the republic a new peculiar institution with incalculable possibilities for evil, — destructive of liberty and constitutional government, degrading the white man as well as the colored, burdening the country with a problem greater and graver than slavery, and securing through this institution enhanced and undue political power, which would be a revolting injustice to every state of the North and West, — then they will make reprisal on Northern capital invested in the South and bring about a race war on the negroes.

However, he will not be able to make good his threat so far as the business interests of the South are concerned, — the good sense of Southern business men will take care of that; but he or his friends can make reprisal on the negroes or make "bonfires" of them at will. But public opinion can be depended upon to stay the hand.

What possible connection is there between the reduction of Southern representation to the proper, constitutional basis and the "hybridizing" of the South?

Such reduction certainly does not bring the races any closer together. It does not alter the status one way or another of a single colored man, nor change the status of a white man.

As to the hybridizing plaint, Mr. Williams should go slow. For all the hybrids in the South are children of white men. All the hybridizing which has been done there is the work of white men. But why denounce the hybrids? They have absolutely no responsibility in the matter. Would Mr. Williams dare to go a step further and pour the vials of wrath and indignation on all the fathers of the hybrids?

The colored man is far more concerned about keeping the white man from entering his back door than he is about knocking at the white man's front door for social recognition. Such good offices as may come to him, he may accept, but he does not clamor for more.

The truth is that "hybridizing" can progress in the South only so far as the whites themselves shall carry it. And the colored man would rejoice in the day when the honor of his wife and daughter shall be respected and they shall become immune from the taint.

The people of the North will not go into hysterics because a white child and a colored child waved the flag of the United States in the presence of ten thousand American patriots. Colored men fought and died for that flag even when threatened with death, if captured, by those for whom Mr. Williams speaks.

The people of the North want the colored child to love and honor "Old Glory" even as the white child honors and loves it. And it may come to pass that the little colored boy, James B. Cashin, the son of a reputable colored citizen, whom Mr. Williams denounces as an Alabama "coon," in his maturity shall fight and die in the defence and honor of the flag of his country. In all the days of slavery colored children and white children, boys and girls, freely played and romped together and ate out of the same plate with their fingers. There was no protest against it.

Another expression of surpassing interest is the plank in the platform adopted at the National Democratic Convention, which reads as follows: "The race question has brought countless woes to this country. The calm wisdom of the American people should see to it that it brings no more.

"To revive the dead and hateful race and sectional animosities in any part of our common country means confusion, distraction of business, and the reopening of wounds now happily healed. North, South, East, and West have but recently stood together in line of battle, from the walls of Peking to the hills of Santiago, and as sharers of a common glory and a common destiny we should share fraternally the common burdens.

"We therefore deprecate and condemn the Bourbon-like, selfish, and narrow spirit of the recent Republican Convention at Chicago, which sought to kindle anew the embers of racial and sectional strife, and we appeal from it to the sober common-sense and patriotic spirit of the American people."

The chief significance of this plank is the fact that it is a demonstration that the reactionists and radical leaders of the South have accomplished the remarkable feat of capturing the National Democratic party, horse and foot, and have "Jim-Crowed" it.

The thoughts in this plank are simply the echo of the speech of Mr. Williams, supplemented by the views of Senator Tillman and Governor Vardaman. The merest glance at the proceedings of this convention will show that it was dominated by the extreme reactionists of the South. For instance: Congressman Williams of Mississippi was the temporary chairman and keynote speech-maker; Congressman Champ Clark of Missouri was permanent chairman; Senator Daniels of Virginia was chairman of the committee on resolutions; Senator Tillman of South Carolina was the "Highcockalorum"; and he and Senator Carmack of Tennessee, Governor Vardaman of Mississippi, and Senator Bailey of Texas were the referees and censors and directors of the entire proceedings from the beginning to the end. It would seem a joke to regard these men as representing Americanism. Who would urge their fitness to fix the standard of American life and shape the destiny of the American republic?

It was an ill omen that this great national gathering should have been, to all practical purposes and intents, turned into a sectional, a Southern pow-wow. And it is noticeable that in this aggregation not once was the commanding voice of an eminent or a trusted Northern leader heard above the din, nor was such a leader assigned an important post. The South was in the saddle and the extreme reactionists held the reins.

What, indeed, could be more preposterous than that this free nation of 80,000,000 people should surrender their government to the control or influence of Tillman and Vardaman and their cohorts that dominated the convention? The thought of it makes the brain reel.

THE NATIONAL DUTY TO THE NEGRO

Mr. James S. Henry, a special and responsible newspaper, correspondent, reports in the Philadelphia *Press* that, "From Pettigrew, of South Dakota, who was a member of the committee (on resolutions), it is learned that the South's only vigorous contention was for something against the 'nigger'." And the South got its "Jim Crow" plank, as predicted by Senator Tillman and Governor Vardaman.

A strange fatuity has followed the Democratic party by reason of overbearing Southern leaders. In the days of slavery it became the helpless tool of the slaveholder. In 1864, in the great crisis of the war, and a year after the chivalric Lee had been hopelessly beaten and driven back from Gettysburg and the invasion of the North, it declared "the experiment of war a failure."

In 1868 it declared the reconstruction of the South as "unconstitutional, revolutionary, null and void."

In 1876 a streak of sanity came to it, and it "recognized the questions of slavery and secession as having been settled for all time to come by the war."

In 1884 Mr. Cleveland saved it from "daftness."

In 1894, in the midst of President Cleveland's second administration, it broke loose from all restraint, and not even the well-known firmness and cleverness of the President could "doctor" its mania. It "pitch-forked" him, repudiated him, threw him overboard, and went wildly daft.

In 1896 it fell a victim to Populism, free silver, and other fads. In 1900 it did likewise. And in 1904 it became the helpless prey to the microbes of "Jim Crowism", and adopted a "Jim Crow" plank which is intended by its sponsors to get the people's endorsement for a new peculiar institution, more dangerous and less excusable than slavery.

Not a word of criticism is here directed against Judge Parker, the eminent New York jurist who was nominated for the presidency of the United States, and not a syllable unfavorable against Senator Davis, the distinguished citizen of

313

West Virginia who was nominated for the vice-presidency, — for they both represent the best class of Americans; and not a word of disparagement to the progressive and prosperous commonwealth of West Virginia, which is rather to be congratulated on having such a worthy and distinguished citizen within her borders.

But the " Jim-Crowing " of the convention was a national misfortune, as it lends plausibility to the Southerner's declaration: " We have got our heel on the neck of the. niggers and we can hold them down ; and we have got a clutch in the craw of the Yankees and we will choke down their throats our views on the negro question."

Successful choking was done when the convention swallowed the " Jim Crow " plank. This plank is a compound of cupidity, cunning, hypocrisy, and mendacity, and will confuse no one. Historically it was not "the race question," but in truth the slaveholders — a minor element of the people, who threatened, at the time of the founding of the government, not to enter the Union unless slavery was recognized, saying that it was temporary, and promising its certain abolition, and who afterwards strengthened and fastened the barbarous institution on the republic — who are responsible for the countless woes to this country.

And it is those who have inherited the ideas of the slaveholders that are now exerting all their powers and chicanery — in defiance of the laws of God and the laws of their country and the moral sentiment of mankind, and regardless of a most costly and bitter experience — along lines which, if continued, will as certainly bring other countless woes to this country. Indeed, the calm wisdom of the American people should see to it, yes, will see to it, that the South is saved from the folly of its leaders, and the republic from the crime of serfdom.

" North, South, East, and West have but recently stood together in line of battle, from the walls of Peking to the hills of Santiago." This is mendacious! Was ever the truth so mutilated in order to serve a mean and base purpose? It is a matter of public knowledge that the very first regiment summoned from the Western barracks to the front in the Spanish-American War, by General Miles, who was at that time at the head of the army, was a colored regiment.

It was ungrudgingly stated at the time and universally accepted, that the chief honors won in the fights around the hills of Santiago were fully shared by colored soldiers, the Ninth and Tenth colored cavalry, and the Twenty-fourth and Twenty-fifth colored infantry. It is not intended to underrate to any degree the invaluable services of their white comrades in arms who contributed to the victory; but while there were of course others, Colonel Roosevelt's Rough Riders and the Ninth and Tenth colored cavalry were the two forces which make forever memorable the Santiago campaign. But for the timely and heroic charge of these colored soldiers, San Juan Hill would to-day mark the greatest defeat and humiliation that American arms have ever met.

Colonel Roosevelt, by far the most heroic figure in that war, said: "I know the bravery and character of the negro soldier. He saved my life at Santiago and I have had occasion to say so in many articles and speeches. The Rough Riders were in a bad position when the Ninth and Tenth Cavalry (colored) came rushing up the hill carrying everything before them."

The New York *Journal*, concerning this battle, said: "The two most picturesque and most characteristically American commands in General Shafter's army bore off the great honors of the day, in which all won honor. No man can read the story in to-day's *Journal* of the Rough Riders' charge on the block house at El Caney, of Theodore Roosevelt's mad daring in the face of what seemed certain death, without having his pulses beat faster and some reflected light of the fire of battle gleam from his eyes.

"And over against this scene of the cowboy and the college graduate, the New York man about town and the Arizona bad man, united in one coherent war machine, set the picture of the Tenth United States Cavalry — the famous colored regiment. Side by side with Roosevelt's men they fought — these black men. Scarce used to freedom themselves, they are dying that Cuba ·may be free.

"Their marksmanship was magnificent, say the eye-witnesses. Their courage was superb. They bore themselves like veterans and gave proof positive that out of natures naturally peaceful, careless, and playful, military discipline and an inspiring cause can make soldiers worthy to rank with Cæsar's legions or Cromwell's army.

"The Rough Riders and the Black Regiment. In these two commands is an epitome of almost our whole national character."

And further: hard by the walls of Peking, and in the Philippine Islands, the colored soldiers, at the command of the Government of the United States, in defence of its flag, have but recently stood together in line of battle with their white compatriots and moistened the parched sands of that tropical land with their warm life-blood.

The late President McKinley, in an address to the State Normal and Industrial School for colored persons at Prairie View, Texas, shortly before his death, said: "In our recent war with Spain your race displayed distinguished qualities of gallantry upon more than one field. You were in the fight at El Caney, and San Juan Hill; the black boys helping to emancipate the oppressed people of Cuba; and your race is in the Philippines carrying the flag, and they have carried it stainless in honor and in its glory." He also said: "Your race is moving on and has a promising future before it. It has been faithful to the government of the United States. It has been true and loyal and law-abiding."

Be true, then, to the truth and history. The colored soldiers are the Southerners who won the greatest glory in the Spanish-American War.

Is it a " Bourbon-like, selfish, and narrow spirit," to demand that no section of the country shall enjoy unfair and undue advantage in representation in the government over any other section? Should it " kindle anew the embers of racial and sectional strife," to equalize representation in a representative government according to the basis and limitations of the Constitution? For what does the Constitution exist? Or is the "solid South" above and beyond the Constitution of the United States?

Are the immense, incalculable business, financial, industrial, and commercial interests of this republic best safeguarded by giving a white man in South Carolina or Mississippi three times as much power at the ballot-box, in the electoral college and in the Congress, as a man in New York, or Wisconsin, or Indiana, or New Jersey, or Connecticut? Did not the " solid South" vote for free silver and free trade in the last two national elections?

The facts and figures given in a previous chapter prove beyond all cavil or question that it was the negro vote that elected Mr. McKinley in 1896 and saved the country from disasters and woes which words can hardly overstate.

The New York *World*, speaking of some of the grave and serious consequences the nation escaped through Mr. Bryan's defeat in 1896 and for whom the " solid South" voted, says: "The 'free-riot' plank was quite as obnoxious as the free-silver plank. The resolution proposing to deny the right of private contract in money transactions was likewise bad. The intimation that the Supreme Court would be packed to secure the reversal of distasteful decisions was scandalous. The postponement of tariff reform 'until the money question has been settled' as the cheap-money men wanted it settled, was a betrayal of the traditional Democratic principle upon which the party has elected its only presidents since the war. The opposition to the use by Federal courts of the writ of injunction was calculated to leave the Government powerless in the face of emergencies requiring prompt action to protect life, industry, and property against mobs and conspiracies."

The votes unjustly wielded by the "solid South" are the greatest menace that faces the nation, and may in a close or doubtful election produce embarrassments bordering on chaos. The South has seized powers unlawfully, by wholesale disfranchisements. And wholesale disfranchisement in the South effects the partial disfranchisement of every Northern state.

The demand, therefore, for equalization of representation in the electoral college and in the Congress, and the preservation of the balance of power among the states of the Union is of vital concern to the whole people.

It is a condition, not a theory, that faces the country.

The combined white population of South Carolina and Mississippi, according to the census of 1900, is 1,199,007, and these two states elect 15 members to the Congress; while the combined white population of the states of Minnesota and Nebraska is 2,793,562, being 1,594,555 greater than the white population of South Carolina and Mississippi, and yet they elect only 15 Congressmen. The states of Maine, New Hampshire, Vermont, Rhode Island, and Connecticut have a total white population of 2,757,262, being 1,558,417 greater than the white population of South Carolina and Mississippi, and yet they elect only 15 members of the Congress.

By this Southern method 1,594,555 white people in Minnesota and Nebraska or 1,558,417 white people in the New England states named above have no voice in their government and are practically disfranchised.

South Carolina, Mississippi, and Louisiana have a total white population of 1,928,719 and elect 22 Congressmen; while Ohio has a white population of 4,060,204, being 2,031,485 greater than that of the three named Southern states, yet elects only 21 members of Congress.

The states of Indiana and New Jersey have a total white population of 4,270,825, being 2,242,146 greater than the combined white population of South Carolina, Mississippi, and Louisiana, and yet elect only 23 members of Congress.

By this Southern method 2,031,485 white people in Ohio or 2,342,106 white people in Indiana and New Jersey are deprived of a political status and are without a share in their government.

By massing the colored population of South Carolina, Mississippi, Georgia, Louisiana, Florida, and Alabama, the injustice and inequality will appear even more flagrant and condemnable.

The total colored population of these states is 4,433,605. The Southern leaders refuse to recognize the colored man as the equal of the white man at the ballot-box in the South, nevertheless they count him, and play him as the equal of the white man in the North in order to secure unfair, undue representation in the government.

By appropriating to themselves full representation for these 4,433,605 colored citizens and playing them against great Northern states, they can effectively achieve the political effacement of the 4,060,204 white citizens of Ohio; or the 4,734,873 white citizens of Illinois; or the 4,270,825 white citizens of Indiana and New Jersey; or the 4,456,474 white citizens of the north central states Wisconsin and Michigan; or the 4,209,881 white citizens of Kansas, Minnesota, and Nebraska, or even completely neutralize, nullify in the electoral college and in Congress the voice of the great Empire City of New York with its imperial interests, together with the states of Connecticut and Rhode Island and Delaware thrown in for good measure.

Furthermore, by taking representation on these 4,433,605 colored people they completely offset, negative in Congress and the electoral college, the entire white population of all the states west of the Rocky Mountains, namely California, Washington, Montana, Idaho, Nevada, Oregon, and Utah, to which we can add North Dakota and South Dakota, and still have 1,153,508 negroes left to overwhelm and negative white voters in other states.

It is as true now as in the days of slavery that the "solid South" grasps the "advantages derived from the unity and identity of action and motive," and would " move in phalanx " over the great states of the North, by dividing them, and catching here and there a few Congressmen and presidential electors.

But will not the methods employed to make and keep a "solid South" also make a solid rather than a divided North? A North solid, however, only for justice, the right, and constitutional government.

The "solid South" wields approximately 50 votes in the electoral college and also in Congress based on its colored citizens. All the New England states taken together have only 29 votes. What freeman of the North, whether Democrat or Republican, Socialist or Prohibitionist, or of whatsoever party, would condone this flaming injustice and crying wrong, which destroys representative government and menaces free institutions? He must regard himself as the third-of-a-man, for the white man in South Carolina or Mississippi is three times as potential at the ballot-box and in the affairs of the government as he.

This question is greater than party. It cannot be smothered or brushed aside by the hypocritical shrieks of sectionalism. The only sectionalism in this republic is that which is fomented, kept alive, and forced on the people by the un-American, perverse attitude of the leaders of the "solid South."

The Constitution of the United States is plain, explicit, mandatory. It imposes on the Congress the duty of equalizing representation in the government. Whether the Southern constitutions which have wrought wholesale disfranchisement of the colored citizen are constitutional or unconstitutional, in whole or in part, is not a matter of particular concern to Congress in equalizing representation in the government. The Southern leaders have proved themselves experts and pastmasters in framing laws for the oppression and degradation of others. They may, by circumlocutory wordings and cunningly devised phrases, and the skilful manipulation of sentences, have succeeded to some extent, at least, in cheating the Constitution of the United States. But it may be discovered that cheating one section by "a grandfather clause," does not invalidate other sections.

But the disfranchising constitutions and laws of the Southern states are not constitutional, for the reason that they are a fraudulent restraint on liberty and representative government, and were so intended to be.

The presiding officer of the Louisiana Constitutional Convention, in his closing address, said: "What care I whether it [the Constitution] be more or less ridiculous, or not? Does n't it meet the case? Does n't it let the white man vote, and does n't it stop the negro from voting? — and is n't that what we came here to accomplish?" Thus these leaders themselves brand their constitutions as frauds, and even glory in the fraudulent work. But Congress is master of the situation.

So that it matters not a particle whether the Southern constitutions are constitutional in whole or in part, if the fact exists that there are bodies of "the male inhabitants, . . . 21 years of age and citizens of the United States" in sufficient numbers to attract attention and destroy the equilibrium of representation in the government, and who have not "participated in rebellion or other crime," and yet are denied "the right to vote"; in whatsoever state such bodies of "male citizens" are denied "the right to vote," it is the imperative duty of Congress to reduce "the basis of representation therein to the proportion which the number of such male citizens shall bear to the whole number of male citizens 21 years of age in such state."

The enforcement of this section of the Constitution of the United States will prevent the republic from being ruled by an oligarchy. For although an oligarchy may seize states and under one pretence or another disfranchise large bodies of the citizens, it cannot count those so disfranchised as a basis of its representation in the government. This too must promote and strengthen the broader liberty of the people.

Mr. Hardwick of Georgia, in a recent speech in the Congress, said : "If Congress should be unwise enough to elect to exercise this discretionary power vested in it by section 5 of Article XIV, it will not only be the most serious strain of the present cordial relations so happily existing between the sections, but it will require a readjustment of the basis of representation that will not start at the Potomac and at Rio Grande, but will stretch from Hatteras to the Golden Gate, from Maine to Florida, and will embrace in its majestic sweep every state and Territory in the Union and even our new islands of the sea." This threat is characteristically Southern.

The only "cordial relations" that can bind together the sections of a republic are based on the equality of representation. Inequality destroys cordiality; they cannot coexist. The fundamental guarantee of "cordial relations," between the sections is the equal obedience of the sections to the Constitution of the United States.

In equalizing representation, it would be fair, wise, and just to yield every Southern state full representation for its entire white citizenship, supplemented by the number of colored citizens actually enrolled as voters. This information is easily accessible. As the laws and constitution of some of the Southern states were made for the expressed purpose, openly and publicly avowed, of disfranchising the colored citizens, it would not be necessary to follow the intricacies, windings, and tricks as to how the details are worked out. The main purpose and results only are worthy of consideration.

The Northern states should have identically the same basis; its entire white citizenship plus its registered colored votes. But as no colored man in the North is disfranchised, practically the whole colored citizenship would be counted.

The South is estopped from all complaints, because it would have the full and unrestricted power to enlarge, at any time, its electorate and thus increase its representation.

Reducing Southern representation would not of course settle the question of suffrage, but it would be a start in the right direction. It would chill the disposition of the states for wholesale disfranchisement. States covet more, not less power. The struggle will go on until impartial laws shall regulate the suffrage in every state. The better South will assert itself. The Fifteenth Amendment is an impregnable fortress, and no law which the reactionist's ingenuity can invent can keep all colored men from the ballot-box. No one who now has the franchise can lose it.

The work of the schoolroom will gradually remove all the artificial barriers which now exist and the approach to the ballot-box will be greatly facilitated.

Some fears have been expressed that the Southern leaders might even accept reduction of representation in order to get rid of the negro vote, and that such reduction might be construed as an endorsement by the nation of wholesale disfranchisement. These fears are illogical and groundless, and are entirely without a basis in reason, political science, or history.

In the first place, the Southern leaders would oppose reduction of representation to the limit of their power, for
the sake of their own political salvation. But even if they
should accept it, it must still be remembered that the Southern *leaders* are not the Southern *people*, but only a very small
fraction of them. A majority of the whites would not view
reduction of representation with the same complacency that
they show for the disfranchisement of the colored race. As
a matter of fact, many Southerners are opposed to wholesale
disfranchisement, and regard the " grandfather clause " as a
subterfuge reproachful to Southern manhood. The inflamed
South is not the sober South. The sober South would never
give up one third of its representatives in Congress and also
in the electoral college in order to uphold a flagrantly unmoral and disastrous policy. More than this — the sober
South would shrink from thus publicly and directly impeach-
ing itself in the eyes of civilization and Christianity.

There should be no temporizing or half-way measures, but
reduction should be based, in full, on that proportion of the
colored population not represented on the list of registered
voters. The South being thus shorn of one third of its
power, it would be much easier to enact such additional laws
as the nation may adjudge necessary to enforce the Fifteenth
Amendment. But nothing can be more certain than that
the sober South will break away from the reactionists at this
point, or before it is reached, rather than provoke the nation
to the enactment of further legislation. It is already realized
that the madness of the reactionists has produced the woes of
the South. As sure as the sun shall shine the Southern people,
under a patriotic, noble-hearted, and broad-minded leadership,
will rise in revolt and overthrow the " Jim Crowites " and
reactionists and wipe out any policy which would thus destroy the power, dignity, and standing of their states, and
which would relegate such states to the position of " pocket-
boroughs," or " sage-brush " communities.

In the second place, the reduction of representation would not be an endorsement of wholesale disfranchisement, but only the application of the penalty. If a man commits a theft or any other offence, and the law is invoked and he is duly punished, no sane person would ever pretend that the invocation of the law and the punishment of the offender is an endorsement of the crime. Such reasoning would overturn civilization. Penalties operate correctionally, and not as endorsements of offences whatever their character. Reduction of representation would punish, and also, at the same time, work out the correction of the offence of wholesale disfranchisement. How? Such reduction would have the immediate effect of making the entire colored population a valuable asset in the political life of the South; whereas, as things stand now, the colored man is a political nonentity.

The reactionists disfranchised him because they saw that under present conditions nothing was to be gained by allowing him the ballot, and that by denying him the ballot nothing was to be lost. The colored man was thus counted, in so far as his own recognition was concerned, simply as a cipher in the political equation of Southern life. In politics, as in other matters, things go by values. In the economy of life, everything of value is put to use. Make the negro of political value to the South, just as he is of industrial value, and the South will protect his ballot because it will serve its interests to do so. Reduction of representation would instantly reverse present conditions and put a political value on the head of every colored man. The reactionists could not then treat the colored man as a cipher, and at the same time profit by the full representation based on the colored population to strengthen their oligarchy. The colored man would have inherent political value; and to secure its benefits, the South would be compelled to recognize his right to cast his own ballot. He would thus be transformed from a cipher into a unit; from a mere abstraction into a political personality. His ballot would be restored under just and equal laws, and he would be protected and assisted in the wise use of it by the conservative and patriotic elements. For it would mean five more votes in Congress and as many in the electoral college for Georgia; four votes each for North Carolina, Texas, South Carolina, Virginia, and Alabama; five more for Mississippi, and a corresponding increase in other states according to the colored population. Is any man crazy enough to believe that a majority of the white people of South Carolina, that old and historic commonwealth, rich in renown and prestige, would surrender four of her seven representatives in the Congress and the electoral college at the beck of Senator Tillman, simply to carry out a degrading, unmoral, and unrighteous policy, injurious alike to its white and colored citizens; or that Mississippi would give up five of her eight Congressmen and electors at the dictation of Governor Vardaman; or that the great state of Georgia would cut her congressional and electoral delegation in half to humor the frenzy of the Honorable John Temple Graves, or as a tribute to the social-equality bogyman?

Such a condition, even if it were possible, would only be transient. It would provoke revolt. The liberal and patriotic elements would desire and could have no better platform than such an issue on which to appeal to the people to save the prestige, power, and honor of their commonwealths and demand fair and equal laws for all the people.

When the white people of the South shall thus approach the suffrage question with honest purposes, and in the broad spirit of patriotism and humanity, and enact fair and honest election laws, taking every needful precaution to insure good government by the rule of intelligence, thrift, character, and property; punishing alike the man who sells his vote and the man who bribes it; prohibiting the use of money in campaigns except for specified purposes; eliminating from politics the ignorant, vicious, shiftless, and criminal classes whether

white or colored ; discarding the unholy and un-American
policy of the reactionists in violating the Constitution and
subjugating the colored race ; assuring the colored man of
the protection of his civil and political rights ; giving him
considerate treatment, recognizing his right to representation in the government and so dividing his vote, — they shall
have the hearty good-will, applause, and benediction of every
honest man and patriotic citizen of the land ; for the race
question will then be solved, and in the only way that it can
be solved, by respecting the ethics of the Christ and by the
due observance of the organic law of the republic ; and it
will be removed from the arena of politics.

The solemn appeals and warnings of two eminent Americans may fittingly close this chapter. One is of the South,
the other of the North. Both are of national reputation,
and represent the best type of American manhood.

Ex-Governor William O. Bradley, of Kentucky, in a recent
address, said : " Men of the North, we come from the battle-
field, consecrated to freedom with the blood of your brave
sons. In their names, and by their memories, the disfranchised South appeals to you for justice. Shall it be said that
your sons marched and fought and died in vain ? Shall it
be said that a nation can exist part slave and part free ?
Are people free who are forced to bear the burden and yet
denied the highest privilege of citizenship ? If it be true
that warrant may not be found in the Constitution to prevent disfranchisement, then we beg that you no longer permit
the disfranchised and oppressed to be estimated for the purpose of increasing the electoral strength of their oppressors."

And the late Mr. James G. Blaine, in the *North American
Review*, after affirming that the South " wrongfully gains "
a " great number of electoral votes," " by reason of its
unlawful seizure of political power," goes on to say : " Our
institutions have been tried by the fiery test of war and have
survived. It remains to be seen whether the attempt to

govern the country by the power of a 'solid South' unlawfully consolidated, can be successful. No thoughtful man can consider these questions without deep concern. The mighty power of a republic with a continent for its possession, can only be wielded permanently by being wielded honestly. In a fair and generous struggle for partisan power let us not forget those issues and those ends which are above party. Organized wrong will ultimately be met by organized resistance. . . . Impartial suffrage is our theory. It must become our practice. Any party of American citizens can bear to be defeated. No party of American citizens will bear to be defrauded. The men who are interested in a dishonest count are units. The men who are interested in an honest count are millions. I wish to speak for the millions of all political parties, and in their name to declare that the republic must be strong enough, and shall be strong enough, to protect the weakest of its citizens in all their rights. To this simple and sublime principle let us, in the lofty language of Burke, ' attest the retiring generations, let us attest the advancing generations, between which, as a link in the great chain of eternal order, we stand.' "

And there may be added these forceful words from the New York *World*: "If the Southern Democrats who are forcing these measures do not perceive their ultimate inevitable consequences, they are lacking in political understanding. The preponderating vote of the Northern states will not consent permanently to representation in Congress and in the electoral college of millions of disfranchised inhabitants in the Southern states. Especially is this true when the disfranchising qualifications apply and are intended to operate not against illiteracy or shiftlessness or unworthiness, but solely against color. . . .

"Back, however, of the questions of political expediency and of the equality growing out of the representation of non-voters is the deeper question of constitutional guarantees and of the anomaly and danger in a republic of an enormous number of citizens disfranchised for their color alone."

Colonel T. W. Higginson read a poem before the Phi Beta Kappa Society at the late Commencement of Harvard College, which concludes as follows : —

> "The humbler friends who ne'er betrayed a trust,
> And never in defeat yet turned their back,
> Stood firm till gunshot strewed them in the dust.
> Why need they pardon ? For their faces black !

> "A hundred thousand negroes filled your ranks,
> When most depleted, with their manhood strong.
> Shall we not still keep warm the nation's thanks
> While lingering days those modest lives prolong ?

> "They saved you ; charged Fort Wagner ; they held out,
> Held the coast safe that Sherman might pass through,
> You built Shaw's statue; can you calmly doubt
> That those who marched with him should vote, like you ?

> "'Not fit to live,' some say ; 'an alien race,
> Oh, set them all aside ! ' advisers cry.
> 'Their birth a shame, their color a disgrace.'
> Not fit to live ? You trusted them to die !

> "Not on these walls your tribute need be paid,
> But in that outer world your teachings rule ;
> Here by your thoughts a nobler conscience made
> Gives to the nation's life a loftier school.

> "To praise one's self by flattering all the great —
> How easy ! Worthier honors then were won
> When Harvard kept her cherished laurels late
> And placed them on a humbler Washington.

> "Within this hall she cried, ' Protect the low,'
> Till all earth's children from this life are whirled
> To see fulfilled the debts we vainly owe,
> And find God's justice in a nobler world."

CHAPTER X
PUBLIC OPINION OMNIPOTENT

PRINCE TALLEYRAND, probably the most resourceful, astute, and remarkable European diplomatist of his day, said : "There is one who is wiser than Voltaire, and has more understanding than Napoleon and all ministers; and that one is — Public Opinion."

In the equitable settlement of complex and vital issues incident to the life of a free and self-governing nation — the arbitrament of the sword being eliminated — public opinion is the court of last resort. Its mandates are imperative and final. From its inexorable decrees there is no escape. It inspires, formulates, and executes the laws of a people. The public opinion of the nation is and of necessity must be paramount : the peace and prosperity, the honor and dignity, the good order and safety, and the perpetuity and sovereignty of the nation are dependent on this. For the laws of a self-governing nation represent the consensus of the public opinion of the nation.

If South Carolina and Mississippi can violate with open defiance and impunity certain sections of the Constitution of the United States at will, what is to prevent Utah and Wyoming from overthrowing other sections, and still other states from nullifying remaining sections? How much of the Constitution is to be left intact?

If this wonderful instrument, the grandest charter of liberty on the face of the earth — "the hope of man" — can thus be torn into tatters and threads, of what avail is the consensus of public opinion, the saving salt of a nation's life? What becomes of national honor, authority, sovereignty? When the public opinion of this nation shall cease to be sovereign — then the republic is dead. The public opinion of this nation, in the free exercise of its plenary and sovereign powers, removed the fetters of slavery, and made the colored people citizens; acknowledging to them the birthright which belongs to every man — " the inalienable rights " of " life, liberty and the pursuit of happiness"; and it is the prerogative and binding duty of the nation to make the full enjoyment of these natural rights and privileges secure and complete.

The United States being a nation, the allegiance and loyalty of the citizen is not to a state or section, but to the nation. It must necessarily follow, as a corollary, that the highest, the supreme, prerogative of the nation is the protection of the citizen. The relation is reciprocal. This involves the very life of the nation itself. In the protection of its citizens the nation finds its own protection.

President Lincoln, in the heat of the antislavery agitation, declared : "This nation cannot continue to exist half free and half slave." He was right.

President Garfield, in his inaugural address, twenty years after the slaveholders' unsuccessful rebellion against the republic, said: "There is no middle ground for the negro race between slavery and equal citizenship." He was right.

There was no peace with the nation half free and half slave. There can be no peace with the nation half free and half serf. " Men may cry peace! peace! but there is no peace." The extreme and unreasonable, the unchristian and un-American attitude of the South is " the fly in the ointment," the disturber of the public peace.

No one will deny that it ought to be, and is, a most ardent and even sacred desire of every good citizen, that peace and concord, unity and good fellowship shall exist between the several sections of the country and among all of its inhabitants. But the essential, the elementary condition of this consummation most devoutly to be wished for, is a fair and faithful, a just and honorable administration of the law for all the people "without regard to race, color or previous condition of servitude."

The policy pursued by the South, and portrayed in these pages and proved by evidence unquestioned and incontrovertible — a policy of mob rule and lynch law ; oppressive, proscriptive, and unlawful legislation ; harsh persecutions and general ostracism; and debasement of all colored people, regardless of their moral worth, their thrift and industry, their superior mental endowments, their value to the community, or their service and sacrifices for the nation in the storm and stress of war — is not constructive of the peace of the nation, but on the contrary is destructive of the very foundations of peace.

When one class of citizens seize local governments and inflict gross wrongs and inhumanities on another class of equal citizens, in defiance of the organic law, it is a matter of concern to the whole people. The familiar phrases " hands off," "no interference," "we will settle the question to suit ourselves," smack of haughtiness but not wisdom, of audacity but not honesty, and will deceive no one.

" Hands off " — when the liberty and hope of ten millions of American citizens are being openly assassinated ?

" No interference " — when these people are being stripped and despoiled of every essential manhood right of a free American ?

" We will settle the question to suit ourselves " — when that settlement leads to serfdom with abuses even blacker and more bestial than slavery ?

If a colored man pre-eminent in character and of superior talent, a high officer of the government is invited to a function at the White House, or another of admitted ability and standing is appointed to a Federal office, the churlish and childish plaint is made : " It is an insult to the white people of the South." A social boycott is flauntingly proclaimed against the President of the United States and the demand made that he shall "be treated in all respects by Southern people precisely as if he were a negro, and with absolute indication that he is not of our race, or in any respect socially an equal with us or a fit associate for us or any of us." The press reports show that many leading Southerners have absented themselves from the social functions at the White House, as if by this childish act they could coerce the President to violate the liberty and rights of citizens whom his oath of office binds him to protect.

If a Northern man has the temerity to make a manly plea for fair and honorable treatment of the colored people and condemns oppression, he is met with the charge of "stirring up sectional strife", "waving the bloody shirt", and is denounced as the "fool-friend" of the negro.

The social and business boycott is rigorously applied to any white person in the South who may treat the educated and cultured negro with the courtesy due a gentleman. The Northern man residing in the South and who is the victim of this un-American code and who does not show the colored man the kindness or courtesy he would show if residing in the North, is paraded as being as hostile as the Southerner to the recognition of the colored man.

Principal Booker T. Washington, admittedly the most distinguished Southerner living—and pronounced by Mr. Carnegie one of the greatest men of the age, registers in an Indiana hotel: the next morning a white chambermaid refuses to make up his bed, because a "nigger" had slept in it. She at once becomes the heroine of every "Jim Crowite" in the South. Letters of congratulation are poured in upon her. Subscriptions are made up in various parts of the South, and thousands of dollars are showered upon her. Her courageous act consisted in offering an unprovoked insult to an unoffending gentleman. Mr. Washington sends his daughter to a Northern boarding-school: the demand is made that Southern white girls shall leave the school.

An Italian, keeping a restaurant in a Mississippi town, sells a colored man a meal; his place is immediately raided and he is driven from his home. Any incident is seized upon to inflame passions against the colored man.

During the riots in New Orleans, a Northern white man was arrested, and fined twenty-five dollars for protesting against the killing of innocent negroes and admitting to the judge he had said that "A negro in body and soul is as good as a white man." At Memphis, Tennessee, a Northern white man who justified President Roosevelt in dining Principal Booker T. Washington was promptly thrashed. And the cry has gone forth that "no quarter" shall be given to any one who shall dare to interpose against this policy. Is this not choking Southern ideas down Northern throats with a remarkable vehemence?

These things are sufficient to cause the patriots of 1861 to turn in their graves. Did they destroy slavery and save the Union only to have the cardinal doctrine of the Southern Confederacy re-enacted into law throughout the Southland, and forced on the nation as slavery was forced on it? This is not a basis which makes for the peace of the republic, nor will the people be silent in the consummation of such a sin against Heaven and crime against humanity.

The American people lack neither courage nor conscience. The issues thus raised must be bravely met and overcome, as have other issues equally perplexing and menacing.

The South was wrong, even if it was united, on the slavery question — but public opinion destroyed slavery.

The South was wrong, even if it was united, in making war on the republic — but public opinion saved the republic.

The South was wrong, even if it was united, in its threats to shoot colored soldiers and their white officers when captured — but public opinion kept the colored soldiers on the firing line and protected them.

The South was wrong, even if it was united, in passing the

Black Code — but public opinion destroyed the Black Code.

The South was wrong, even if it was united, in its hostility to the great measures of reconstruction — but public opinion achieved the reconstruction it wanted.

The South *is* wrong, even if it is united, in the extreme un-American, and unholy attitude assumed to-day — and public opinion will be found equal to the task of dealing with it.

Public opinion spoke through the ballot-box in the national election held in the fall of 1904. The overwhelming vote given in support of the victorious candidate attests the adherence of the people to the principles advocated in these pages. Never before in the history of the republic have the people, the true American sovereigns, given such an emphatic demonstration of their power through the instrumentality of the ballot-box, and so splendidly and gloriously confirmed their devotion to the principles of liberty and constitutional government.

Every state in which there was a free and fair expression of public opinion was carried by President Roosevelt by majorities which daze the political mind. New York gave 175,000 majority, Illinois 300,000, Michigan 206,000, Kansas 126,000, Minnesota 126,000, Wisconsin 130,000, Nebraska 85,000, Massachusetts 92,000, California 125,000, Ohio 240,000, Connecticut 75,000, Indiana nearly 100,000, Washington 72,000, and Pennsylvania over 500,000. In ten states his majority ranged from 100,000 to more than 500,000; and his combined majorities in fifteen states exceeded Judge Parker's total vote.

The total vote cast in the thirteen Southern states, including Maryland, which Judge Parker carried, was 2,033,226, of which he received 1,238,878. The total vote polled in the thirty-two states carried by President Roosevelt was 11,475,270. But it must be remembered that the South, while casting only 15 per cent of the whole number of votes polled, nevertheless has 34 per cent of the presidential electors. About one-third of these electors are based on the colored population, who in large measure are disfranchised by trick election laws. This is like killing the sheep, and yet still expecting to possess and be benefited by the annual crop of wool.

The continuance of such gross inequality invites' gravest consequences in case of a close election. It is a most impressive fact that President Roosevelt's majorities alone in the four states of New York, Illinois, Ohio, and Pennsylvania were greater in the aggregate than the total vote cast for Judge Parker in the thirteen Southern states, including Maryland. President Roosevelt's popular majority, at large, was 2,547,578, being more than twice as great as the whole number of votes polled by his opponent in the "solid South."

The political cataclysm struck and shook to the centre the border states, and West Virginia and Missouri enrolled themselves on the side of progress and humanity; Maryland half yielded, and "Old Kentucky" weakened.

The former seceding states stand alone, isolated, embittered, out of touch with the liberal and progressive ideas of the sister states, without reconciliation to the popular will, and refusing to keep step in the march of civilization and to the "music of the Union." The following post-election expressions from leaders of the "solid South" will disclose the poverty of the South, in its public life, in capable, sober, constructive, statesmanlike leadership. The Louisville *Courier-Journal* says: "From Theodore Roosevelt we ask no quarter and expect none. He is infinitely a worse enemy of the white men and women of the South than any of the radical leaders of the past."

In the Huntsville, Alabama, *Mercury*, Mr. Robert T. Bently says: "It appearing that Theodore Roosevelt, the head and front of the Republican party, which represents the dangerous policies of civilization, protective tariff, imperialism, and social equality, has been elected President of the United States by a strictly sectional vote, and has established an insurmountable barrier between the North and South, I feel constrained to express my humble opinion, as a true and patriotic American citizen of the South, that, if the Republican party should continue its dangerous policies for the next four years and should triumph in the next national election, the thirteen states which voted for Alton B. Parker should secede from the union and by force of arms resist an oppression which means the early fall of our great republic."

In an interview, General John W. A. Sanford, one of the oldest and best-known citizens of the South, says that " the South is practically ostracized. There is one policy for the South to pursue that it may retain its prestige, its honor, and all it holds dear in its social as well as political life. Abjure national politics, participate in no future national political conventions. Allow the Northern Democrats and Northern Republicans to hold their own conventions and vote their own tickets. Let the South select and elect its own electoral ticket and vote in the electoral college for that party or candidate whose principles are more in accord with our own policies, and whose policies will promote in the greatest degree the peace, power, and prosperity of the Southern people. And when we become more populous and more wealthy, the Northerners will court the Southerners, our interests will be more respected, and our views of government will receive greater consideration from the political parties of the Northern states."

The Atlanta *Journal* says : " Let the South remain true to its traditions, true to the principle of white supremacy, true to the principles of democracy, and let it stand by itself in national politics until its support is sought on *its own terms*."

The *Journal* and the Atlanta *Constitution* also demand that the South shall nominate its own candidate for the presidency at the next election.

Judge J. M. Chilton says : " We had as well recognize this position and make the best of it. In my opinion the South ought never again, at least for several years to come, enter a national Democratic convention or any sort of national political convention. The Southern states which have been thus driven to solidification should hold a Southern convention and align themselves with that one of the Northern parties which will promise us most. Let them fight it out with their own reds and socialists. Let the South give its aid to that one of the parties which is least objectionable. In such a position the South will hold the balance of power, and it will not be long before we will be accorded the position and influence to which we are justly entitled."

The *News and Courier*, Charleston, South Carolina, says : " The North was also solid, and solid without cause ; solid on sectional lines for a sectional party, a sectional candidate, and for sectional purposes."

The Columbia *State* declares that, " if trouble is provoked, the negroes will be the chief sufferers, and a dozen Roosevelts cannot help them."

Senator Carmack of Tennessee denounces " the pharisaical people of New England," and " the rotten politicians of the North," and " the press of the North " for " misrepresenting the Southern people."

The Honorable John Sharp Williams of Mississippi goes to South Carolina, the cradle of the former secession, and preaches a new rebellion against the republic. This time, however, thanks to his discretion, it is to be a bloodless war. He advises the South to uphold its nullification of the Constitution of the United States by refusing to obey any law the sovereign people of the republic may enact through their representatives in Congress to equalize representation.

The New York *World* makes the following comment on Mr. Williams' speech : " Martyrdom was joined to nullification in the doctrine of ' passive resistance ' which John

Sharp Williams, the Democratic leader of the House, preached to the people of Spartanburg, South Carolina, Friday night.

"On the assumption that Congress might reduce Southern representation in accordance with the provisions of the Fourteenth Amendment, Mr. Williams proceeded to lay out a programme of 'passive resistance' for the South. 'I know of no power on earth or in heaven, except a direct intervention of God,' he said, 'that can force a state legislature to pass a bill redistricting a state so that it shall contain four or five or six Congressional districts instead of seven or eight.'

"Mr. Williams then advised the Southern states to pay no attention to an act reducing representation, if one should be passed, but to elect their Representatives on the old basis and send them to Washington. The House would refuse to seat them and would withhold the payment of salaries. Judicial proceedings could then be instituted to determine whether the act of Congress was constitutional. In the mean time all the Southern states would be without representation and would stand as 'a visible object-lesson' to the flinty-hearted brethren of the North. . . .

"But if the question of reducing representation in accordance with the Fourteenth Amendment were under serious consideration in Republican councils, the blame would rest upon the South alone — or, more specifically, upon the sinister cunning that devised 'the grandfather clause' and the other discriminating franchise provisions in the new state constitutions.

"Nobody in the North is disposed to quarrel with the South for disfranchising ignorance, for disfranchising viciousness, or for disfranchising shiftlessness. The objection is to a policy that disfranchises only negro ignorance, viciousness, and shiftlessness, while assuring the franchise to the most worthless 'white trash' that can prove a voting grandfather or get a political committee to pay his poll taxes. . . .

" Mr. Williams gives his whole case away when he says that he and his friends would be willing to submit gracefully to reduced representation if the country would repeal the Fifteenth Amendment. What the Southern politicians wish to do is not to withhold the suffrage from the elements that pollute it, but to disfranchise forever such men as Booker T. Washington and Professor Du Bois, along with the most depraved levee loafers, for the crime of not having white skins.

" To such a programme the country will never give its consent, and Mr. Williams wastes his breath in suggesting it. The American people are not yet ready to surrender the fundamental principle of their institutions — that in respect of political rights ' all men are created equal,' and that ' the republic is opportunity.' When the South asks this surrender it is asking the impossible."

The plan of Congressman 1–4–33 Williams (the numerals indicate the total number of votes he received in his canvass for Congress) has about as much common-sense in it as that of the man who attempted to drain the ocean by emptying buckets of water on the beach. The republic will not be coerced, nor can the government be destroyed by sulking. A way will be found under the Constitution to elect delegations at large, and voters will be found to vote for them. The South must repeal its "grandfather" constitutions and other trick election laws which defraud the people of an equal share in their government, and enact fair laws, or representation must be reduced.

These leaders present the South in a pitiable plight before the eyes of the world. It is indeed a matter for deep lamentation and profound regret that a land so wonderfully blessed by nature, and with the members of one class of its population, at their best, so hospitable and chivalric, and with the other class so peaceful, responsive, and hard-toiling, should become the prey of unbalanced leaders and wild reactionists. The justice which man owes to man ; the righteousness which God exacts of all ; the peace and fraternity which are the nation's meed ; and the love, charity, and helpfulness which the Christ teaches apparently find no place in their minds, hearts, or works.

Why does not the South accept with the same heartiness ˉand in the same spirit of patriotism and fraternity the result of the election that has been made manifest in every hamlet of other sections of the republic ? Why should it remain offensively sectional, to its own detriment and the marring of the peace of the nation ? Why does it cling so tenaciously to the barbarous traditions of slavery which are out of harmony with the age, repugnant to the national conscience and ideals, and frowned upon and disowned by the whole civilized world ?

The Honorable Thomas E. Watson of Georgia, candidate of the People's party for president in the last campaign, gives the philosophy of the matter in a recent speech in saying : " The politicians keep the negro question alive in the South to perpetuate their hold on public office. The negro question is the joy of their lives. It is their very existence. They fatten on it. With one shout of ' nigger ' ! — they can run the native Democrats into their holes at any hour of the day." Nevertheless, the tremendous uprising of the people on election day and the unprecedented avalanche of ballots which carried Mr. Roosevelt to the presidential chair, after a campaign of abuse and detraction, cannot fail to have a sobering effect ; and the prophecy may even be ventured that a show of firmness in upholding the Constitution by an aroused public opinion will mark the opening of a new era in the Southland — the beginning of the end of the dominion of incapable, rancorous, implacable reactionaries. The handwriting is on the wall. The people have spoken. The meaning of the election is plain.

It means that the Thirteenth, Fourteenth, and Fifteenth Amendments to the Constitution of the United States are incontestable; that the liberty and citizenship of the colored man are no longer open to challenge and are not to be the foot-ball of "cheap-John" politicians; that he shall take his place before the law in common with other races and thus work out his destiny. It means the overwhelming condemnation of wholesale disfranchisement, lynch-law and burnings at the stake, proscriptive laws, the attempt to inaugurate a new form of slavery, and the rampant and unbridled "Jim Crowism" which was constantly flaunted in the face of the nation and offered gross insults and indignities to the President of the United States.

For, indeed, it was not the tariff, nor the gold standard, nor the trusts, nor imperialism, nor the Philippines, nor large expenditures for the army and navy, nor all of these combined that aroused and rallied the sovereigns of the land to the Roosevelt standard. The party in opposition did not propose any summary or radical changes along any of these lines. But it was because "the people loved him for the enemies he has made," and because he stood as firm as adamant against the assaults and traducings of the reactionists and proclaimed his ceaseless devotion to the ideals of liberty as held by Abraham Lincoln, and for a republic of law, orderly government, equal rights and opportunities, and "the door of hope" for all Americans without regard to race, color, or creed, or whether rich or poor — because his personality embodied the American ideal.

The New York *World*, which has been repeatedly quoted, is generally regarded as the leading Democratic organ of the country. It has always been friendly to the South and has rendered it invaluable services. No one would accuse it of leaning toward the colored man or fawning upon him. But in its discussion of the race question it has been fair, firm, and fearless. It has emphasized some thoughts since the election which the white people should ponder over, calmly weigh, and digest. In various issues it says:

PUBLIC OPINION OMNIPOTENT

" The American people will never accept the dictum that a negro scholar is the inferior of a white ignoramus, that a negro gentleman is the inferior of a white blackguard, that a man's title to consideration rests on the color of his skin and not on his character and his achievements.

" The *World* hopes that this little lesson has finally been thoroughly learned. . . .

" Never before in our history were so many votes cast for a candidate for office. Black and white, Protestant and Catholic, Jew and Gentile, vied with one another in testifying at the ballot-box their faith in Mr. Roosevelt's purposes and their confidence in his statesmanship. . . .

" If the South wishes to take the negro question out of national politics the quickest way is to stop burning negroes at the stake and to abandon the un-American notion that the meanest of white scoundrels is better than the most industrious, intelligent, honorable negro.

" If the race question played any part in the recent campaign, the South alone is to blame. It was the South that raised the Booker T. Washington issue. It was the South that advanced the monstrous doctrine that the better qualified a negro was to hold a Federal office the more objectionable was his appointment. . . .

" You cannot convince the people of the North that it is a heinous crime for a President of the United States to lunch with a Booker T. Washington, whatever the color of the Washington's skin may be. They will no more worry about equality between American and African than about equality between American and Chinese, when the President invites the Chinese Minister to dinner."

The white people of the South must come back to the first principles of liberty, constitutional government, and fraternity. They are in fact and by right, and should be in spirit, a harmonious part of the Union — cheerfully co-operating with other sections in enacting and administering just and equal laws and adding to the moral grandeur of the republic. Isolation is a mistaken policy. It bodes no good to the South. It keeps alive sectionalism and bitterness. The South is the chief sufferer. The policy is childish. It rests absolutely in the power of the South, and it alone, to destroy sectionalism. This will be a truly harmonious nation and the last vestige of sectionalism will disappear when the white people of the South, like the people of the North, shall accept in good faith the constitutional amendments which manumitted the slave and restored him to his place in the brotherhood of men. And in recomposing the relations between the races there are two elemental truths which will count mightily in an honorable, a righteous, and lasting settlement.

The first of these is, that the white people, deep down in their hearts, do not hate the colored people. As paradoxical as it may sound, they really love them. They would not exchange them for any class of laborers in the wide world.

The second is this: The colored people do not hate the whites; on the contrary, they cherish genuine friendship and affection for them. The races are not as far apart as it may seem.

The excessive bitterness, rank intolerance and contempt, and the extreme and violent forms of prejudice displayed toward the whole colored race are not an expression of the true heart of the whites. They are rather due to the artificial conditions and influences purposely created by the Bourbons, the pernicious and mischievous leaders, to strengthen and aggrandize their political power and establish an oligarchy. The entailments of slavery made it possible for them to inflame the whites beyond reason and drive the mass of them into stark madness on the race question. To undo their work : the repeal of all proscriptive laws ; the enactment of impartial suffrage and acknowledgment of the right of its rewards to office based on good citizenship and merit; the protection of life, liberty and property; the due punishment of all criminals according to law and not color; the protection of the laborer and the elimination of all forms of peonage; the overthrow of mob-rule and the guaranty of equal rights before the law for all, white and colored alike — these should become the self-imposed task of the best and decent elements of the South. Thus could they bring peace to the nation, and reconciliation between the races; thus could they vindicate the honor of the South and emancipate its name from shame.

From the womb of the South itself, there surely will come men with the honesty, courage and statesmanship of those beacon lights in the early history of the nation — men like Henry and John Laurens, Pinckney and Gadsden of South Carolina; Jefferson, George Mason, Madison, and Randolph of Virginia; and Luther Martin of Maryland — who cried out against the wrong of oppression and servitude at the very incipiency of the nation's birth. What they denounced as a wrong then is a crime in the light of to-day.

The advent into public life of men of their mental calibre, political honesty, and moral courage — men broad in statesmanship, liberal-minded, invincible to passion and prejudice, devoted to free institutions — will be the harbinger of better days for both the white and colored people of the Sunny South, as it will also mean the overturn and banishment into political oblivion of the reactionists, the negrophobists, the "Jim Crowites" and the whole brood of those who fatten on public office or public patronage by preaching hatred and strife between the races, and who are the worst enemies the Southern people have to fear.

The nation longs for peace, but peace which is purchased at the sacrifice of the dictates of justice and humanity and the vital principles of Christianity is not only too costly in price but it is a worthless peace. It is worthless because the conscience of the American people will not accept it. It

would not even bridge over matters. The mere announcement of peace purchased at such a price would open wide
the flood gates of agitation and strife.

The dominant leadership of the South is endeavoring to
turn back the hands of the dial of time and engraft on the
republic the leading principles of the Southern Confederacy.
Thus they would achieve by indirect action what failed of
accomplishment by open rebellion, — the perpetual subjugation and servitude of a people.

The Honorable Alexander H. Stephens, Vice-President of
the Confederacy, made this historical declaration in a speech
delivered at Savannah, Georgia, on the 21st of March, 1861,
less than a month before "Old Glory" was fired on at Fort
Sumter: "The new Constitution has put at rest forever all
the agitating questions relating to our peculiar institution—
African slavery as it exists among us, the proper status of
the negro in our form of civilization. This was the immediate cause of the rupture and present revolution. Jefferson,
in his forecast, had anticipated this, as the 'rock upon which
the old Union would split.' He was right. What was con-
jecture with him is now a realized fact. But whether he
fully comprehended the great truth upon which that great
rock stood and stands may be doubted.

"The prevailing ideas entertained by him and most of the
leading statesmen at the time of the formation of the old
Constitution, were, that the enslavement of the African was
in violation of the laws of nature; that it was wrong in
principle, socially, morally, and politically. It was an evil
they knew not well how to deal with; but the general
opinion of the men of the day was that, somehow or other
in the order of Providence, the institution would be evanescent
and pass away. This idea, though not incorporated in the
Constitution, was the prevailing idea at the time.

"The Constitution, it is true, secured every essential
guarantee to the institution while it should last; and hence

no argument can be justly used against the Constitutional guaranties thus secured, because of the common sentiment of the day. These ideas, however, were fundamentally wrong. They rested upon the assumption of the equality of races. This was an error. It was a sandy foundation, and the idea of a government built upon it : — when the 'storm came and the wind blew,' it fell. Our new government is founded upon exactly the opposite ideas. Its foundations are laid, its corner-stone rests, upon the truth that the negro is not equal to the white man; that slavery, subordination to the superior race, is his natural and normal condition.

"This, our new government, is the first, in the history of the world, based upon this great physical, philosophical, and moral truth. This truth has been slow in the process of its development, like all other truths in the various departments of science. It has been so even among us. Many who hear me, perhaps, can recollect well that this truth was not generally admitted, even in this day."

Mr. Stephens emphasizes the statement that the Confederate government was "the first in the history of the world" to make human slavery its foundation-stone. It will probably be the last.

He lived to learn, however, that no government in the history of the world ever had such a fitful, transient, and malodorous existence. It died a-borning, in the very throes and agonies of its own travail, and without the pity of a single civilized nation. The Almighty did not permit it to darken the earth or curse humanity with its presence — save as a scourge and punishment to the nation, and to cleanse and purge it of the sin and crime of slavery.

When the storm came and the wind blew, it fell. But the government based on the immortal and divine principles of justice and equality for all stood the severest tests and shocks of the greatest war of these ages, and vindicated the principles held by Jefferson and most of the leading statesmen of his time that "the enslavement of the African was in violation of the laws of nature; that it was wrong in principle, socially, morally, and politically."

It may also be noted that Mr. Stephens further said of the Southern Confederacy, that "its foundations are laid, its corner-stone rests, upon the great truth that the negro is not equal to the white man ; that slavery, subordination to the superior race, is his natural and normal condition."

The principles enunciated by Mr. Stephens are monstrously inhuman. The people of the United States are superior in many things to the people of the Latin republics of South America, but does that give the right to North America to conquer or deport the inhabitants of South America and hold them in "slavery, subordination to the superior race," as their "natural and normal condition"?

Some nations in Europe are distinctly superior to other nations. But what nation, arrogating its superiority would dare to make the attempt to conquer or deport the inhabitants of a weaker country and make slaves of them?

Mr. Stephens, however, speaking in 1861, was uttering the exact thoughts and even words that are proclaimed by Southern leaders to-day, on the floors of the Congress, in the halls of legislation, on the lecture platform, sometimes in the pulpit, and frequently in the public press. Truly, some neither learn nor forget.

Mr. Lincoln was far wiser than Mr. Stephens ; he said: "If slavery is not wrong, then nothing is wrong."

And it would seem to follow that "if outraging and oppressing a man on the ground of color is not wrong, then nothing is wrong."

The truth of God, the sentiment of civilization, and the public opinion of the country were with Mr. Lincoln; and because of this, in the Constitution of the United States it is written : "Neither slavery nor involuntary servitude, except as a punishment for crime whereof the party shall have

been duly convicted, shall exist within the United States."
— "All persons born or naturalized in the United States
and subject to the jurisdiction thereof, are citizens of the
United States and of the state wherein they reside." —
"No state shall make or enforce any law which shall abridge
the privileges or immunities of citizens of the United States."
— "Nor shall any state deprive any person of life, liberty,
or property without due process of law, nor deny to any
person within its jurisdiction the equal protection of the
laws." — "The right of the citizens of the United States to
vote shall not be denied or abridged by the United States or
by any state, on account of race, color, or previous condition
of servitude."

There are also guaranties for the right to the writ of
habeas corpus; for freedom of speech; for a free press;
to keep and bear arms; for a public and speedy trial; to
be informed of the nature and cause of the accusation; to
be confronted with the witnesses; to compulsory process for
the attendance of one's own witnesses; to have counsel; to
trial by jury; immunity from bill of attainder; from *ex
post facto* laws; from unreasonable searches and seizures;
from trial for a capital or otherwise infamous crime
unless on presentment or indictment of a grand jury;
from being compelled to testify against one's self; from
excessive bail; from excessive fines; from cruel or unusual
punishment.

Not one of these righteous, humane laws is honestly observed in the South with regard to the colored man. There
is, on the contrary, a general repudiation of them; and in
many essential respects, the South is governed by the galvan-
ized corpse of the Southern Confederacy rather than by the
Constitution of the United States. It has often been demonstrated that the life of a colored man is not held as sacred in
the South as the life of a robin on the Boston Common, or
a swan on the lakes of Lincoln Park in Chicago.

But two vital considerations may apply here: one divine; one human.

First, "the thunderbolts of God are still hot," and "righteousness and judgment are the habitation of his throne."

Second, the American people have shown in their history that when they make up their minds to do a thing, they do it; when they determine to accomplish a result, they will find a way or make it.

The particular manner of the co-operation between the divine and the human powers may not be thoroughly understood. The fact of the co-operation, however, human history abundantly illustrates. God's hand can be plainly seen in the history of this republic. There is more than euphony in these words of Holy Writ: "Righteousness exalteth a nation; but sin is a reproach to any people." Sin is not without its wages.

Thomas Jefferson wrote: "Indeed I tremble for my country when I reflect that God is just; that His justice cannot sleep forever."

The hour came; God's justice did awaken; the country was convulsed and shocked from centre to circumference, and the best blood of the nation paid the atonement. The lesson should not be forgotten.

The humiliations, outrages, and inhumanities now forced on the colored man, contrary to law, human and divine, are a sin and a reproach to the nation. Public opinion is the remedial agent; it is all-potent because the truth and God are behind it.

A cloud of witnesses speak from the skies. Some of these were "workmen who laid the keel," and were on the deck at the launching of the Ship of State. Others were at quarters, on guard, and at the wheel through all the trying ordeals and the perilous voyages of a century and a quarter. The voices of the most eminent men and women now living are also heard with no uncertain sound. They plead for right-

eousness, for justice, for humanity; and in the name of
God.

Fundamentally, a nation is wise in so far as it is righteous;
it is strong and powerful in so far as it is just; it is safe and
invincible in so far as it has the favor of the God of battles.

From the depth of hearts warmed with the fire of liberty,
and with love for their country, faith in humanity, and
abiding confidence in the Almighty and Righteous Ruler
of the universe — the illustrious fathers and the glorious sons
of the republic speak out. Will the South give ear? Will
the nation take heed? Hear them!

Thomas Jefferson says: "And with what execration
should the statesman be loaded, who, permitting one half the
citizens thus to trample on the rights of the other, transforms
those into despots, and these into enemies; destroys the
morale of the one part, and the *amor patriae* of the
other. . . . And can the liberties of a nation be thought
secure when we have removed their only firm basis — a conviction in the minds of the people that these liberties are the
gift of God, — that they are not to be violated but with His
wrath?"

Mr. Bancroft, writing of Mr. Jefferson says: "The heart
of Jefferson in writing the Declaration, and of Congress in
adopting it, beat for all humanity; the assertion of right
was made for all mankind and all coming generations, without any exception whatever; for the proposition which
admits of exceptions can never be self-evident."

The last public act of Benjamin Franklin was the signing
and presentation of a memorial to Congress as President of
the Pennsylvania Abolition Society, in which these words
occur: "That mankind are all formed by the same Almighty Being, alike objects of His care, and equally designed
for the enjoyment of happiness, the Christian religion teaches
us to believe, and the political creed of Americans fully coin-
cides with the position. They have observed, with real

satisfaction, that many important and salutary powers are vested in you for 'promoting the welfare and securing the blessings of liberty to the people of the United States'; and as they conceive that these blessings ought rightfully to be administered without distinction as to color, to all descriptions of people, so they indulge themselves in the pleasing expectations that nothing which can be done for the relief of the unhappy objects of their care will be omitted or delayed.

"From the persuasion that equal liberty was originally the position, and is still the birthright, of all men, and influenced by the strong ties of humanity and the principles of their institutions, your memorialists conceive themselves bound . . . to promote a general enjoyment of the blessings of freedom."

To General Lafayette, who denounced slavery as "a crime blacker than any African's face," and labored for its abolition, George Washington wrote: "Would to God a like spirit might diffuse itself generally into the minds of the people of this country."

Washington also declared that, "the propitious smiles of Heaven can never be expected on a nation that disregards the eternal rules of order and right."

The Honorable Henry Laurens of South Carolina, President of the Continental Congress, minister to Holland, and commissioner with Franklin and Jay to negotiate peace with Great Britain, left on record these emphatic words: "I am not one of those who arrogate the peculiar care of Providence in each fortunate event; nor one of those who dare trust in Providence for defence and security of their own liberty, while they enslave and wish to continue in slavery thousands who are as well entitled to freedom as themselves."

The Reverend Isaac Backus of Massachusetts, says: "The American Revolution was built upon the principle that all men are born with an equal right to liberty and property."

The voices of George Mason of Virginia, and Livingston of New York; Gadsden of South Carolina, and the Adamses of Massachusetts; Alexander Hamilton of New York, and John Tyler of Virginia; Roger Sherman of Connecticut, and Luther Martin of Maryland; Joshua Atherton of New Hampshire, and George Tucker of Virginia; Rufus King of Massachusetts, and Edmund Randolph of Virginia, and a host of others — these all express the sentiment of liberty and humanity.

Of special significance are the declarations of the Honorable John Jay, the first Chief Justice of the Supreme Court of the United States, and thus the first final authority in interpreting the Constitution and laws under it; he says: " I believe that God governs the world; and I believe it to be a maxim in His as in our Court, that those who ask for equity ought to do it." And again: " Till America comes into this measure her prayers to Heaven for liberty will be impious." And further: " To contend for our own liberty and to deny that blessing to others involves an inconsistency not to be excused. . . .

" What act of public or private justice and philanthropy can occasion more pleasing emotions in the breast of Christians, or be more agreeable to Him who shed His blood for the redemption of men, than such as tend to restore the oppressed to their natural rights, and to raise unfortunate members of the same great family with ourselves from the abject situation of beasts of burden, bought and sold and worked for the benefit and at the pleasure of persons who were not created more free, more rational, more immortal, nor with more extensive rights and privileges, than they were."

Concerning the discordant note of Chief Justice Taney, which was the embodiment of the slaveholders' idea, that the negro " had no rights which the white man was bound to respect," Mr. George Livermore, in his *Historical Research*, says: " It shocked the moral sentiment of our own community, and excited the indignant rebuke of some of the most eminent jurists and statesmen of Europe, who declared the sentiments to be 'so execrable as to be almost incredible.'" The Honorable George Bancroft says: "He has not only denied the rights of manhood, the liberties of mankind, but has not left a foothold for the liberty of the white man to rest upon. . . . No nation can adopt that judgment as its rule, and live; the judgment has in it no element of political vitality."

If black men can be put into practical slavery, or be oppressed, the same kind of power can force white men into practical slavery, or under the rod of oppression.

> "Fleecy locks and dark complexions,
> Do not alter nature's claim ;
> Skins may differ, but affections
> Dwell in black and white the same."

This idea of Justice Taney, however, is the central idea in the plan of campaign of Southern leaders. And this accounts for the "Jim Crow" laws and the "Jim Crowism" which disgraces the South and is the shame of the nation.

A press despatch recently reports: "Thomas Grades, a well-dressed negro, is more familiar to-day with the 'Jim Crow' laws of Virginia than he was when he left New York. He was dragged from a train at Alexandria and taken to the station house, where he said he was unfamiliar with the law, and on payment of $10 collateral for his appearance was released. Grades had travelled from New York in comfortable fashion, but at the Virginia end of the long bridge the conductor requested him to go forward to the little pen set aside for negroes. He refused, and at Alexandria the entire force was employed to drag him from the car. After depositing the $10 he proceeded on his journey in the 'Jim Crow' pen."

Is this civilization? Is it Christianity? Is it not barbarous? Yet every colored person regardless of the excellence of his inner life, or outward behavior, whatever his talents, possessions, or high standing in the republic, is subject to these barbarous laws of the South. A colored woman or schoolgirl is treated the same way. In every case first-class fare is demanded and paid, and "Jim Crow" accommodations are forced on them. Sad, indeed, that the ineffable meanness of it does not appeal to the higher sense of justice, the spirit of humanity or the Christian ethics of the white people of the South.

A colored man travels from the city of Washington, the nation's capital, to the Pacific coast. The time required is about five days, and the distance is over three thousand miles. He may be a high official of the government, despatched on public business. The train stops at various places for breakfast, for dinner, for luncheon, for supper. Every person on board of the train, except a colored person, can freely buy refreshments or meals. But no colored person, not even the Register of the Treasury of the United States, who is a colored man, can cross the threshold of a single dining-room, or even slake his thirst with a cup of coffee, or munch a sandwich at a lunch counter. And yet it is written in the Holy Scriptures: "And whosoever shall give to drink unto one of these little ones a cup of cold water only, in the name of a disciple, verily I say unto you he shall not lose his reward." "Inasmuch as ye have done it unto one of the least of these my brethren, ye have done it unto me."

The colored man, government official, minister, or bishop of a great denomination, with money in his pockets, cannot buy food and drink to refresh his body. Not in all civilization outside the boundary of the South is such a condition possible, nor even among semi-civilized people, and hardly among the savages. The negro has "no right which the white man [that is, the Southern white man] is bound to respect."

The harsh and discordant words of Chief Justice Taney may, however, serve to emphasize the strength of the spirit of liberty in the American heart. That spirit has survived every assault and is the abiding heritage of the American people.

But the sons of the republic, like the fathers, also speak for liberty and humanity. President Garfield said : " And this thing we will remember ; we will remember our allies who fought with us. Soon after the struggle began, we looked behind the army of white rebels, and saw four millions of black people condemned to toil as slaves for our enemies ; and we found that the hearts of these four millions were God-inspired with the spirit of liberty, and that they were our friends. We have seen white men betray the flag, but in all that long, dreary war we never saw a traitor in a black skin. Our prisoners escaping from the starvation of prisons, fleeing to our lines by the light of the North Star, never feared to enter the black man's cabin and ask for bread. In all that period of suffering and danger no Union soldier was ever betrayed by a black man or woman. And now that we have made them free, so long as we live we will stand by these black allies. We will stand by them until the sun of liberty, fixed in the firmament of our Constitution, shall shine with equal ray upon every man, black or white, throughout the Union."

General Sherman said : " The South went out of the Union ; it came back with five-fifths voting power based on the negro population. And it is not fair ; it is not just ; it is not honorable for the South to suppress the negro vote."

Mr. Blaine said : " No human right on this continent is more completely guaranteed than the right against disfranchisement on account of race, color, or previous condition of servitude, as embodied in the Fifteenth Amendment of the Constitution of the United States." And he further says : " Without the right of citizenship his (the negro's) freedom could be maintained only in name, and without the elective franchise his citizenship would have no legitimate and no authoritative protection."

356

PUBLIC OPINION OMNIPOTENT

General Grant in his Memoirs, said : " Four millions of human beings held as chattels have been liberated; the ballot has been given to them ; the free schools of the country have been opened to their children. The nation still lives, and the people are just as free to avoid social intimacy with the blacks as ever they were, or as they are with white people."

. President Benjamin Harrison said: " As long as free suffrage shall be held by our people to be a jewel above price ; as long as each for himself shall claim its free exercise and shall generously and manfully insist upon an equally free exercise of it by every other man, our government will be preserved and our development will not find its climax until the purpose of God in establishing this government shall have spread throughout the world — government of the people, for the people, and by the people."

And with the voices of these sons of the republic are heard the voices of Logan, John Sherman, Stanton, Chase, Sheridan, Longfellow, Whittier, Joshua R. Giddings, McKinley, and a mighty host of others — a glorious company speaking as it were from the skies to the American people.

The vast body of the American people to-day think the same thoughts and would say the same words. And their voice is the voice of God speaking through the human heart.

Public opinion is omnipotent. Let it speak in thunder tones ! Its commanding voice will be heard, respected, and obeyed.

It will prevail because it carries with it the grandeur of noble conviction, the majesty of the truth, the sovereignty of the right, and the power and determination of execution.

Kipling's " Recessional," penned in celebration of the fiftieth anniversary of the reign of Victoria, that most gracious queen and sovereign of a world empire, in essentials perhaps the most illustrious ruler the world has ever seen, embodies at once the hopes, doubts, vanities, and fears; the struggles, triumphs, and prayers of a people.

It points the way to greatness and glory because it points the way to the mind of God.

Its lesson cannot fail to impress the American heart.

> "God of our fathers, known of old,
>   Lord of our far flung battle line,
> Beneath whose awful Hand we hold
>   Dominion over palm and pine —
> Lord God of Hosts, be with us yet,
> Lest we forget — lest we forget!
>
> "The tumult and the shouting dies;
>   The captains and the kings depart:
> Still stands Thine ancient sacrifice,
>   An humble and a contrite heart.
> Lord God of Hosts, be with us yet,
> Lest we forget — lest we forget!
>
> "Far-called, our navies melt away;
>   On dune and headland sinks the fire:
> Lo, all our pomp of yesterday
>   Is one with Nineveh and Tyre!
> Judge of the Nations, spare us yet,
> Lest we forget — lest we forget!
>
> "If, drunk with sight of power, we loose
>   Wild tongues that have not Thee in awe,
> Such boasting as the Gentiles use,
>   Or lesser breeds without the Law —
> Lord God of Hosts, be with us yet,
> Lest we forget — lest we forget!
>
> "For heathen heart that puts her trust
>   In reeking tube and iron shard,
> All valiant dust that builds on dust,
>   And guarding calls not Thee to guard,
> For frantic boast and foolish word —
> Thy mercy on Thy people, Lord!
>   "*Amen.*"